Children's Literature

Volume 13

Volume 13

Annual of
The Modern Language Association
Division on Children's Literature
and The Children's Literature
Association

Yale University Press
New Haven and London
1985

Children's Literature

Editor-in-chief: Francelia Butler
Editor, Volume 13: Margaret R. Higonnet
Book Review Editor: John Cech
Editorial Assistant: J. Craig Robertson
Advisory Board: Robert Coles, M.D.; Lois Kuznets; Alison Lurie; William T. Moynihan; Sam Pickering, Jr.; Albert J. Solnit, M.D.
Consultants for Volume 13: Gillian Adams; Ruth Angress; Marilyn Apseloff; Robert Bator; Warner Berthoff; Kathleen Blake; Benjamin Brockman; Stephen W. Canham; Geraldine DeLuca; Robert Dupree; John M. Ellis; Jacques Guicharnaud; Edward Guiliano; Elizabeth Keyser; Kathleen McCormick; David Mann; Leonard Marcus; Mitzi Myers; Deborah Nord; Thomas Riggio; Richard Rotert; Stephen Roxburgh; Mary Shaner; Susan Suleiman; Diane Wolkstein

The editors gratefully acknowledge the support of the journal by the University of Connecticut. Editorial correspondence should be addressed to the Editors, *Children's Literature*, Department of English U-25, University of Connecticut, Storrs, CT 06268. Manuscripts should conform to the new *MLA* style sheet. An original on nonerasable bond and two copies must be accompanied by a self-addressed envelope and return postage.

Volumes 1–7 of *Children's Literature* can be obtained directly from John C. Wandell, The Children's Literature Foundation, Box 370, Windham Center, Connecticut 06280. Volumes 8–13 can be obtained from Yale University Press, 92A Yale Station, New Haven, Connecticut 06520, or from Yale University Press, 13 Bedford Square, London WC1B 3JF, England.

Library of Congress catalog card number: 79-66588
ISBN: 0-300-03319-2 (cloth), 0-300-03362-1 (paper)

Set in Baskerville type by The Saybrook Press, Inc., Old Saybrook, Conn. Printed in the United States of America by Vail-Ballou Press, Binghamton, N.Y.

10   9   8   7   6   5   4   3   2   1

Contents

Children's Literature

Resisting Growth through Fairy Tale in Ruskin's
The King of the Golden River

U. C. Knoepflmacher

"How things bind and blend themselves together!" mused a seventy-year-old John Ruskin in the last paragraph of *Praeterita*, the lyrical autobiography concluded in 1889. In this remembrance of things past, Ruskin's most resolute attempt to come to terms with his origins, realism blends with an intense wishfulness. A lifetime's desire to retrieve the emblems of cultural wholeness and purity now takes the shape of a personal quest as an old man rummages through the residual layerings of his backward-looking, richly evocative mind. Young faces dissolve into old ones. Landscapes interpenetrate, merged by memory. Juxtaposition, always Ruskin's forte, yields likeness in unlikeness. Though the final vision is, appropriately enough, one of approaching darkness, a golden radiance also confers eternity on a moment in time: "Through the sunset that faded into thunderous night as I entered Siena three days before, the white edges of the mountainous clouds still lighted from the west, and the openly golden sky calm behind the Gate of Siena's heart, with its golden words, 'Cor magis tibi Sena pandit,' and the fireflies everywhere in the sky and cloud rising and falling, mixed with lightning, and more intense than the stars."[1]

Ruskin is alone as he imaginatively crosses this golden gate. But, in the previous paragraph, when he reconstructs still another refuge from darkness, his garden at Denmark Hill, he becomes rejuvenated by the company, not of one, but of two small Eves: "I draw back to my own home, twenty years ago, . . . and the Elysian walks with Joanie, and Paradisiacal with Rosie, under the peach-blossom branches by the little glittering stream which I had paved for them" (35:560). Here, too, nature and artifice fuse. Yet the awed observer of a skyscape is presented as lord of his own garden. He can pave the glittering brook. And he can screen the entering inmates. For it is significant that Ruskin's two companions should be remembered as children only, still "girlish" figures (542). His cousin "Joanie" Agnew is not yet Mrs. Arthur Severn, the matronly caretaker of Ruskin's

later, tormented years. Similarly, "Rosie" La Touche remains closer
to the ten-year-old he first met in 1859 than to the young woman
whose painful references to the "Eden-land" they so briefly shared
now sting the "sorrowful" old man and remind him of having ever
since "lost sight of that peach-blossom avenue" (561). He can reopen
that avenue only by retreating into a precarious realm of imagined
innocence.

Almost half a century before he composed *Praeterita*, Ruskin
fashioned another golden blending of art and nature as a preserve
for the desexualized purity of childhood. If *Praeterita* enlists the
nostalgia of memory, *The King of the Golden River*, though similarly
retrogressive, activates those "forward-looking thoughts" and "stir-
rings of inquietude" which the growing child evokes, according to
Wordsworth, in the maturing adult.[2] The little book ostensibly
intended for the thirteen-year-old Euphemia Gray (then known as ·
"Phemy," but later as "Effie") was written in 1841 before Ruskin's
delayed graduation from Oxford and before his propulsion into
eminence with the publication of the first two volumes of *Modern
Painters* (1843, 1846). Yet despite his later disparagement of the
work, it contained in embryonic fashion many of the ideas Ruskin
was to develop in his more serious theoretical writings.

Still, as Jane Merrill Filstrup has rightly suggested, *The King of the
Golden River* also "gives a glimpse" of the incipient fears that beset
Ruskin during his "early manhood."[3] And these fears not only
stemmed from doubts about his "aesthetic appreciation of nature,"
as Filstrup shows, but also involved far more elementary insecurities
about assuming the identity of an adult male. "Phemy's fairy tale," as
its youthful author called it at the time, acted as an important
emotional outlet for the over-nurtured only child of Margaret and
John James Ruskin. By casting himself as a deprived and parentless
child in Gluck, the boy-Cinderella, Ruskin could indulge emotions
that did not fully erupt into his consciousness until 1863, when
cloaked self-pity turned into open anger and recrimination. Only
then did he squarely blame his parents for having made him unfit
"for the duties of middle life."[4] Instead of having been taught how
to be steeled against adversity, "severely disciplined and exercised in
the sternest way," forced "to lie on stone beds and eat black soup," he
had—he complained—been raised as an overindulged middle-class

child: "You fed me effeminately and luxuriously." A parental insistence on the religious denial of "all the earnest fire of passion and life" was what presumably had rendered him so volitionless.

Ruskin's 1863 denunciation of the supposed "mistakes" that his parents had committed in supervising his growth was written, significantly enough, from the precincts of Winnington Hall, the girls' school in which he had assumed the role of avuncular guardian and educator of his "little birds." But the young Ruskin who authored *The King of the Golden River* in 1841 was not yet a child-lover. He accepted the lively Phemy Gray's challenge to write a fairy tale because he was eager to ward off personal anxieties about change and death. They were both in need of therapeutic relief. She had just lost three younger sisters who died of scarlet fever; he, then twenty-two, was convalescing at Leamington after a bout of what his ever-solicitous parents feared might turn into fatal tuberculosis.

Still, if *The King of the Golden River* was composed at Euphemia Gray's request, it was primarily intended for Ruskin's parents (and, especially, for his father). For the elder Ruskins, who made sure to retain a manuscript copy for themselves before forwarding Phemy her own, appreciated the story as a reassuring token of their son's uncorrupted—and uncorruptible—"innocence." *The King of the Golden River* ends on a note of submission. Only by obeying the paternalistic King can Gluck, the passive young protagonist, bring about a process of refertilization: "And thus the Treasure Valley became a garden again, and the inheritance, which had been lost by cruelty, was regained by love."[5] Margaret Ruskin wrote to John, "I like your Fairy Tale amazingly." And, as if to signify that she had fully grasped the implications of that ending about an inheritance regained by love, she added: "The latter part I think quite equal to the beginning—did I mention this before?"[6] John James Ruskin proudly concurred: "I almost wish Fairy Tale was printed . . . —very moral and descriptive."[7]

On the surface, then, "Phemy's fairy tale" was addressed to a double audience of child and adult by a writer whose delayed adolescence caused him to continue to hover between the opposed states of innocence and experience. Despite his eagerness to obtain the approval of this dual readership through the story of an obedient and effeminate boy rewarded for charitable behavior, Ruskin was not wholly able to prevent quite contrary emotions from piercing his fable's emphasis on acquiescence. The rebelliousness that would surface in his later career lurks in *The King of the Golden River* as half-submerged as those threatening black rocks over which the swirling waters "rose wildly into the night" (1:339, 342; D, 54, 59).

I

That Ruskin sensed some of the subversiveness concealed in *The King of the Golden River* seems evident from his repeated attempts to distance himself from this early production. When the story appeared in December of 1850, nine years after its composition, lavishly illustrated by Richard Doyle, its author was no longer a youth writing for a private audience, fit though few. At work on *The Stones of Venice*, he had become a literary celebrity with the appearance of the first two volumes of *Modern Painters* and *The Seven Lamps of Architecture* (1849), issued by Smith, Elder, and Company, who now also published his fairy tale. There was a further change in circumstances. Little Phemy Gray had turned into sensual Effie Ruskin. For Ruskin's 1841 child-reader had become the alluring young woman he married on April 10, 1848, the day of one of the largest Chartist political protests, after he had overcome the initial opposition of his reluctant parents.

The story of Ruskin's ill-fated marriage to Effie, of its annulment on grounds of his failure to consummate it, of her remarriage to John Everett Millais, has been often and well told.[8] There is no need to rehearse it once more. But one question remains. By the time *The King of the Golden River* appeared in print, Ruskin's disaffection for his young wife had become more than manifest. The flirtatious woman he continued to treat as a desexualized "Sweet Sister" now belonged to the same "adult reality" he had resisted in his fairy tale, where his exaltation of an "unquestioning innocence" was intended to bind him to a thirteen-year-old.[9] But the effeminate little Gluck could no longer act as an emblem for their bond. Why, then, did Ruskin agree to publish a book written at such a markedly different phase of his emotional life?

The 1850 version of *The King of the Golden River* carried a prefatory "Advertisement" by its "Publishers" rather than an introduction by its "Author." This author, who is characterized as having composed "solely" the story to amuse an anonymous reader described as a "very young lady," as having never wanted to reach a wider audience, as giving even now a merely "passive assent" to a nameless "friend" who has suggested publication, and as relying on the aid of Doyle's art to bring out his "ideas with characteristic spirit," appears distanced, without any affective or ideological involvement in his own handiwork. The suppressions make the "Advertisement" seem suspect. There is no hint that the "very young lady" has since become the author's own wife, a touch that would certainly have endeared the project to sentimental Victorian readers. Nor is there any identification of the equally anonymous friend who had retained the manuscript, only recently surmised to be none other than Ruskin's father (1:310; D, 7).[10] The two figures seem unrelated, purposely kept apart from each other as well as from an author somehow unwilling to be identified in his relation as husband and son.

When decades later in *Praeterita* Ruskin was forced to take a stance toward *The King of the Golden River*, he continued to play down all emotional associations. Only after a seeming digression on the "comforts and restoratives" he found in Dickens's writings,[11] he at last assesses his own handiwork as a fabulist, yet quickly dismisses it and its "restorative" aims in self-deprecatory fashion:

> *The King of the Golden River* was written to amuse a little girl; and being a fairly good imitation of Grimm and Dickens, mixed with a little true Alpine feeling of my own, has been rightly pleasing to nice children, and good for them. But it is totally valueless, for all that. I can no more write a story than compose a picture. [35:303—04]

Ruskin's derogation of his book is excessive, as is his characterization of its derivativeness. That *The King of the Golden River* is highly imitative of the form of a Grimm märchen is certainly true, as Filstrup has noted by valuably linking it to "The Water of Life."[12] But Ruskin's adaptation of this and of several other of the tales he had found, as a child, in Taylor's *German Popular Tales* (1823, 1826) involves some revealing departures. These departures, to be scrutinized in the next two sections of this essay, suggest the existence of aggressive underpinnings that he still took great pains to conceal.

Back in 1850, however, by giving his "passive asent" to his father's renewed plea that he publish *The King of the Golden River*, Ruskin hoped to erase internal fissures that had become all the more pronounced after his marriage. The Edenic purity he coveted so ardently required this last gesture of reaffirmation. From 1850 onward, Ruskin chose to adopt the guise of a maturer self, the sophisticated critic of architecture and culture, in his search for a pristine Treasure Valley. Instead of resettling Gluck in a "paradisiacal" garden, he could guide adult readers to the remnants of an organic past still embedded in the present, still attainable as the visible emblems of an earlier era of untainted, childlike belief. Instead of reducing Gluck's overgrown brothers into two huge black boulders, he could animate the stones of medieval Venice by stripping them free from the accumulated detritus of subsequent layers of civilization. Magic could be carried into history. The imaginative man who professed to be wholly unable to tap his creativity ("I can no more write a story than compose a picture") could at least signify his socialization through the extraordinary powers of *re*creativity by which he managed to distill a cultural "innocence" from the anxious manifestations of modernity. Not until *Praeterita*, near the very end of his writing career, would he again devise a narrative construct to recover his threatened, special childhood self.

Ruskin's eagerness to protect such a childhood self, with a fierceness that often bordered on falsification, provides a key to that long and rich career. Read in that context, *The King of the Golden River* was a crucial undertaking. In 1841, the young Ruskin had naively thought that he might remain perennially virginal if could "bind and blend" himself with an unspoiled young girl; as yet barely conscious of the misgivings his story betrayed, he had proudly offered this fictional blending to his parents. By 1850, though considerably chastened, Ruskin still tried to tell himself that not only the manuscript of his fairy tale, but also his better childhood self, had somehow "remained" intact "in the possession" of friends more precious than any wife. It was a pious myth. But by believing in it Ruskin only succeeded in delaying one more time the encroaching recognition that his adult development had been severely stunted. If he could subsequently acknowledge that fact and turn his wrath on modernity's adulterations, he could also remain steadfast in clinging to his earlier idealization of innocence. Childhood still needed to be insulated from a destructiveness which Ruskin persisted in identifying with an adult modality: "Children should laugh but not mock," he asserted in "Fairy Stories" in 1868, "and when they laugh it should not be at weaknesses and faults of others" (19:234).

Unlike the Thackeray of *The Rose and the Ring* and the Carroll of the Alice books, Ruskin thus felt repeatedly compelled to deny the subversiveness of his own fairy tale for "nice children." Instead of acknowledging the anger that lurked in the book or transmuting that anger into the controlled aggression of satire, as Thackeray or Carroll would do, he preferred to turn his negativity on the book itself. But was the tale just as "valueless" a creative endeavor as he maintained? Is it really akin to those earlier eighteenth-century didactic productions designed to confirm nice children in their niceness? The story can certainly be read in that fashion. My students give *The King of the Golden River* their rather unenthusiastic respect. They value it for its craftsmanship: its symmetry and control, its evocative descriptions of landscape, its color and design. A handful even praise the work for its quasi-Christian "message" about the rewards of charity. But the majority find the tale to be too pietistic. They particularly dislike Gluck as an excessively bland and bloodless protagonist whose acquiescence they unfavorably contrast to the behavior of later Victorian child heroes and heroines, Thackeray's Giglio and Rosalba, Carroll's Alice, Kipling's Mowgli, Burnett's Mary Lennox, all figures capable of indignation and spunk, as well as of considerable ingenuity and self-reliance. Their response seems justified. And yet they fail to recognize that the story's ostensible tameness is in conflict with the extraordinarily powerful violence which the tale activates and then barely subdues in order to reward its "nice" child-hero.

II

At first glance, the oppositions that Ruskin establishes at the start of *The King of the Golden River* seem familiar. Innocence is juxtaposed to experience. The fecund Eden "commonly called the Treasure Valley" is immediately set apart from the "broad plains" and "populous cities" that lie on the other side of the mountains sheltering this agrarian enclave. And, just as predictably, the youngest of the "three brothers, called Schwartz, Hans, and Gluck," who own the "whole of this little valley," is "completely opposed" to his "seniors" both in "appearance and character" (1:314, 315; D, 14, 16). As in those Grimm märchen which Ruskin so well remembered from his boyhood reading of *German Popular Tales*—stories such as "The Water of Life," as well as "The Golden Goose," "The Queen Bee," and "The Golden Bird"—a youngest brother epitomizes the trust and openness of the Innocent.[13]

Schwartz and Hans are powerful adult males who exhibit distrust as well as a ruthless delight in maintaining their superior station. Their masculinity is shown to be repulsive. They are described as "very ugly men, with over-hanging eyebrows and small dull eyes, which were always shut, so that you couldn't see into *them*, and always fancied they saw very far into *you*" (1:314; D, 15). In thus portraying them, the narrator assumes the vantage point of a powerless child who vainly tries to fathom the thoughts of the domineering adult who towers over him. That such an identification is taking place is soon confirmed by the description of "little Gluck" himself. As a child, "not above twelve years old" (like Phemy at the time), "fair, blue-eyed" (like John Ruskin), he is still unmarked by suspicion, still unworldly, and, above all, still unmasculine in his state of prepubescence.

The contrast between child and adult is reinforced by Richard Doyle's carefully differentiated drawings of the three brothers.[14] Depicted by Doyle as highly developed athletic figures whose short-cropped hair accentuates their muscularity, the ugly older brothers are exposed in Ruskin's text as rapacious sadists who kill "everything that did not pay for its eating": blackbirds, hedgehogs, crickets, even the harmless cicadas, "which used to sing all summer in the lime trees" (1:314; D, 15). With the exception of the sketch in which a shackled Schwartz is brought before the magistrate, every drawing of the two men portrays them as holding on to staffs, flagons, sticks (with which they beat Gluck), rolling pins (with which they try to beat their first visitor, "the little gentleman"), and swords and daggers (with which they fight each other).

Gluck, by way of contrast, respects the ways of a more feminine Nature. Unlike Hans and Schwartz, he is "kind in temper to every living thing" (1:315; D, 16). While they hoard both corn and gold, and will later display their acquisitiveness by adulterating metals in

Richard Doyle (1824−83) had been as precocious as Ruskin himself, having joined the staff of *Punch* at the age of 19. Here he renders Hans and Schwartz as brutal adults whose sadism is a male intensification of the cruelty shown to Cinderella by her older sisters.

"the large city," the boy-Cinderella is forced to "clean shoes, floors, and sometimes the plates, occasionally getting what was left on them, by way of encouragement, and a wholesome quantity of dry blows, by way of education" (1:326, 315; D, 33, 16). Drawn by Doyle as a decidedly girlish figure, with a soft swelling breast and long flowing hair, Gluck curiously anticipates Tenniel's far more famous rendering of the young Alice. Even when transported to the city by his brothers, Gluck is shown, in one illustration, in the pose of a sequestered Rapunzel, nostalgically looking out from an ivy-encased window in the direction of the lost Treasure Valley. In three other drawings, in each of which he stands against the open concavity of the goldsmith's furnace (so like the even more huge concave of the fireplace against which he is depicted in the first chapter), Gluck disregards a sword that leans, unused, next to him. The same sword will soon be seized by one of his fighting brothers. Gluck, however, in the last of these three drawings, prefers to peek in amazement into the hollow furnace out of which he has previously extracted the baby-sized King of the Golden River. The midget had arrived in a

The femininity of Ruskin's boy-Cinderella is evident in these three renditions of Gluck.

kind of breech-birth ("instead of a liquid stream, there came out, first, a pair of pretty yellow legs" [1:329; D, 39]). He now "deliberately" and mysteriously disappears again into the hollow (1:332; D, 43).

As the first and foremost of the oppositions on which Ruskin relies for his plot, the contrast between Gluck and his two brothers would seem to be clear-cut. For Ruskin quite overtly prepares readers conditioned by the traditional form of the märchen to expect that the youngest and weakest of three brothers would eventually be allowed to obtain some prize above his more powerful elders. That this rewarded innocent should be called "Gluck" rather than "Dummling" (or Simpleton), as in the story of "The Golden Goose," also seems in keeping with established conventions. In the fifth volume of *Modern Painters* Ruskin would rightly recall that the "latest descent" of a "youngest child" was habitually regarded as "a sign of fortunateness" in the "Northern traditions," the Scandinavian and Germanic sagas on which so many Grimm folktales are based (*Works*, 7:396). The German word for such luck or "fortunateness" is, of course, "Glück." The noun by which the boy is called thus also helps to separate him from the unfortunate fates of Schwartz, the oldest brother whose adjectival name acts as a surname for both "Black Brothers," and of Hans, the middle brother, who pushes himself ahead of Schwartz by becoming the first of the three questers.

Yet, as even the specificity of this symbolic naming suggests, Ruskin departs quite markedly from the German models he later professed to have followed as submissively as Gluck follows the authority of his superiors. In the Grimm stories, the fortunate youngster who vies with his brothers not only bests them but invariably acquires the power explicitly associated with an even stronger father figure. In "The Golden Goose," for example, Dummling, "despised and ill-treated by the whole family," dutifully asks his father's permission to replace the brothers who had ventured into the enchanted forest. Yet the woodcutter cruelly reminds the boy of his inferiority to the favored elder children: "Your brothers have lamed themselves; you had better stay at home, for you know nothing of the business." When Dummling insists on being given the same opportunity accorded to the "brighter" brothers who nonetheless have maimed themselves with their father's sharp ax, the woodcutter relents "at last" but gruffly dismisses him: "Go your way; you will be wiser when you have suffered your folly."[15] He regards the boy as valueless. Whereas the older sons had been given cake and wine by their parents, Dummling is merely granted some stale bread and sour beer. But by sharing his coarse fare with one who seems as powerless as he has been, a "little old man" much like Gluck's two little supernatural visitors, Dummling soon excels his crippled brothers. Moreover, by winning a princess and becoming *her* father's heir, he becomes the recipient of a power far greater than that which his own surly father has withheld from him.

If, as Bruno Bettelheim contends, tales such as "The Golden Goose" encourage a growing child to overcome its feelings of insignificance by making it trust that "small real achievements are important," they also tend to equate such achievements, much more than either Ruskin or Bettelheim wants to allow, with a gained male potency that has decided sexual overtones.[16] When Dummling cuts down an old tree to find the golden goose "in a hollow under the roots," his ax-wielding produces results that neither his father nor his father's male heirs could have obtained. His prowess does not stem from the acquisition of adult skills but relies instead on a more

primal and instinctual energy that makes him the sharer of the
forest dwarf's own powers. He can thus reverse the rules of primogeniture that operate in a social organization.

The same pattern of reversal also operates in "The Queen Bee"
and in "The Golden Bird." In the first story, the youngest and
weakest of three princes (he even assumes the shape of a "little
insignificant dwarf" in the Taylor translation that Ruskin read as a
child) wins the "youngest" but "best" of three princesses. Although
he generously grants the two other princesses to the brothers he
rescues, it is he who will rule as "king after her father's death."[17]
Again, a princess, a golden steed, and a golden bird deservedly go to
the kindly youngest son of the king's gardener in "The Golden
Bird." In the German original, the protagonist is himself a "Königs-
sohn" or prince, and it is his royal father who executes his treacherous older brothers and allows him to reign in their stead as his sole
successor to the throne.[18]

If *The King of the Golden River* follows the formula established by
these fantasies of magically achieved power, it nonetheless greatly
qualifies that male power. It is true that the meek and feminized
Gluck will, by the story's end, inherit the earth his violent brothers
have turned into sterile "red sand and grey mud" through their
unnatural behavior (1:234; D, 30). Yet Ruskin pointedly departs
from his German models by omitting two of their prime features. He
carefully removes any reference to the father figure who, in the
märchen, is always needed to confirm the fantasy of mastery: Gluck
is a brother but never a son. Although he eventually recovers,
through love, the "inheritance" which "had been lost by cruelty,"
that inheritance, though called a "patrimony," is given distinctly
female characteristics. At the same time, Ruskin refuses to award
Gluck the prize habitually bestowed on the younger son as a token of
his sexual maturation, a princess. Indeed, in its total avoidance
of any female figure whatsoever, *The King of the Golden River* differs
not just from the three stories just mentioned (or from "The Water
of Life" and "The King of the Golden Mountain," which contain
parallels to be discussed later) but also from most other Grimm
folktales. Given the fact that Ruskin wrote the fairy tale for his
father, mother, and little Phemy, the absence of either parents or of

a female mate from the plot of his story seems an omission that must be regarded with considerable suspicion.

Why did the tale written by a dutiful son seemingly omit the elementary identification of child with parent, so central, as Bettelheim and others have shown, to the basic format of the fairy tale? And why did this offering "to a very young lady" have to remain so ostensibly desexualized by avoiding the obligatory use of both genders? The answer to both questions is simple. Ruskin tried to rid his story of the "impurities" of aggression and sexuality. And yet he merely managed to disguise or displace those elements so much more overtly handled in the folktales which he wanted to refine.

Indeed, displacements occur throughout the plot of *The King of the Golden River*. Previous questers in the Grimm märchen were rewarded with totemic objects of power—golden animals or artifacts with magical properties; even the Water of Life in the story of that title has curative powers. But the "Golden River" of the book's title yields no tangible hoard; as a waterfall that merely looks "like a shower of gold" and does not even fall into the the Treasure Valley itself, it remains a fluid metaphor. Initially, the valley does not need this stream to fertilize it but relies instead on the humidity of hovering clouds for its moistness. When Gluck finally undertakes his quest, near the end of the story, he still assumes, after the manner of his petrified brothers, that he will be rewarded with a literal store of gold, the traditional source of power. What he will gain, however, is something else. Freed from the rigidity of his older brothers—and, correspondingly, from the rigidity that is identified as the result of a lust for power—Gluck merely benefits from a natural diversion of waters: "Behold, a river like the Golden River, was springing from a new cleft of the rocks above it, and was flowing in innumerable streams among the dry heaps of sand" (1:347, D, 67).

The feminized boy is thus rewarded by the waters that emanate from this "new cleft." He can return to a renovated Eden better by far than that which his brothers, but not he, had lost. He has remained as pure as before. No princess is needed to mark his final maturation as a male, for he can bypass the very process of maturation. He has not altered. Like the "fresh grass" and "moistening soil" around him, he has merely become refertilized. Like the little King whose "pretty yellow legs" Gluck had poured out of the "liquid stream" of the goldsmith's furnace, he can be reborn as a child. It is his older two brothers who must remain forever frozen as "two black stones," the hardened emblems of their callous male rigidity.

III

Despite the harmoniousness of its ending, *The King of the Golden River, or, The Black Brothers* owes its imaginative energy less to Gluck's beatification than to the harsh punishment meted out to his brothers by the boy's two supernatural allies. Ruskin's reliance on two such characters to replace the single figure who operates in stories such as "The Golden Goose" and "The Golden Bird" befits his use of parallelism throughout the meticulously crafted five-part structure of his tale. The success of Gluck's quest in the last chapter obviously builds on the failure of the expeditions undertaken by Hans and Schwartz in chapters 4 and 5. Yet these two chapters also form a paired pendant that contains its own pleasing variations-within-repetition. And if, as noted, the opening chapter sets up the contrast between the older and younger brothers that informs the entire book, it also introduces Gluck's first visitor, South West Wind Esquire, to prepare the reader for the appearance of the King of the Golden River in chapter 2.

   These figures are sufficiently alike to be occasionally confused with each other by unwary readers. (Since the name of South West Wind is not made known until the very last line of the first chapter, the expectation that he might be the King of the book's title is actually encouraged.) Each visitor is presented as small in size and hence associated with the boy called "little Gluck." When the first one appears, he strikes Gluck as "the most extraordinary looking little gentleman he had ever seen"; when the second one assembles his legs, arms, and "the well-known head" of Gluck's golden mug into a unified body, he rises "in the shape of a little golden dwarf" (2:316, 329; D, 19, 39). Yet despite their minuteness and drollness, each figure also assumes an authoritative stance that makes Gluck behave just as "submissively" toward them as he has behaved toward Schwartz and Hans (2:330; D, 41). The first visitor speaks "petulantly," "gruffly," and "drily" to the boy, although he initially addresses the older brothers "very modestly" (2:317, 318, 319, 320; D,

20, 22, 23, 26). The second one soon proves to be equally "pertina-
cious" and "intractable" in speech as in demeanor (2:329; D, 40).
Each figure thus combines Gluck's physical slightness with the superior strength of his brothers. Indeed, by prevailing over the older
brothers, each ally can enact a hostility which Gluck is not allowed to
display. Whereas the dwarf who leads Dummling to the Golden
Goose or the fox who secures treasures for the youngest brother in
"The Golden Bird" may indirectly cause the maiming or punishment of the older siblings, Ruskin's two little magical figures take an
open delight in their far more active role as avengers.

Despite their similar roles, South West Wind Esquire and the King
of the Golden River nonetheless differ considerably both in their
appearance and in the extent and nature of their power. Gluck's first
visitor is as grotesque as the older brothers he will so relentlessly
humiliate. Though only "about four feet six in height" and hence
slightly smaller than Gluck, South West Wind relies on a series of
protuberances greatly to enlarge his actual size. He wears "a conical
pointed cap" of "nearly" his own "altitude," further extended by a
"black feather some three feet long," and drags an "enormous black,
glossy-looking cloak" which might have been "much too long" even
in calmer weather but which the powerful gusts spread out horizon-
tally "to about four times his own length" (2:316; D, 19). What is
more, "the old gentleman" sports "a very large nose, slightly brass-
coloured," which Ruskin originally went on to describe as "expand-
ing toward its termination into a development not unlike the lower
extremity of a key bugle" (2:316, 316*n*; D, 18). When Richard Doyle
accordingly drew that nose as a long and metallic, trumpetlike snout,
a suddenly prudish Ruskin deleted the description and insisted that
the phallic proboscis shown in three illustrations be redrawn and
considerably shortened and naturalized. Yet he retained sufficient
allusions to the "dripping" appendages of Gluck's visitor to prepare
the reader for his eventual mode of confronting Schwartz and Hans.

Unlike his predecessor, Gluck's second supernatural visitor is
described as "exquisitely delicate." Only the features of his face
are "rather coarse, slightly inclining to coppery in complexion,
and indicative, in expression," of his own pugnacious temperament
(2:329; D, 40). He thus retains merely the "very fierce little face" on
the original drinking mug, which an uncle (rather than a father) had

In the redrawn version of this scene the nose of South West Wind no longer resembles a "key bugle," but Schwartz's rolling pin still faces that nose.

The redrawn nose once again: the earlier version better befits all the other protrusions—the conical cap, the enormous feather, the flowing cape, and the extended door knocker.

given "to little Gluck, and which he was very fond of" (1:326; D, 34). Having never drunk "anything out of it but milk and water," Gluck is appalled when commanded to melt down his "old friend." Unlike Schwartz, who has been made uncomfortable by the "intense gaze" that animated the mug when he used it to quaff Rhenish wine, the mild boy seems oblivious to the "malicious" glare of those lifelike eyes. Noting that the "flowing hair" (so like his own golden locks) has disappeared into the melting-pot, Gluck regards the eyes, which now "looked more malicious than ever," as those of a fellow-victim: " 'And no wonder,' thought Gluck, "after being treated in that way' " (1:327; D, 35). Though incapable of voicing any resentment over his own mistreatment, the boy finds himself shocked by the pugnacity the King adopts as soon as he regains the fluidity already associated with the bellicose South West Wind. The disabled King may have been, as Gluck still is, paralyzed: "The shape you saw me in," he explains, "was owing to the malice of a stronger king" (1:331; D, 42). But, unlike Gluck, he has now regained full command of his former might. And, what is more, he will not hesitate to rely on that might to impose on the boy's "wicked brothers" the same arrested condition from which he has been released.

Ruskin carefully contrasts the sizes of Gluck's two "little" visitors. If South West Wind is four and a half feet tall, the golden dwarf is exactly one third in size, "about a foot and a half high." Yet the tinier of these two visitors actually possesses greater magical powers. South West Wind's destructive energies are purely natural. He overpowers Gluck's brothers and ravages the Treasure Valley. Although he spares Gluck, he is unconcerned with the boy's ultimate fate. The King of the Golden River, on the other hand, by turning Hans and Schwartz into boulders and then rewarding Gluck, mixes violence with beneficence by liberating his own unwitting liberator. What is more, by allowing Hans and Schwartz one further chance before each man's self-destruction, he grants them free will. This Lilliputian deity thus seems at least superficially kindlier than the South West Wind who resentfully rends an Eden. Still, each figure is acerbic and quarrelsome and thus paradoxically displays the same aggressiveness that Ruskin's narrator condemns in Hans and Schwartz. Just as in Doyle's drawing a nervous, finger-biting Gluck stands by passively as the first of his surrogates is about to engage his pugnacious brothers, so does the story's narrator dissociate his meek male Cinderella from the contentiousness that he attributes to the boy's virile enemies and allies.

Yet Ruskin undeniably relishes sadistic manifestations, not just in his portrayal of the Black Brothers, but also in the manner of their disablement. South West Wind overwhelms them, not once, but twice. He first vanquishes them in combat and then, in a sequence given unmistakable sexual overtones, violates the enclosure into which Gluck had so reluctantly admitted him. The first encounter ends swiftly. When Schwartz seizes the rolling-pin to beat Gluck for letting the dripping stranger sit by the hearth, "the old gentleman" removes the huge conical cap he had previously stuck "up the chimney" to parry the blow and sends the weapon "spinning like a straw" into a corner. When Hans tries to grab the intruder, he is sent flying after the pin, and soon a "very angry" Schwartz follows him, hitting "his head against the wall as he tumbled into the corner" (1:318, 320, 321; D, 21, 25, 27).

On his second visit, South West Wind produces far greater damage. For he now not only batters the house in which he has been so inhospitably treated but also reduces the paradisiacal Treasure Valley into "one mass of ruin, and desolation" (1:324; D, 30). The mighty gale that makes the barred door "burst open with a violence" which shakes the entire structure also rips off the roof of the bedroom of the older brothers and drenches their beds:

> The two brothers sat up on their bolster, and stared into the darkness. The room was full of water, and by a misty moonbeam, which found its way through a hole in the shutter, they could see in the midst of it, an enormous foam globe, spinning round, and bobbing up and down like a cork, on which, as on a most luxurious cushion, reclined the little old gentleman, cap and all. There was plenty of room for it now, for the roof was off.
>
> "Sorry to incommode you," said their visitor, ironically. "I'm afraid your beds are dampish; perhaps you had better go to your brother's room; I've left the ceiling on there." [1:328; D, 29–30]

The symbolism speaks for itself. Two adults are commanded to take refuge in a child's room. The bed of the virginal Gluck is not "dampish"; no conical cap has deflowered the enclosure into which his older brothers, "wet through, and in an agony of terror," flee for their safety. The situation reverses that in which a small child, on awaking either in discomfort or in terror over some overpowering "bad" dream, seeks shelter in the warm, dry bed of reassuring parents presumably better equipped, as grownups, to defuse anxiety or shame. It is Schwartz and Hans, however, who have suffered from an excess of something not unlike what Wordsworth (who yoked the imagination to "the sexual appetite, and all the passions connected with it") called a "spontaneous overflow of powerful feelings."[19] As their sarcastic visitor reminds them, the brothers have met their match.

Still, Gluck too, though physically spared, is not immune to the aftereffects of this imaginative overflow. The waters emitted by South West Wind's spillage have, after all, "gutted" the rest of the house in which Gluck has so docilely labored as a domestic; outside, they have "swept away trees, crops, and cattle" (1:323, 324; D, 30, 31). The Treasure Valley has turned sterile: "What had once been the richest soil in the kingdom, became a shifting heap of red sand" (1:325; D, 33). All three brothers must be exiled from an Eden that has turned into a "desert." Although the youngest and most feminine can retain a "paradise within," he too must suffer the deprivation caused by a violent and violating masculinity. Only his charity—and the agency of a more benign supernatural protector—will again cause fecund ground waters to spring from that "new cleft."

Yet even the kindlier King of the Golden River displays none of the charitable feelings that he ostensibly rewards in Gluck. It is no coincidence that the boy's crowning act of goodness—to the dying dog who will, once its thirst is slaked, turn into the King himself—should be presented as his only mild act of defiance in the entire book. On deciding to give the animal the last drops of the water he has saved for his quest, Gluck denounces the instigator of that quest: "Confound the King and his gold, too." Although, ironically enough, he has just nurtured the very figure he purports to condemn, it is noteworthy that Gluck at last displays some of the anger from which he has, until then, so carefully been screened. When the King materializes immediately thereafter, the boy is scared by his act of defiance. After reassuring Gluck not to feel guilty for having cursed him, the dwarf gives vent to his own far more unencumbered irascibility: "Why didn't you come before," he demands, "instead of sending me those rascally brothers of yours, for me to have the trouble of turning into stones? Very hard stones they make too." When Gluck protests, horrified, "Oh dear me! . . . Have you really been so cruel?" the dwarf-king becomes "stern." His cruelty, he insists, befitted the crime of those who failed to heed "the cry of the weary and dying" (1:346; D, 64, 65).

IV

In an epilogue to *The King of the Golden River* that he decided not to print, Ruskin shifted from the earnest biblical cadences of the book's conclusion to the adoption of a more satirical, Thackerayan tone as the narrator now mocks the efforts by several "old people," fictitious adult commentators, to interpret the "mysterious" circumstances which led to the punishments of the Black Brothers and to Gluck's reward. At the heart of the story, this new speaker hints, lies a core of meaning that such grownup interpreters somehow cannot fathom. And yet the narrator provides his own clue to that core when he agrees with the general consensus that three appeals of "increasing strength" led to the doom of the older brothers while only appeals *"diminishing* in their claims" could bring about Gluck's ultimate reward (1:348; Ruskin's italics).

Diminution is, in *The King of the Golden River* as much as in *Alice's Adventures in Wonderland*, both an imaginative feature as well as a primary mode of defense against growth. Ruskin created his fantasy of "little Gluck" and the "little" supernatural allies who disable the boy's overgrown tormentors as a gift for the prepubescent Phemy Gray. Yet, as I have been suggesting, he also relied on the regressive form of the fairy tale in order to confront potentially disabling childhood conflicts he had never fully resolved in the process of growing up. As an only child, Ruskin saw himself as the weakest member of a tightly knit trinity formed by himself and his adoring parents. The security he derived from their total and unqualified support was both an asset and a liability. The strength of their backing helped to reassure him of his own election as a special and favored dweller in some paradisiacal "Treasure Valley." At the same time, however, he could not help regarding that very strength as a form of domination that accentuated, for him, his own Gluck-like debility and overdependence.

Ruskin's fairy tale thus explores a childhood wholly unlike that which he had experienced as the coddled child of Margaret and John James Ruskin. His early reading of *German Popular Tales* had peopled his fantasy life with a rich and variegated series of alternate identities. He could not only relocate himself as a Dummling spurned by parents yet rewarded by "fortunateness" but also could translate himself into figures who, even when maligned, abandoned, or deceived, might remain steadfast in their allegiances. The protagonist of "The Water of Life," still another youngest son of three, risks his own life to bring the sick king, his father, a potion "that he might drink and be healed."[20] The hero of "The King of the Golden Mountain," an only son, does not resent being given to a dwarf by the impoverished merchant father who wants to replenish his sagging fortunes. As victims of injustice, both of these figures resemble Gluck. If Gluck harbors no resentment toward his powerful brothers, the youths in Grimm remain all the more strongly attached to fathers whose powerlessness they pity—the sick king who mistakes his youngest son's deep love for a parricidal enmity and the imprudent merchant who cannot protect the only son he turns "adrift." Yet each of these dispossessed sons overcomes the obstacles placed in his way through a charity and self-reliance that are far more active than Gluck's.

If Gluck hesitantly feeds South West Wind and accidentally restores life to the frozen King, the protagonist of "The Water of Life" embraces the role of nurturer with great determination. Not only is he resolved to resurrect his dying father but he also manages, on his return, to feed three entire countries "laid waste by war and a dreadful famine" with a magical loaf of bread he has found, together with a sword, at the same spot where he obtained the vial with the Water of Life. His kindness knows no bounds. If Gluck accepts the dwarf-king's decision to turn Hans and Schwartz into stones, this hero pleads and pleads until a dwarf who has similarly immobilized his own older brothers agrees to release them, despite warning the young man about their "bad hearts." He is promptly betrayed by them when they take credit for his achievement and substitute a nearly fatal, "bitter sea-water" for the elixir he presents to his father as a token of his devotion. Only the proof of his earlier prowess—brought by emissaries from the countries the young man fed with his magical bread and liberated with his magical sword—and the steady devotion of a princess who refuses either of his brothers finally help convince the Lear-like patriarch that it was his youngest child who loved him best.

A potential victim also overcomes betrayal in "The King of the Golden Mountain." Through the agency of a powerful ring, the deserted son proudly returns to his merchant-father, bringing with him his wife, a princess, and their own seven-year-old son as tokens of his maturity. But, like the hero of "The Water of Life," this protagonist, too, is stripped of his accomplishments at the parental home to which he has come back. Deserted by his wife and ashamed to stay at his father's house, he must acquire new sources of power. Through his ingenuity, he deprives three gigantic brothers of an invisible cloak, seven-mile boots, and a magical sword which, like that in "The Water of Life," permits him to decapitate enemies "whenever the wearer gave the words 'Heads off !' "[21] Confronting his unfaithful wife and the suitors who have gathered at her palace, the returning Ulysses slays all of his rivals and once again reigns as King of the Golden Mountain. The Cruikshank drawing, quite possibly one of those illustrations that Ruskin diligently copied as a boy, depicts with gory realism the culmination of this fantasy of male omnipotence.

Both of these tales fulfill a child's need to assuage its guilt for desiring to feel itself stronger than its parents. And so, of course, does *The King of the Golden River*, with its adoption of elements found in each (there is even a "water of life" in "The King of the Golden Mountain"). Yet despite this similarity, Ruskin's tale remains far more tentative in its resolution. Its attempts to subdue a deep uneasiness over the conflict between strength and weakness remain, as I have been suggesting, essentially unreconciled. The trinity formed by Ruskin and his two strong parents is incarnated, at first, by the trinity formed by Gluck and the two brothers who exhibit to such an exaggerated degree the mercantile mode of thinking that Ruskin came to resent in his father. In a letter in which he reproached the wine merchant for an excessive concern with status, the son protested that as a child he had been encouraged to prefer high-placed "brutes" to the company of humbler folk "whose life is as pure as an archangel's."[22]

To vindicate Gluck's purity was an easier task for Ruskin than to endow his fictitious surrogate with a princess or a magical sword. By placing Gluck into a second male trinity created through the boy's association with his two "little" avengers Ruskin introduced the aggressive masculinity so much more directly enthroned in a tale such as "The King of the Golden Mountain." South West Wind Esquire represents the primal energies or "laws of nature" that Ruskin felt his parents might have harnessed to make "a man out of me" while in rugged Wales (35:96). Yet by reducing this figure and by rendering him as a grotesque, snout-faced intruder Ruskin also reveals his misgivings about adopting such raw powers. He refuses to create a giant such as the one whom the protagonist of "The King of the Golden Mountain" cleverly strips of his phallic sword. Still, though ridiculous, the "old gentleman" must act as a link between Ruskin and his own father.

As *The King of the Golden River* shows, Ruskin identified masculinity with an aggression he both courted and feared as being too "profane and rebellious"(35:35). Gluck thus must rely on a fellow-victim, the dwarf-king, to rid himself of his overpowering brothers. The final identity he obtains as a result is that of a matriarchal provider who lacks the masculine traits of his fellow-nurturer, the hero of "The Water of Life." No potent overspill but a mere "three drops of holy dew" convert Gluck into the harvester of the feminine Treasure Valley over which he presides, still unmarried, delicate, and pure. That Margaret Ruskin should have stressed her pleasure over the tale's outcome should hardly have been surprising.

In an important 1933 essay, "The Early Development of Conscience in the Child," Melanie Klein relied on her "numerous analyses of children of all ages" to propose that the "evil monsters out of myths and fairy-stories" that take such a hold on the child's imagination did not just stem, as even Freud had until then supposed, from primal fears of "being devoured, or cut up, or torn to pieces" or from "repressed impulses of aggression," but could also be attributed to the growing child's fully conscious censorship of its asocial and destructive feelings. She remarked: "I have no doubt from my own analytic observations that the real object behind those imaginary, terrifying figures are the child's own parents, and that those dreadful shapes in some way or other reflect the features of its father and mother, however distorted and fantastic the resemblance may be."[23] Her observation applies in interesting ways to *The King of the Golden River*, a fantasy which confirms Ruskin's own failure to resolve,much earlier in his development, issues at a stage of character-formation which Klein, in still another essay, calls the boy's "femininity-phase," and which, in her view, leads to a gradually channelled expression of "excessive aggression" that results from the anxious subjection to "the tyranny of a super-ego which devours, dismembers, and castrates and is formed from the image of father and mother alike."[24]

By feminizing "little Gluck" and by making him the impotent

recipient of the King's gift, Ruskin deflected an aggression that needed to be acknowledged more overtly in a parable concerned with the acquisition of a properly balanced male identity. Gluck thus most resembles, not the male protagonists of the Grimm märchen that Ruskin continued to hold out as "innocent"—because innocuous—models for growing children,[25] but rather the younger sister in oriental tales such as that of "The Golden Water" in *The Arabian Nights*, a story which he on one occasion covertly identified with his own *The King of the Golden River* and which he, in a sequel to *Praeterita*, professed to regard as "quite a favourite" that had exercised an "immense power over my own life."[26]

Ruskin's decision to write a fable about rewarded innocence has a significance that is both personal and cultural. By screening his child-protagonist from an adult reality portrayed as "cruel" and competitive, Ruskin hoped to proclaim that even as a young adult he could somehow stay unsullied by the acquisitive, mercantile world of his father—a male-dominated bourgeois existence that had, in effect, carefully nurtured him and provided him with the privileged education he had received. In his fairy tale, he tried out an alternative identity as Gluck, abused, orphaned, uneducated, yet favored still. But Gluck fails to grow. Instead, like the King frozen on the golden mug, he remains arrested in his aureate purity, merely shuttled out of Eden into the City of Experience and deposited back into his native paradise. Ruskin's later derogation of his tale for "nice children" was surely excessive; it fails to acknowledge the story's imaginative energies, soon recognized by other Victorian writers for children. And yet Ruskin correctly saw that, for all its emphasis on the fluidity of melted gold and flowing waters, his tale sadly bypasses the natural flow that metamorphoses the growing child into an adult.

After the manner of Wordsworth who held that both children and rustics were closer to "the essential passions of the heart" or Coleridge who insisted that the early reading of fairy tales habituated the mind to an organic "love of the great and the whole,"[27] Ruskin, as a latter-day Romantic, profoundly believed in, and zealously defended, the purity of a form that would preserve the "child's unquestioning innocence" (19:235). He thus resented the intrusion of an adult point of view in "the best stories recently written for the young" (19:233). His remark, made in 1868, suggests that he was possibly thinking of specific works by Thackeray, Carroll, and Mac-Donald, his immediate successors, whose work he seemed to underestimate as much as his own. For if Ruskin's eagerness to block out such an adult perspective leads him to make shrewd observations on the ways in which writers for children may adulterate their work by imposing alien values or a diction foreign to the child, his defensiveness also leads him to veer into improper extremes. His radical separation of innocence from experience denies the important interplay between stages which, in true Romantic fashion, he prefers to regard as absolute contraries. Whereas, in their own "best stories written for the young," Ruskin's Victorian successors soon tried to capitalize on that interplay by seeking out the common interests binding childhood and adult selves, he chose to insist on their incongruity. And his obsessive need to insist, in particular, on the "child's unquestioning innocence" led him to negate what more realistic observers of the child promptly recognized, namely, its own pressing hunger for the adult power that comes with adult experience.

Notes

1. *Praeterita* in *The Complete Works of John Ruskin*, ed. T. E. Cook and Alexander Wedderburn, 39 vols. (London: George Allen, 1903–12), 35:561–62. Unless otherwise noted, all references in the text are to this edition.

2. "Michael," lines 148–49.

3. "Thirst for Enchanted Views in Ruskin's *The King of the Golden River*," *Children's Literature* 8(1980):77–78. Filstrup's emphasis on the "aesthetic morality" of Ruskin's fairy tale is shared by George P. Landow in "And the World Became Strange: Realms of Literary Fancy," *Georgia Review* 33(Spring 1979):12–15.

4. To John James Ruskin, 17 December 1863, in *The Winnington Letters: John Ruskin's Correspondence with Margaret Alexis Bell and the Children at Winnington Hall*, ed. Van Akin Burd (Cambridge: Harvard Univ. Press, 1969), 459. The citations in the remainder of the paragraph are taken from pp.458–59.

5. *The King of the Golden River*, in *Works*, 1:347; the passage occurs on p. 67 of the Dover edition (New York: Dover, 1974), cited as "D" hereafter for the convenience of readers consulting this modern paperback.

6. To John Ruskin, 7 October 1841, in *The Ruskin Family Letters*, ed. Van Akin Burd, 2 vols. (Ithaca: Cornell Univ. Press, 1973), 2:695.

7. To John Ruskin, 9 October 1841, ibid. 700. In the previous paragraph, Ruskin's father to his twenty-two-year-old "boy": "*Eat slowly masticate well* especially minced Collops."

8. See, especially, Mary Lutyens, *The Ruskins and the Grays* (London: John Murray, 1972), and Jeffrey L. Spear, "Ruskin on His Marriage: the Acland Letter," *Times*

Literary Supplement, 10 February 1978, as well as the same author's *The Dreams of an English Eden: Ruskin and His Tradition in Social Criticism* (New York: Columbia Univ. Press, 1984), 54–64. For the most recent of the popularized accounts of the marriage, see Phyllis Rose, *Parallel Lives* (New York: Random House, 1983), 45–94.

9. Mary Lutyens, *Young Mrs. Ruskin in Venice: Her Picture of Society and Life with John Ruskin, 1849–1852* (New York: Vanguard Press, 1965) 8, 21; Ruskin, "Fairy Stories" (1868), *Works,* 19:236.

10. See James S. Dearden, *"The King of the Golden River:* A Bio-Bibliographical Study," in *Studies in Ruskin: Essays in Honor of Van Akin Burd,* ed. Robert E. Rhodes and Del Ivan Janik (Athens, Ohio: Ohio Univ. Press, 1982), 32–59.

11. Ruskin remembers how, "from the first syllable" in *Sketches by Boz,* Dickens became "altogether precious and admirable to my father and me" (35:303). Although Dickens had not yet begun to write his Christmas stories and Christmas books, there are affinities between *A Christmas Carol* and Ruskin's fairy tale that are briefly discussed in my introduction to *"A Christmas Carol" by Charles Dickens and Other Victorian Fairy Tales by John Ruskin, W. M. Thackeray, George MacDonald, and Jean Ingelow* (New York: Bantam Classics, 1983), vii–xvii.

12. "Thirst for Enchanted Views," 69, 71, 73–74.

13. The lifelong impact on Ruskin of Taylor's translation of the Grimm fairy tales is evident from his frequent use of individual stories as a frame of reference both in his published work and in his private letters. His allusions always assume that his readers possess his own intimate familiarity with the tales. Yet the impact of *German Popular Tales* on Ruskin was as visual as it was literary. In *Praeterita,* he recalled how he copied as a boy "Cruikshank's illustrations to Grimm, which I did with great, and to most people now incredible, exactness, a sheet of them being, by good hap, well preserved, done when I was between ten and eleven" (35:74–75). When Ruskin decided to reissue (albeit in larger print suited for child readers) the original 1823 and 1826 volumes of Taylor rather than to embark on a new Grimm collection, he also retained Cruikshank's designs, which he hailed in his preface as belonging "to the best period of Cruikshank's genius" (19:239). He regarded his preface, which he reprinted separately in 1885 under the title of "Fairy Stories," as one of his very own best pieces of prose.

14. Ruskin's choice of the young illustrator for the work he had written at the age of twenty-two was well premeditated. Doyle had succeeded Cruikshank (Ruskin's childhood favorite) as illustrator of a new translation of the Grimm stories, *The Fairy Ring,* five years earlier, in 1845. At the time, in a review in which he stressed the "child-like simplicity and wonder" which he held out as the "main charm" of all fairy tales, Thackeray had praised Doyle's illustrations by taking note of the artist's own youth and capacity for wonder *(William Makepeace Thackeray: Contributions to the "Morning Chronicle,"* ed. Gordon N. Ray [Urbana: Univ. of Illinois Press, 1966], 98). Doyle's only fault, according to Thackeray—a trait which Ruskin, however, would have regarded as a virtue—is an excessive "gentleness of disposition" which leads the artist to soften his drawings of hags and witches. When Doyle adopted a more satirical style in his later work, Ruskin became predictably cooler.

15. *Grimms' Fairy Tales Translated by Edgar Taylor and Illustrated by George Cruikshank,* reproduced in facsimile from the first English edition, 2 vols. (London: Scolar Press, 1979), 1:180. In the German version, Dummling's folly is more pointedly contrasted to the behavior of the older brothers, ironically called "klug" and "verständig"—that is, clever. For the German text of the tales I rely on *Grimms Märchen: Vollständige Ausgabe,* 2 vols. (Zürich: Manasse Verlag, n.d.).

16. *The Uses of Enchantment: The Meaning and Importance of Fairy Tales* (New York: Knopf, 1976), 73, 186.

17. *Grimms' Fairy Tales Translated by Edgar Taylor*, 1:86, 90.

18. The implausibility of a gardener's son becoming heir to the king, his master, stems from Taylor's excessive condensation of "Der Goldene Vogel." As elsewhere in his translations, he also greatly softens the fate of the older brothers. By converting "ergriffen und *hingerichtet*" into "seized and *punished*" (1:27), Taylor robs the story of its parallelism: in the German version, the "godless" brothers executed by their father are immediately replaced by the kindly fox, who, when granted his wish to be slaughtered, turns into the princess's own long-lost brother. He and the prince and their sister/wife thus form a new trinity: "Und nun fehlte nichts mehr zu ihrem *Glück*, solange sie lebten" (italics added).

19. Preface to the second edition of *Lyrical Ballads* (1800).

20. *Grimms' Fairy Tales Translated by Edgar Taylor*, 2:121.

21. Ibid., 1:176.

22. To John James Ruskin, 12 August 1862, in *Winnington Letters*, 370.

23. *Love, Guilt, and Reparation and Other Works* (New York: Dell, 1977), 249.

24. "Early Stages of the Oedipus Complex," ibid., 189, 190.

25. See, for instance, Letters 16 and 50 in *Fors Clavigera*. In the first of these, entitled "Gold Growing," Ruskin indulges in the wish that lawyer's clerks "were appointed to write down for us words really worth setting down—Nursery Songs, Grimm's Popular Stories, and the like"; the result, he maintains, would be "not, perhaps, a cheap literature; but at least an innocent one" (27:284). In the second, "Agnes's Book," he opposes books produced by secular and religious didacticists and upholds the narrower but purer store on which the child could draw if raised, "with instruments suited to her strength," in his ideal St. George's Company (28:266).

26. Even in that lengthy story, which Sir Richard Burton reprinted, heavily annotated, under the title of "The Two Sisters Who Envied Their Cadette," the Princess Perizadah is given, like Carroll's Alice or later Victorian heroines, a far more active role than that accorded to Gluck. For further links between "The Golden Water" and *The King of the Golden River*, see Spear, *The Dreams of an English Eden*, 52, 247*n*.

27. Preface to the second edition of *Lyrical Ballads* (1800); S. T. Coleridge to Thomas Poole, 16 October 1797.

Tests, Tasks, and Trials in the Grimms' Fairy Tales

Maria Tatar

In Shakespeare's *As You Like It*, Le Beau launches a speech with the words, "There comes an old man and his three sons—" only to be cut short by Celia's repartee, "I could match this beginning with an old tale."[1] Both Le Beau and Celia were no doubt aware that many old tales—most notably fairy tales—feature a man with his three sons. Shakespeare himself based the play in which these two characters match wits on the classical fairy tale plot in which a naive young man triumphs over his two older brothers.[2] In these tales, as in tales of an old woman and her daughters, there is essentially only one figure who stands at the center of events and who commands both our sympathy and attention: the youngest and the humblest in a trio of siblings.[3]

As numerous critics have pointed out, two radically different types of heroes grace the pages of the Grimms' collection of tales. The first is especially prominent: the dim-witted numbskull, the fatuous simpleton who despite all the odds succeeds in winning a kingdom and a bride. Generally the youngest of three sons, he does not seem seriously handicapped by his boundless naiveté. The second class of male protagonists comprises far more sophisticated fellows: these are the tricksters, knaves, and swindlers who triumph over their adversaries by outwitting them.[4] In theory the opposition of simple/clever or naive/cunning seems to serve as a useful guide for classifying fairy tale heroes. Yet in practice it is not always easy to determine whether a figure exhibits a low or high level of intelligence. What at first blush appears to be a perfectly straightforward choice is in the end fraught with complexities. The happy-go-lucky simpleton who appears to succeed without trying is not always as doltish as the first sentence of his tale would lead us to believe, even as the roguish trickster does not always live up to his reputation for shrewd reasoning.

Despite their jaunty artlessness and unadorned narrative style, fairy tales are not without ironic touches that subvert surface meanings. In particular, the epithets and predicates reserved for their protagonists often highlight utterly uncharacteristic traits. The eponymous heroine of "Clever Else" ranks high on the list of dull-witted characters; the tale "Hans in Luck" charts a steady decline in its hero's fortunes; and the courageous tailor in the tale of that title displays more bravado than bravery.[5] In the world of fairy tales, a simpleton can easily slip into the role of the cunning trickster; a humble miller's son can become a king; and a cowardly fool can emerge as a stout-hearted hero. Character traits display an astonishing lack of stability, shifting almost imperceptibly into their opposites as the tale unfolds. Bearing this in mind, let us take the measure of male protagonists in the Grimms' collection to determine what character traits they share and to assess the extent to which the plots of their adventures possess a degree of predictability.[6]

Identifying fairy tale heroes by name is in itself no mean feat. It is hardly a secret that the most celebrated characters in fairy tales are female. Cinderella, Snow White, Little Red Riding Hood, and Sleeping Beauty—these are the names that have left so vivid an imprint on childhood memories. With the exception of Hansel, who shares star billing with his sister, male protagonists are exceptionally unmemorable in name and deed.[7] Lacking the colorful descriptive sobriquets that accord their female counterparts a distinctive identity, these figures are presented as types and defined by their parentage (the miller's son), by their station in life (the prince), by their relation to siblings (the youngest brother), or by their intelligence (the simpleton).

If the female protagonists of fairy tales are inevitably as good as they are beautiful, their male counterparts generally appear to be as young and naive as they are stupid. Snow White's stepmother may be enraged by her stepdaughter's superior beauty, but the fathers of male heroes are eternally exasperated by the unrivalled obtuseness of their sons. To the question "Who is the stupidest of them all?" most fairy tale fathers would reply, "My youngest son." Yet that son is also the chosen son, the son who ultimately outdoes his older and wiser siblings. In an almost perverse fashion, fairy tales featuring male protagonists chart the success story of adolescents who do not even have the good sense to heed the instructions of the many helpers and donors who rush to their aid in an effort to avert minor catastrophes and disasters. "You don't really deserve my help," declares one such helper in frustration after his sage advice has been disregarded on no less than three occasions.[8]

In fairy tales the world over, the least likely to succeed paradoxically becomes the most likely to succeed. Merit rarely counts; luck seems to be everything. Aladdin, the prototype of the undeserving hero who succeeds in living happily ever after, begins his rise to wealth and power under less than auspicious circumstances. The introductory paragraphs of his tale give the lie to the view that classical fairy tales reward virtue and punish evil. "Once upon a time," so the story of "Aladdin and the Enchanted Lamp" begins, "there lived in a certain city of China an impoverished tailor who had a son called Aladdin. From his earliest years this Aladdin was a headstrong and incorrigible good-for-nothing."[9] When he grows older, he refuses to learn a trade and persists in his idle ways until his father, "grieving over the perverseness of his son," falls ill and dies. Yet this same Aladdin, who becomes ever more wayward after sending his father to the grave, ultimately inherits a sultan's throne. As one critic astutely points out, the story of Aladdin and his enchanted lamp exalts and glorifies a figure who stands as "one of the most undeserving characters imaginable."[10]

The many male simpletons of fairy tales may be unlikely to win prizes for intelligence and good behavior, but they are even less likely to earn awards for courage. Their stories chronicle perilous adventures, but they themselves remain both cowardly and passive. When summoned to discharge the first in a series of three tasks, the simpleton in the tale known as "The Queen Bee" (62) simply sits down and has a good cry. In "The Three Feathers" (63), a folkloric cousin of that same simpleton sits down and "feels sad" instead of rising to the challenges posed by his father. Fairy tale heroines have never stood as models of an enterprising spirit, but it is also not rare for fairy tale heroes to submit to their plights in a hopelessly passive fashion.

For all their shortcomings, the simpletons in the Grimms' fairy tales do possess one character trait that sets them apart from their fraternal rivals: compassion. That compassion, however, is not bestowed on kinsmen or even on compatriots; instead it is reserved for those natural allies and benefactors who inhabit the earth, the waters, and the sky.[11] Even before the simpleton embarks on his journey to foreign kingdoms or undertakes various tasks to liberate a princess, he must prove himself worthy of assistance from nature by displaying his compassion for wildlife. Of the various tests, tasks, and trials imposed on the hero, this first test figures as the most important, for it establishes the privileged status of the young simpleton. Once he displays the virtue of compassion—with its logical concomitant of humility—he can do no wrong, even when he violates interdictions, disregards warnings, and ignores instructions. This test of the hero's character serves the dual function of singling out the hero from his brothers and furnishing him with potential helpers for the tasks that lie ahead.

Two fairy tales from the Grimms' collection illustrate the extent to which compassion for fish, fowl, and other fauna is richly rewarded. In "The Queen Bee" (62), the youngest of three sons defends an ant hill, a bevy of ducks, and a beehive from the assaults of his mischievous brothers. "Leave the animals alone," he admonishes his elders on three occasions. Compassion pays off in the end, for he is the only one to escape being turned to stone—a punishment that perfectly suits the crimes of his callous siblings. With the help of his newly won allies, the simpleton son of the family discharges the three tasks spelled out for him on a stone slab. He gathers a thousand pearls that lie strewn about the forest; he fetches the bedroom key of a princess from the sea's depths; and he succeeds in identifying the youngest of three "completely identical" sisters. Or, to be more precise, the ants gather the pearls, the ducks fetch the key, and the bees identify the sister. Yet the simpleton is credited with disenchanting the palace in which the trio of princesses reside, and he thereby wins the hand of the youngest and earns the right to give the two other sisters in marriage to his brothers.

The hero of "The White Snake" (17), like the simpleton of "The Queen Bee," hardly lifts a finger to win his bride. Once he displays compassion for wildlife by coming to the rescue of three fish, a colony of ants, and three ravens, he joins the ranks of the chosen heroes who receive assistance from helpers as soon as they are charged with carrying out tasks. Although male fairy tale figures are generally celebrated for heroic exploits and feats, their greatest achievement rests on the successful passing of a character test.

Passing the preliminary test distinguishes the hero from his brothers and eliminates all other rivals in the general competition for the desired object or person destined in the end for the hero alone. The test singles out the hero, but it does not always suffice to make him singular. Compassion and humility, coupled with simplicity or even stupidity, do not, after all, represent an exceptional combination of character traits. But what the tale makes clear through this preliminary test is that compassion and humility are prerequisites for attaining the virtues associated with the hero's accomplishments in the course of his tale.[12] By enshrining compassion and humility, which are both acquired characteristics rather than innate traits, the fairy tale suggests to its audience that even the least talented of youths is equipped with the potential to rise to the top.

Once the hero has succeeded in passing the preliminary test, he is entitled to receive advice, assistance, or gifts from the beneficiaries of his compassionate acts and humble deeds. These grateful beneficiaries are quick to even out the balance sheets. As soon as the hero finds himself faced with an impossible task—emptying a lake with a perforated spoon, building and furnishing a castle overnight, devouring a mountain of bread in twenty-four hours—help is at hand. For every task that requires wisdom, courage, endurance, strength, or simply an appetite and thirst of gargantuan proportions, there is a helper—or a group of helpers—possessing the requisite attributes. And ultimately the achievements (and the attributes) of the helper redound to the hero, for he is credited with having drained the lake, built the castle, and consumed the bread.

Passing the preliminary test and carrying out the basic tasks are in themselves sufficient to secure a princess and her kingdom. Nonetheless, a number of fairy tales mount a third act in keeping with the ternary principle governing their plots.[13] This final trial which the hero must endure is motivated by the reappearance of the fraternal rivals who vexed the hero in his earlier, preheroic days. These rivals seize the earliest opportunity to pilfer the hero's riches, alienate him from his beloved, malign his good name, or banish him from the land. Yet they are no match for the hero, who deftly succeeds in outwitting them and in surviving their murderous assaults. Although the hero is rarely instrumental in carrying out the tasks imposed on him, he nevertheless acquires the attributes of his help-

ers and possesses the strength, courage, and wit needed to defeat his
rivals.

Just as the humble male protagonist matures and is elevated to a
higher station in life, so his blustering antagonists are demoted and
demeaned in the final, optional segment of the tale. If the hero
distinguishes himself from the start by showing mercy and compassion for animals, he remains singularly uncharitable when it comes
to dealing with human rivals. Even brothers are dispatched without
a moment's hesitation once their deceit comes to light. Treachery is
punished as swiftly and predictably as compassion is rewarded. This
third phase of the hero's career endows his story with the symmetry
and balance for which all tales strive. Like the first two acts, the final
act stages a contest between a brother and his two older, but morally
inferior, brothers. Both dramatic conflicts culminate in the rewarding of good will and the punishment of treachery; the last act simply
intensifies the reward (a princess and a kingdom) and the punishment (death). In doing so, it not only gives added moral resonance
but also a measure of finality to the tale. The hero has attained the
highest office in the land and also eliminated his every competitor.
For that office, he was singled out in the tale's first episode, made
singular in the tale's second part, and celebrated as the sole and
single heir to the throne in the tale's coda.

The trajectory of the hero's path leads him to the goal shared by
all fairy tales. In keeping with the fundamental law requiring the
reversal of conditions prevailing in its introductory paragraphs,
the fairy tale ends by enthroning the humble and enriching the
impoverished. The male heroes of fairy tales are humble in at least
one, and often in both, senses of the term. More often than not they
are low men on the totem pole in families of common origins. But
whether born to the crown or bred on a farm, they are also humble
in character: without this special quality they would fail to qualify for
the munificence of helpers and donors. Humility therefore seems to
be the badge of the fairy tale hero. And since humility, in one of its
shades of meaning, can inhere in members of any social class, both
princes and peasants are eligible to assume the role of hero.

Humility may be an innate characteristic of fairy tale heroes, but it
also comes to color the psychological makeup of fairy tale heroines.
Female protagonists are by nature just as humble as their male

counterparts, but they display that virtue in a strikingly different fashion. Fairy tales often highlight psychological characteristics by translating them into elements of plot, and in the case of female heroines, this proves especially true. Daughters of millers and daughters of kings alike are not merely designated as humble; they are actually humbled in the course of their stories. In fact, humbled is perhaps too mild a term to use for the many humiliations to which female protagonists must submit.

Since the majority of fairy tales end with marriage, it would seem logical to assume that a single tale suffices to illustrate the contrasting fates of male and female protagonists. Although there is often a happy couple at the end of a fairy tale, the fate of only one, central person is at stake as the tale unfolds. That pivotal figure stands so firmly rooted at the center of events that all other characters are defined solely by their relationship to him and thereby lack an autonomous sphere of action. In "Cinderella," for instance, even the bridegroom—for all the dashing chivalry attributed to him by Walt Disney and others—remains a colorless figure. The tale tells us nothing more about him than that he is the son of a king. Lacking a history, a story, and even a name, he is reduced to the mere function of prince-rescuer waiting in the wings for his cue. The brides in stories of male heroes fare little better. Relegated to subordinate roles, they too fail to engage our interest. Still, the Grimms' collection provides one noteworthy exception to the rule that only one character can occupy center stage in fairy tales. "The Goose Girl at the Well" (179) weaves together the fates of both partners in the marriage with which it concludes. To be sure, there are signs that the tale is not of one piece, that at some historical juncture it occurred to one teller of tales to fuse two separate and distinct plots.[14] Nonetheless those two plots conveniently dovetail to create a single narrative. The story of the humble count and the humbled princess who marries him offers an exemplary study in contrasts between the lot of males and females culminating in marriage ceremonies.

"The Goose Girl at the Well" commences with an account of the heroine's future bridegroom. Although this young man is handsome, rich, and noble, he must—like the most lowly fairy tale heroes—prove his mettle by displaying the virtues of compassion and humility. Without these twin virtues, his otherwise impeccable credentials would prove utterly worthless. And indeed, we learn that the young count is not only able to "feel compassion," but that he is also, despite his noble station in life, not too proud to translate compassion into action. Once he demonstrates his humility by easing the burdens of a feeble old hag shunned by everyone else, he earns a passport to luck and success. Like his many artlessly benevolent folkloric kinsmen, the count becomes the recipient of a gift that accords him a privileged status among potential suitors of a princess. The emerald etui he receives as a reward from the old hag ultimately leads him to his bride, a princess masquerading as a shepherdess.

Neither the count nor his rustic bride can boast humble origins. The unsightly girl tending geese at the beginning of the tale is not at all what she seems. At the well, she peels off her rural costume along with her rough skin to reveal that she is the daughter of a king. Despite her aristocratic origins, she too can in the end ascend to a higher position, for her fairy tale days have been spent in the most modest of circumstances. Unlike her groom, she did not voluntarily prove her innately humble nature but was pressed into assuming a humble position when her own father exiled her from the household. Like countless folkloric heroines, she suffers a humiliating fall from grace that reduces her from a princess to a peasant, from a privileged daughter to an impoverished menial. Fairy tale heroes receive gifts and assistance once they actively prove their compassion and humility; heroines, in contrast, become the beneficiaries of helpers and rescuers only after they have been abased and forced to learn humility.

There are many well-known tales of victimized female heroines who rise to or return to the ranks of royalty once they have been humbled and humiliated.[15] But no two tales spell out more explicitly that humiliation is a prerequisite to a happy ending than "King Thrushbeard" (52) and "The Sea-Hare" (191). The bride of King Thrushbeard furnishes the classic example of the heroine who earns a king and a crown as soon as straitened circumstances break her arrogance and pride. It is not enough that she curses the false pride that led to her downfall; her husband must also solemnly state: "All of this was done to crush your pride and to punish you for the haughty way in which you treated me." When King Thrushbeard generously offers to reinstate her to a royal position, she feels so deeply mortified that she declares herself unworthy to become his bride. The princess in "The Sea-Hare" also finds herself humbled by her prospective husband. Nonetheless, she takes the defeat in stride and declares to herself with more than a touch of satisfaction: "He is cleverer than you!" Male heroes demonstrate from the start a meekness and humility that qualify them for an ascent to wealth, the exercise of power, and happiness crowned by wedded bliss; their female counterparts undergo a process of humiliation and defeat that ends with a rapid rise in social status through marriage, but that also signals a loss of pride and the abdication of power.

In tales recounting the fortunes of the youngest of three sons, compassion and humility count among the hero's most prominent character traits—in part because they accord well with the status of the third-born in a family of three. In a number of tales, however, particularly those lacking preliminary tests, the heroes display virtually no trace of these attributes. Instead they possess a quality that is frequently defined in negative terms: they are "without fear." In accordance with the fairy tale's general tendency to avoid endowing its male protagonists with heroic traits, these figures cannot be described as bold, courageous, or intrepid. As one hero bluntly puts it, he has simply not yet learned the art of being afraid. To be sure, this specific character defect can stand the protagonist in good stead once he determines to seek his fortune in the world. The less fearful and the more foolhardy the hero, the more likely he is to rise to the challenge of the various tasks devised to foil the suitors of a princess. But heroic feats performed by a figure with a clear character defect—utter lack of fear—can also end by producing a comic effect. The hero rushes into perilous situations simply because he is so naive that he knows no better, and he escapes harm only because his naiveté completely disarms his opponents. He may succeed in accomplishing the tasks laid out for him, but there is more than a touch of vaudeville to his every move.

The burlesque effect produced by tales chronicling the deeds of fearless heroes is perhaps most pronounced in "The Fairy Tale of One Who Went Forth to Learn Fear" (4). The hero of that tale tries in vain to learn to be afraid, or more precisely, to shudder. Through one hair-raising episode after another he preserves his equanimity and coolly turns the tables on his would-be terrorizers. In one last desperate attempt to discover what it is to feel fear, he spends three nights warding off and ultimately exorcising the demons haunting a castle. His reward is the hand of a princess, but still he feels no fear. Only in his marriage bed does he finally learn to shudder, when his resourceful wife pulls off his covers and pours a bucket of live minnows on him. Bruno Bettelheim is surely right to read psychosexual implications into this final act of the fairy tale, particularly since the art of shuddering rather than the actual experience of fear constitutes the overt tale value. The hero's inability to feel fear ought not to be construed as a totally negative trait: Bettelheim asserts that "the hero of this story could not shudder due to repression of all sexual feelings."[16] But it is precisely the absence of the capacity to fear that enables the sprightly hero to withstand the horrors of the haunted castle and consequently to win the hand of his bride. Indeed, the inability to fear comes so close to courage in this tale that the protagonist begins to take on, for all his unflinching artlessness, heroic attributes. Unlike his humble and helpless kinsmen in classical fairy tales of three sons, he breezily accomplishes one task after another without resorting to aid from friendly foreign agents. As one critic has noted, "The more marvelous (or heroic) the hero, the less he is in need of the assistance of a helper."[17] Were it not for the comic resolution to the adventures of this fairy tale hero, it would seem entirely appropriate to place him in the class of sly heroes who live by their courage and wits.

In much the same way that fearlessness can shade into courage in fairy tales, naiveté can translate into cunning. Both processes become clear if we look at a tale known as "The Crystal Orb" (197). The hero of that story combines the attributes of humble heroes and fearless fools: he possesses the simplicity that goes hand-in-hand with his familial status as the youngest of three sons, and he has "a heart without fear." It is above all his foolishly dauntless spirit that gives him the audacity to line up as the twenty-fourth suitor to seek out an enchanted princess imprisoned in the Castle of the Golden Sun and to undertake her liberation. And it is solely his slow-wittedness that provides him with the means for arriving in the kingdom inhabited by the princess. In the course of his search for her castle, he encounters two giants engaged in a dispute over a magical hat. Generously offering to serve as referee in the quarrel, he proposes that the two giants run a race for the hat and heads down the road to post himself at the finish line. On the way to his station, he becomes ever more absorbed in thoughts of the princess, sighs deeply, utters the wish that he be transported to her castle, and finds himself at its gate. In fairy tales, brashness can clearly accomplish more than bravery; naiveté can be more effective than craft. The manifest lack of a virtue often translates into its possession. Just as Cinderella proves to be the fairest and the noblest of them all despite her shabby attire and her station at the hearth, so the simpleton of the family ultimately prevails over his older and wiser antagonists.

Since the class of tales featuring fearless heroes dispenses with the test of compassion, it also usually does away with the animal helpers who reward charity with good deeds. Instead the heroes of these tales must rely on their own mental and physical resources—however modest they may be. Those resources are put to the test in the opening paragraphs of the tale. Since the hero without fear displays a greater measure of self-reliance than his humble kinsmen, the plot of his adventures contains the potential for greater realism. Gone are the magical woodland helpers, counselors, and agents; in their place appear human agents in the form of brides, brothers, fathers of the bride, or even figures from a wider social milieu, such as peasants, millers, and hunters. The setting too shifts from an enchanted forest to a commonplace village or town. And the hero himself is often designated by the occupation he practices rather than by the general epithet of son, brother, or youth. These many realistic touches point to the close connection between tales of fearless, naive heroes (in which the classical ternary structure—test, task, trial—found in tales of humble heroes remains intact) and tales of tricksters (in which an open-ended episodic principle organizes the plot).[18] The trickster cycle, after all, gives us tinkers, tailors, soldiers, and youths of various callings who conspire to thwart their ubiquitous human opponents and to come out on top through ingenious ingenuousness.

While the generic term *trickster cycle* emphasizes only the cunning of the protagonists and, on the surface, establishes a contrast with tales of naive heroes, cunning and naiveté are, as we have seen, close synonyms in the lexicon of fairy tale values.[19] Indeed, the more hopelessly naive and obtuse the hero of a tale, the more likely it is that he will triumph over his adversaries and that his adventures will be crowned with success. "The Courageous Tailor," who decorates himself for having dispatched seven flies with one blow, seems to stand as the very incarnation of fatuous vanity. Yet his bravado endows him with the power to outwit giants, to accomplish the tasks posed by his bride's belligerent father, and to subdue a blueblooded wife who is repelled by the thought of a marriage below her own social station. In this tale, the line dividing naiveté from shrewdness and bravado from bravery has been effaced. The naive hero without fear is virtually indistinguishable from the trickster.

Fairy tales charting the adventures of male protagonists posit from the start one dominant character trait that establishes a well-defined identity for the hero even as it proclaims his membership in the class of heroic figures. The verbal tag attached to the character ("dummy," "the youngest of three sons," "blockhead") ensures that he is recognized as the central character of the narrative. But in the course of the hero's odyssey, his dominant character trait begins to shade into its opposite through a process that can be termed inversion. The humble hero weds a woman of royal blood; the brazen fool proves his mettle; and the naive simpleton outwits giants, ogres, and witches. Just as the least likely to succeed becomes the most likely to succeed, so the youth lacking a good pedigree, a stout heart, and a sharp wit is precisely the one who wins himself a princess and a kingdom.

Inversion of character traits is a common occurrence in fairy tales. A reversal of the conditions prevailing at the start is, after all, manifestly the goal of every tale. The folktale in general, as Max Lüthi has observed, has "a liking for all extremes, extreme contrasts in particular." Its characters, he further notes, are either beautiful or ugly, good or bad, poor or rich, industrious or lazy, and humble or noble.[20] Yet much as readers and critics insist on the fairy tale's low tolerance for ambiguity and stress the inflexibility of the attributes assigned to heroes and villains, the frequency with which inversion appears suggests that they overstate their case. Cinderella is beautiful at the ball and homely at the hearth; the youngest of three sons can be both a simpleton and a sage, a humble lad and a prince, a coward and a hero. Both character attributes and social conditions rapidly shift from one extreme to the other.

That character traits are not as standardized or programmed as would appear becomes evident if we analyze the fate of one character who does not figure prominently in the pantheon of fairy tale heroes. The eponymous protagonist of "Hans in Luck" (83) might, in fact, well be called an antihero. In the course of his travels, he outwits no one—instead he becomes the victim of numerous transparently fraudulent transactions. His fortunes, rather than rising, steadily decline. And at the end of his journey, he seems no wiser or more prosperous than he was at its beginning. Still, Hans is said to be lucky, and he feels himself to be among the happiest men on earth. The steps of Hans's journey to felicity are easy enough to retrace. After serving his master loyally and diligently for a period of seven years, Hans winds his way home with a weighty emolument: a chunk of gold the size of his head. Hans happily barters this monetary burden for a horse that will speed him on his way home. In the further course of his journey, he exchanges the horse for a cow, the cow for a pig, the pig for a goose, and the goose for a grindstone and rock. Even after these two worthless rocks land at the bottom of a well, leaving him nothing to show for his labors of seven years, Hans remains undaunted. He literally jumps for joy and praises God for liberating him from the burdens that slowed his journey homeward. Unencumbered by earthly possessions and with a light heart, Hans heads for his mother's home.

Conventional wisdom has it that the happy-go-lucky hero of this tale stands as the archetypal benighted fool. The very title of the tale, "Hans in Luck," is charged with irony: only a fool would delight in parting with his wages of seven years. Yet on closer inspection, it becomes clear that the story of Hans may also celebrate freedom from the burden of labor. On the last leg of his journey, Hans jettisons grindstone and rock—the tools of the trade that was to secure for him a steady flow of cash; at the outset, he rids himself of the gold with which his labor was compensated. In a stunning reversal of the value system espoused in fairy tales, Hans's story not only substitutes rags for riches but also supplants marriage to a princess in a foreign land with a return home to mother. In short, it ends where most tales begin. Instead of charting the course of an odyssey toward wealth and marriage, it depicts the stations of a journey toward poverty and dependence. But by freeing himself from the drudgery of labor, Hans displays a kind of wisdom that invalidates ironic readings of his tales's title. Bereft of material possessions yet rich in spirit, he turns his back on the world of commerce to embrace his mother.[21]

The story of lucky Hans dramatically demonstrates the impossibility of establishing a fixed set of character traits shared by male heroes. Like Hans, who is both foolish and wise, poor and rich, unfortunate and lucky, the heroes of numerous fairy tales possess attributes that imperceptibly shift into their opposites. All the same, it is clear that certain oppositions (humble/noble, naive/cunning, timid/courageous, compassionate/ruthless) are encoded on virtually every fairy tale with a male hero. It is, then, difficult to draw an inventory of immutable character traits largely because a single figure within a tale can—and usually does—possess one character trait and its opposite. But it is also equally difficult, for different reasons, to establish precise models for the plots of tales featuring male heroes. For every score of heroes who wed princesses and inherit kingdoms, there is one who returns home as an impoverished bachelor. For ten heroes who receive assistance and magical gifts by demonstrating compassion, there is one who acquires aid and magical objects through an act of violence. For every animal bridegroom who is released from a curse through the love and devotion of a woman, there is one who is disenchanted by the callous treatment he receives at the hands of his bride. To be sure, there is a measure of predictability in these plots, but only if we bear in mind that every narrative norm established can be violated by its opposite. Thus the preliminary test of good character at the start of tales with ternary plot structure can be replaced by a demonstration of the hero's ruthlessness. The story of a hero dependent on magical helpers in carrying out appointed tasks can exist side by side with the tale of a hero who acts autonomously and takes on the characteristics of helpers.[22]

Recognizing and appreciating the fairy tales's instability—its penchant for moving from one extreme to another—is vital for understanding its characters, plots, and thematic orientation. Fairy tale figures have few fixed traits; they are totally re-formed once they reach the goals of their journeys, when they become endowed with the very qualities in which they were once found wanting. Male protagonists may adhere slavishly to the ground rules of heroic decorum, or they may break every rule in the book; either way, their stories end with the accession to a throne. And finally, the conditions prevailing at the start of tales are utterly reversed by the end. The fairy tale, in sum, knows no stable middle ground. Inversion of character traits, violation of narrative norms, and reversal of conditions are just a few of the ways in which it overturns notions of immutability and creates a fictional world in which the one constant value is change.

In this context, it is worth emphasizing the stark disparities between folkloric fantasies and social realities. The radical reversals that lift fairy tale heroes from humble circumstances to a royal station in life were unknown during the ages in which fairy tales developed and flourished, but they undeniably correspond to childhood fantasies of past ages and of our own day. If in real life the youngest of three sons rarely had the wherewithal to succeed in life or to transcend his station, fairy tales held out the promise that humility and other virtues might well outweigh the benefits of an inheritance. But beyond offering consolation to underprivileged sons who lived in an era when primogeniture was custom or law, fairy tales more generally respond to the insecurities of every child. Even the eldest child is likely to perceive himself as the least gifted or least favored among his siblings and can thereby readily identify with simpleton heroes. Although specific social realities may have colored fine points of detail in tales featuring a man and his three sons, psychological realities of a more fundamental nature seem to have given rise to the general plot structure of those tales.

If fairy tales enact psychological truths, then it would be logical to expect from them some insights into the mental life or moral climate of a culture. Robert Darnton has observed that the trickster figure is especially prevalent in French folklore and literature.[23] By contrast, the simpleton or (to use a more flattering term) the guileless youth figures prominently in the Grimms' collection but also in such hallowed German literary vehicles as the *Bildungsroman*. These differences between the folkloric heroes of the two cultures

are, however, more apparent than real, for the roguish Gallic trickster and his naive Teutonic counterpart have more in common
than one would suspect. Even the names most frequently bestowed
in the Grimm's collection on the two types ("Dummling" and "Daum-
ling") suggest that they are kindred spirits. Both the simpleton and
the trickster ultimately make good by outwitting or outdoing their
seemingly superior adversaries. Still, Darnton's observations, even
when crudely reduced to the view that the French celebrate cleverness and audacity while the Germans enshrine naiveté and guile-
lessness, ring true after a fashion.

Fairy tales artfully weave realistic details, cultural values, and
psychological truths into a single narrative strand. While the realistic
details and cultural values may vary from one epoch to another and
from one geographical entity to another, the core of psychological
truths that generate the tales' plots remains remarkably stable and
endows all fairy tales with a special charm and magic.

Notes

1. *As You Like It*, I. ii. 111–12.

2. Helen Gardner, "As You Like It," in *More Talking of Shakespeare*, ed. John
Garrett (London: Longmans, 1959), 17–32.

3. According to Axel Olrik, the last item in a series of three always carries the
greatest weight in fairy tales. See "Epische Gesetze der Volksdichtung," *Zeitschrift für
deutsches Altertum* 51 (1909):1–12.

4. See especially Vincent Brun, "The German Fairy Tale," *Menorah Journal* 27
(1939):147–55, and Louis L. Snyder, "Cultural Nationalism: The Grimm Brothers'
Fairy Tales," in *Roots of German Nationalism* (Bloomington: Indiana Univ. Press,
1978), 35–54.

5. Constance Spender makes this point. See "Grimms' Fairy Tales," *The Contemporary Review* 102 (1912):673–79.

6. The stereotypical view of fairy tale heroines and heroes is succinctly expressed
by Simone de Beauvoir: "Woman is the Sleeping Beauty, Cinderella, Snow-White,
she who receives and submits. In song and story the young man is seen departing
adventurously in search of woman; he slays the dragon, he battles giants" (*The Second
Sex*, trans. H. M. Parshley [New York: Bantam, 1952], 271–72). More recently, Jack
Zipes has stated that the male protagonist of the Grimms' tales "leaves home to
reconstitute home." Along the way he learns to be "active, competitive, handsome,
industrious, cunning, acquisitive." See *Fairy Tales and the Art of Subversion: The Classical
Genre for Children and the Process of Civilization* (New York: Wildman Press, 1983), 57.

7. Max Lüthi asserts that the disproportionately large number of female heroines
in fairy tales can be traced to the prominent role played by women in shaping the
plots. See "The Fairy-Tale Hero," in *Once Upon a Time: On the Nature of Fairy Tales*,
trans. Lee Chadeayne and Paul Gottwald (Bloomington: Indiana Univ. Press, 1976),
135–46.

8. These are the words of the fox in the Grimms' version of "The Golden Bird" (57). Numbers in parentheses refer hereafter to the tale numbers of the Grimm collection.

9. *Tales from the Thousand and One Nights*, trans. N. J. Dawood (Harmondsworth: Penguin, 1973), 165.

10. Robert Crossley, "Pure and Applied Fantasy, or From Faerie to Utopia," in *The Aesthetics of Fantasy Literature and Art*, ed. Roger C. Schlobin (Notre Dame, Indiana: Univ. of Notre Dame Press, 1982), 176–91.

11. On the ethnographic significance of animals in fairy tales, see Lutz Röhrich, "Mensch und Tier im Märchen," *Schweizerisches Archiv für Volkskunde* 49 (1953):165–93.

12. Eugen Weber finds that the celebration of compassion in fairy tales reflects the rareness of that virtue during the age in which the tales flourished: "Kindness, selflessness is the greatest virtue (perhaps because there is so little to give, perhaps precisely because it is so rare)." See "Fairies and Hard Facts: The Reality of Folktales," *Journal of the History of Ideas* 42 (1981):93–113.

13. On the three phases of action in classical fairy tales, see E. Meletinsky, S. Nekludov, E. Novik, and D. Segal, "Problems of the Structural Analysis of Fairytales," in *Soviet Structuralist Folkloristics*, ed. P. Maranda (The Hague: Mouton, 1974), 73–139. The authors divide the action of fairy tales into a preliminary test, a basic test, and an additional test.

14. Note the use in the tale of such heavy-handed transitions as "Aber ich muss wieder von dem König und der Königin erzählen, die mit dem Grafen ausgezogen waren." On the presence of a single, sharply defined plot in classical fairy tales, see Max Lüthi, *The European Folktale: Form and Nature*, trans. John D. Niles (Philadelphia: Institute for the Study of Human Issues, 1982), 34. Lüthi uses the term *Einsträngigkeit* (single-strandedness) to designate the absence of digressive plot lines in fairy tales. *Einsträngigkeit* is the term that Walter A. Berendsohn also uses to characterize the fairy tale's single-track plot structure in *Grundformen volkstümlicher Erzählkunst in den Kinder- und Hausmärchen der Brüder Grimm: Ein stilkritischer Versuch* (Hamburg: W. Gente, 1921), 33.

15. On abasement as "a prelude to and precondition of *affiliation*" in "Cinderella," see Madonna Kolbenschlag, *Kiss Sleeping Beauty Good-Bye: Breaking the Spell of Feminine Myths and Models* (New York: Doubleday, 1979), 72.

16. Bruno Bettelheim, *The Uses of Enchantment: The Meaning and Importance of Fairy Tales* (New York: Random House, Vintage Books, 1977), 281.

17. Meletinsky, "Problems of the Structural Analysis of Fairytales," 134.

18. Variants of the tale of the courageous tailor demonstrate that a single theme can lend itself to two different types of narratives: a tale that focuses on the tasks required to win the hand of a princess and a tale that focuses on the pranks played by a trickster. See the seven variants of "Das tapfere Schneiderlein" in Leander Petzoldt, *Volksmärchen mit Materialien* (Stuttgart: Ernst Klett, 1982), 42–72.

19. Stith Thompson emphasizes the ambiguous nature of the trickster's intellect: "The adventures of the Trickster, even when considered by themselves, are inconsistent. Part are the result of his stupidity, and about an equal number show him overcoming his enemies through cleverness." See *The Folktale* (1946; rpt. Berkeley: Univ. of California Press, 1977), 319. In *World Folktales: A Scribner Resource Collection* (New York: Charles Scribner's Sons, 1980), Atelia Clarkson and Gilbert B. Cross confirm the ambiguity when they point out that "the most incongruous feature of the American Indian trickster is his tendency to become a dupe or play the buffoon even though he was the wily, clever trickster in a story told the day before" (285).

20. Lüthi, *European Folktale*, 34–35.

21. For a reading of the story along similar lines, see Roderick McGillis, "Criticism in the Woods: Fairy Tales as Poetry," *Children's Literature Association Quarterly* 7 (1982):2–8.

22. As Vladimir Propp puts it, "When a helper is absent from a tale, this quality is transferred to the hero." See *Morphology of the Folktale*, trans. Laurence Scott (Austin: Univ. of Texas Press, 1968), 83.

23. Robert Darnton, *The Great Cat Massacre and Other Episodes in French Cultural History* (New York: Basic Books, 1984), 9–72.

Iconographic Continuity in Illustrations of "The Goosegirl"

Ruth B. Bottigheimer

The Tale (Grimm No. 89)

Once upon a time there was a queen, whose daughter was to marry a prince in a faraway land. She gathered a rich dowry and gave it to her daughter together with a handkerchief with three drops of her own blood. Then the princess—riding her speaking horse, Falada—set off with her maid. The maid soon became haughty and refused to serve her mistress, making her fetch her own water. Witnessing the princess's humbling, the handkerchief twice intoned:

> Ah, Heaven! If this your mother knew,
> Her heart would break in two.

When the handkerchief fell into the stream, the maid knew that the princess, now weak and powerless, had lost her royal prerogative. Compelled to change places and sworn to silence, the princess was sent off with the gooseboy, Conrad, to herd geese, while the faithless maid married the prince and ordered Falada beheaded. But the goosegirl had Falada's head nailed up in the gateway through which she passed every day, and there she greeted him:

> Alas, Falada, hanging there

to which he replied:

> Alas, young Queen, how ill you fare!
> If this your mother knew,
> Her heart would break in two.

Conrad, captivated by her beauty, tried again and again to snatch a lock of her long golden hair, but each time he tried, she invoked the wind:

> Blow, blow, thou gentle wind, I say.
> Blow Conrad's little hat away,

49

And make him chase it here and there,
Until I have braided all my hair
And bound it up again.

Fretting about the goosegirl's daily exchanges with Falada and his
own hat-chasing, Conrad complained to the prince's father, the old
king, who followed them the next day and saw and heard everything. Because of her oath to the maid to tell no one at the royal court
about their reversal during the journey, the goosegirl could not
explain herself; but the wise old king led her to an old oven, to which
she told her tale while he hovered nearby. He then arrayed the
goosegirl in royal robes and took her to a great banquet, where the
false bride sat with her royal husband. Not recognizing her former
mistress, she was asked what punishment should be meted out to a
person who had usurped her mistress's position. Naming a dreadful
sentence, she was immediately executed according to its terms. But
the true bride and her husband reigned over their kingdom in peace
and happiness.[1]

I

In diction, theme, and motif this tale stands out from most of the
Household Tales. It is one of the few which opens, "Once upon a time
there was an old queen . . ." The figure alluded to in the opening
lines of these stories is usually a male, whether or not he appears and
functions subsequently in the tale. Moreover, this tale is among the
very few of the Grimms' tales in which the magic powers of a female
character have withstood conversion into the malevolent abilities of
a witch-figure. Neither the queen with her handkerchief nor the
princess with her incantations bears the slightest trace of the godless
sorcery associated with witch-figures in the *Household Tales*.

In the recurring verses with their archaic vocabulary—the horse's
name, Falada, and *geschnatzt*, the medieval Germanic word for
"braided"—we recognize the keystone of the tale's structure.
Wilhelm Grimm himself composed many of the verses sprinkled
throughout the *Household Tales* to lend them a more folkloric air; but
the verses in "The Goosegirl" appear in very similar form in many
variants of the tale, attesting to their antiquity. Removing or altering
the verses' content would free the teller to initiate change in other

aspects of the tale, but as long as these verses remain intact, the tale itself retains its traditional form and resists change.[2]

This centuries-old thematic and lexical invariance is all the more surprising when contrasted with the fluidity of structure and plot elements in the past four hundred years, perceptible in familiar tales such as "Sleeping Beauty," "Cinderella," and "Little Red Riding Hood," which historically lacked stabilizing verses or incantations.[3] Cinderella, for example, unites the following traditional folk motifs: wicked stepsisters, impoverished beauty, supernatural assistance, a tiny shoe, and a brilliant marriage. These can be and have been shifted in relation to one another so that different tellings result in varying thematic emphasis. The three verses in "Cinderella," each repeated two or three times, vary significantly from version to version, suggesting that these verses ornament and sum up the text rather than anchor and determine it, as in "The Goosegirl," where the presence of recurring verses appears to be responsible for the tale's structural and thematic continuity over the course of many centuries.

The same stability is evident in the history of the illustration of the tale. We might expect great variety in the "text visualized," since dramatic moments and sensuous images abound: the gleaming gold and glorious linens of the dowry treasure; the queen cutting her finger; the three drops of blood on the handkerchief; the princess taking sorrowful leave of her mother; the princess quenching her thirst, while the maid haughtily refuses to assist her; the loss of the talismanic speaking handkerchief; the forced oath taken by the princess to tell no one at the royal court; their arrival at the court; the knacker cutting off Falada's head and nailing it inside the gateway; the princess speaking with the horse's head; the princess combing out her hair as she invokes the wind; the old king watching and listening; the princess opening her heart to the iron oven; the feast at which the princess appears in royal glory; the false bride revealed; the ghastly punishment of the false bride.

Each of these images marks a critical stage in the dramatic development of the tale, yet the illustration of the tale has solidified around the two narrative moments defined by the verses spoken by the goosegirl and by Falada.[4]

In collections of the Grimms' tales containing more than one tale, the pattern of ornamenting each tale with a single woodcut, copper-plate, or lithograph predominates. It was undoubtedly the total cost of production which dictated the one-picture-per-tale pattern. In addition to the expense of printing several black-and-white or color illustrations, the artists' fees had to be taken into account. The name of a well-known illustrator on the dustjacket must have been thought to increase sales, for fairly frequent pirating and false attributions surface in nineteenth century editions of the Grimms' tales.

Illustrations perform various functions with reference to the text in which they are embedded. At the simplest level they decorate the text and dramatize the action or mise en scène. Illustrations can also interpret the text by portraying characters as dismayed or joyful, weeping or brave, moods which in the psychological flatness of most fairy tale plots take on great importance. Illustrations may even reformulate the text by supplying information different or absent from the text. For the reader who glances at the illustration and even more for the listener whose eyes linger on pictures while someone else reads, the power of pictures to recast the text into memorable images is formidable.

What sets the illustrations of "The Goosegirl" apart from other illustrated tales is the persistence of two "elaborated" images or image clusters, which artists have chosen for edition after edition over more than 150 years. The first of these two elaborated images consists of five elements—the goosegirl combing her hair, geese, wind, Conrad running, and his hat—while the second consists of only three—goosegirl passing through gateway, geese, and Falada's severed head. Each of these image constellations expresses a theme.[5] The first represents the goosegirl in her strength, conjuring up the forces of nature to do her bidding. Though Falada's ability to speak marks her powers, she could not prevent either her own displacement or the horse's beheading, and thus the second emphasizes her humbling.

The first elaborated image illustrates the verse that consists of three imperatives: adjuring the wind to blow, to take Conrad's hat away from him, and to make him chase it until the goosegirl has braided her hair. Her incantation reminds us that ancient beliefs associate royal station with power over nature, just as, inversely, her power over nature betokens her royal heritage.

The second image, that of the goosegirl passing through the gateway and speaking with the head of her horse, emphasizes her misery and powerlessness or, at the very least, her temporary loss of power. Falada, though decapitated, retains his ability to speak, one of many such partial fairy tale creatures who preserve certain abilities of the whole being. Yet unlike most animal helpers he cannot intervene directly on the goosegirl's behalf. His speech is the attenuated means of revealing the goosegirl's true identity, attenuated because he speaks only to her, not directly to a third person, and because his speech can only be effective if a third person overhears the plaint and acts upon it. All of this heightens the reader's awareness that the goosegirl is suffering great deprivation—"how ill you fare"—and that she is constrained from revealing her true nature, unless—as with Falada—a third person arranges to overhear her. This stands in stark contrast to the first image, where she acts directly on the world around her, effecting her own rescue from Conrad's unwanted attentions. Passing through the gateway can also be thought to represent the goosegirl's passage from the world in which she may not speak—the court where her maid holds sway and her intended husband does not recognize her—to the world of nature where her powers remain undiminished. Even though passage and transition inhere in this image, it remains an integral part of her powerlessness, because of her humble task and Falada's severed head.

The verse which elicits the second image grows out of two laments, "Alas, Falada, hanging there," followed by the mournful refrain:

> Alas, young Queen, how ill you fare!
> If this your mother knew,
> Her heart would break in two.

Here it is not the imperative but the counterfactual subjunctive that predominates in a construction that mirrors the disjunction in the goosegirl/queen's situation. On the one hand she is addressed as "young Queen," although her place as queen has been usurped by the faithless maid. And on the other hand, the nearly identical structure in the German of the two lines, "O du Falada, da du hangest," and "O du Jungfer Königin, da du gangest," differing principally in the name of the person addressed, causes the reader to associate the

deposed state of Falada with the goosegirl/queen. The horse has
been despoiled of his bodily life while retaining his magical ability to
speak, whereas the queen has been muted and deprived of her
sovereign life, while retaining her conjuring abilities.

The illustrator's choice of image points to an interpretation of the
goosegirl and of the entire tale: either strong despite her circumstances or suffering because of her circumstances.

II

The imagery of strength characterizes illustrations of "The Goosegirl" until the 1880s in England and the 1890s in Germany. Together George Cruikshank, one of the dominant illustrators of the
nineteenth century, and Ludwig Emil Grimm fixed the iconography
for several of the tales. In 1823 Edgar Taylor sent volume one of his
edition of *German Popular Stories*, illustrated by Cruikshank, to Wilhelm Grimm, who was inspired to commission his younger brother
Ludwig's illustrations for the Small Edition of 1825, fifty stories
chosen specifically for children in the hope of a commercial success
greater than that of the scholarly Large Editions of 1812–15 and
1819.

For "The Goosegirl" Ludwig Emil Grimm chose the scene of her
power, twin peaks in the background, Conrad's hat in the air, trees
bent in the wind, geese, the goosegirl, and her hair. The landscape is
free of buildings, reflecting the Grimms' collectively held conviction
that these tales represented an amalgam of innocence and nature
incompatible with urban life. The figure of Conrad himself—about
to try to pluck a strand of her hair—faces the goosegirl while the hat
appears to levitate above and behind his head.

In its curiously static qualities, Grimm's illustration differs from
Cruikshank's depiction of the same scene for volume two, which
appeared in 1826. Full of motion—the hat flying through the air,
Conrad rushing after it, his staff reaching in vain for it, the geese
honking and stretching their necks—this scene accentuates the relative serenity of the goosegirl, who sits, arms above her head, combing her "silvery locks." The foliage of a tree frames the foreground
and top edge, and two peaks behind a walled city define the horizon.
For Cruikshank, in whose nineteenth-century England walled towns
had long since disappeared, the image of a walled town would

Illustrator Ludwig Emil Grimm, *Kinder- und Hausmärchen gesammelt durch die Brüder Grimm* (Berlin: Reimer, 1825).

Illustrator George Cruikshank, *German Popular Stories*, trans. Edgar Taylor, 2 vols. (London: C. Baldwyn, 1823; London: Robins, 1826). This picture appears in volume 2, 1826.

connote the distant past, whereas the Grimms in Germany would have had lively youthful memories of towns surrounded by ramparts, many of which had been destroyed by Napoleon's invading armies less than twenty years before these illustrations were created. Thus in the one illustration the walled town connotes the distant past, while in the other the absence of the same walled town suggests a distant mythic era.

In spite of these differences, the many parallel details suggest that the 1825 German illustration by Grimm served as a prototype for Cruikshank's 1826 drawing. For more than twenty-five years, Ludwig Emil Grimm's illustrations accompanied the texts of the Small Edition, but immediately after Wilhelm's death, his Berlin publisher replaced Ludwig Emil's charming but static illustrations with those by Ludwig Pietsch.[6] Gone are the mountains and the depth of landscape; the whole exists now in a timeless foreground whose components have been reduced to the goosegirl combing her hair, the geese and the goslings, blowing wind, and Conrad chasing his hat. Like Ludwig Emil Grimm's drawings, Pietsch's enjoyed a long run—from 1858 to the 1870s.

With Wilhelm, Ludwig Emil, and Jacob's deaths within a few years of each other, there occurred a veritable explosion of editions of the *Household Tales* in Germany. The texts were nearly all based on the 1857 edition, the one generally regarded to represent Wilhelm's last thoughts on the text. The illustrators differed from publisher to publisher, but the components of the illustration for this one tale remained remarkably constant, with minor variations. Some artists included a few horses and a pollarded tree in an adjacent field as in P. Grot Johann and R. Leinweber's full-page illustration (1894).[7] In Hermann Vogel's visual quotation from Cruikshank, he returned a staff to Conrad's hand as he chased his flying hat (1894).[8] The elements remain the same in Otto Ubbelohde's 1907 drawing, with its impassive goosegirl and expressionless Conrad, but a terror-struck goose rushes at the viewer against a background of wind-driven clouds and bent trees.[9] When Max Slevogt in the 1920s elaborated on the image of the goosegirl and her hair, he raised her arms above and behind her head, lifting her bosom in a sensual depiction that reminds us of the enormous shift in publicly espoused values in Germany during the Weimar Republic.[10] But the same decade also saw confirmation of traditional values in illustrations with the same image set, which emphasized physical modesty (Karl Mühlmeister)[11] or ignored the goosegirl's physical outlines altogether (Elsa Dittmann).[12] The image survives during World War II, when Ubbelohde's and Grot Johann's drawings were republished in enormous printings, and when new illustrators joined the ranks, such as Lizzie Hoseus-Berlin with her updated, twentieth-century peasant-clad goosegirl.[13] In the postwar period the image persists, sometimes making the geese an auxiliary of the goosegirl's magic power, as in Nikolaus Plump's 1966 watercolor,[14] sometimes broken down into its components and spread out over several pages, as in Werner Klemke's 1967 drawings, which show Conrad's hat in triple image tumbling through the air on the pages preceding the picture of the goosegirl's streaming black hair being combed out.[15]

Since the content of these illustrations remains constant over so long a period, shifting styles in book illustration reveal themselves with startling clarity and deviations from this general pattern leap off the page.

III

Because a firmly established iconographic tradition existed from a very early point, we may assume that a departure from it represented a conscious choice on the part of the artist, especially in editions in which a single illustration appears in conjunction with the tale. A single illustration focuses the effect of the pictorial (as opposed to written) text on the reader/listener.[16] Remarkably, in nearly every instance where the artist has discarded the elaborated image of hair—geese—wind—Conrad—hat, he or she renders instead an aspect of the tale linked to the goosegirl's loss of power and her relative helplessness.

Paul Meyerheim seems to have been the first to amalgamate both images into one, the foreground dominated by the goosegirl braiding her hair, Conrad chasing his hat off the page in the right background, while in the left background, smaller but providing a backdrop, Falada's head hangs limply from the rough stone gateway. Meyerheim's other illustrations also manifest a similarly integrated imagery, which exposes a complex response by the illustrator to the texts of the *Household Tales*. For instance, in "Hansel and Gretel," he portrays an aged and impoverished witch whose house

Illustrator Paul Meyerheim, *Kinder- und Hausmärchen* (Gütersloh: Bertelsmann, 1893).

the two hungry children are blithely eating. The viewer senses that
the witch, too, is a victim.[17] Meyerheim's sensuously rendered flesh
tones and the plump unblemished outlines of his Cinderella, his
Snow White, and his Goosegirl contrast sharply with the blemishes,
shadows, and roughness of male arms and faces, marking a gender
awareness which might point toward images of female figures so
strongly formed in his own mind that showing the Goosegirl only in
her strength would be for him an impossibility.[18]

Heinrich Vogeler-Worpswede's illustration of "The Goosegirl"
marks a further development in the process of offering a more
complex image (1907). He adopted the traditional mode of nineteenth-century German broadsheets, the *Bilderbogen*, which often
offered a dominant image from a fairy tale together with several
other images within a single frame or construct. In Vogeler-Worpswede's illustration the viewer initially perceives the hair—geese—
wind—Conrad—hat image framed by a wide border and crowned
by a castle. Yet closer inspection shows diminutive figures riding
through the woods—the beginning of the princess's loss of power—
and in the lower right corner, the goosegirl passing through the
gateway. Also in the border, Falada's head, at which she is gazing, is
obscured by the corner of the large central illustration. The mixed
imagery of the border enters into the main illustration, for there we
see the goosegirl being watched by the old king, whose intervention
will provide the turning point in the tale. Thus our perception of the
goosegirl's strength is vitiated not only by the presence of the border
elements but by the relatively unusual presence of the old king in the
otherwise fixed iconography of hair—geese—wind—Conrad—hat,
for he is part of the narrative which revolves around the goosegirl's
deprivation of the power to reveal her identity, that is, to speak as a
queen at court. The attenuation of the goosegirl's mythic powers
also evident in the goosegirl's obscured face and bowed head, so
unlike her posture in other representations, parallels the social
strictures placed on female figures in other tales where restraint and
modesty characterize Vogeler-Worpswede's female figures. It must
be stressed that the thematic complexity of this illustration, as of
Meyerheim's, is unusual in the history of editions of Grimm.

The intellectual and artistic ferment evident in so much fin-
de-siècle painting, sculpture, and graphic work also emerges as a

Illustrator Heinrich Vogeler-Worpswede, *Kinder- und Hausmärchen* (Leipzig: Hesse und Becker, 1907).

restructuring of the dominant image with a consequent redefinition of the tale within that image. Thekla Brauer's 1895 illustration clearly develops in the same artistic climate. She pictures the maid humiliating the princess by refusing to fetch water from the stream for her, an act which ultimately leads to the princess's loss of the talismanic handkerchief given her by her mother.[19] When we turn to the other illustrations in this volume we find that their orientation is of a piece with this one. In "Our Lady's Child," the mute queen stands bound to the stake, flames burning high (a heightening of the text's information that the faggots have just *started* to burn), her dress falling from her shoulder in a complex of violence, eroticism, and Christianity, the Virgin Mary appearing in the distance, and a look of despair on the queen's face as she faces imminent death.[20] In "The Sleeping Beauty" the torso and legs of the supine figure are outlined, emphasizing her sexual vulnerability;[21] Snow White appears before us in her glass coffin;[22] and the maiden in "Rumpelstilzchen" is in despair just before the dwarf offers his help.[23] In other words, Thekla Brauer visualizes female figures as helpless, frequently unconscious objects in the power of other beings even when, in the course of the narrative development of a tale, the female figure outwits her adversary, is restored to her promised position, or triumphs in one way or another. In speculating about the reasons why one of the first prominent female illustrators should repeatedly emphasize female powerlessness, one could conclude that she, more so than her male colleagues, understood the painful nature and extent of social and personal constraint and restraint imposed upon women, which is represented in these illustrations.

A similar erotic victimization is stressed by Erich Kuithan, roughly contemporary with Thekla Brauer, whose intricately detailed illustrations reflect the influence of the Wiener Werkstätte. All of his four images emphasize the goosegirl's powerlessness.[24] First she kneels among ferns, drinking from the brook; then in a frame uniting text and illustration, the nude princess is forced to exchange clothes with the perfidious maid; in another page of integrated text and picture, Falada is trussed and hauled to his death as the knacker stands next to him, sharpened knife in hand, and the princess looks on hopelessly and helplessly; and finally, the goosegirl passes through the emblematic gateway. Unable to ignore the significant verse and the princess's extraordinary powers over the wind, Kuithan inserts a thumbnail-sized picture of the goosegirl combing her hair, but in the opposite corner Conrad watches, his hat firmly on his head, her gesture without consequence in the depicted world. The prurience and violence of "The Goosegirl" illustrations keep close company with Christianity in Kuithan's illustration of another tale, "Our Lady's Child."[25] There the viewer reexperiences the shock of the first showing of Manet's *Dejeuner sur l'herbe*, as a fully dressed prince carries off a mute, naked, nubile girl.

In the Swiss Jakob Ritzmann's spare line drawing for "The Goosegirl" (1927), Falada's head, nailed to the wooden framework of the gateway, its mouth open, speaks to the goosegirl while Conrad watches wonderingly. Like Thekla Brauer, Ritzmann stresses suffering and powerlessness in his other illustrations: Snow White lies in deathlike repose and Cinderella appears in filthy poverty. Ritzmann's images consistently represent the moment before the female protagonist's elevation, but regularly evoke instead a sense of degradation unmixed with glory.[26]

That Josef Hegenbarth should choose to illustrate the goosegirl raising her head to meet Falada's doleful gaze as the only illustration to the text comes as no surprise to those familiar with the unremitting violence of his other 1969 illustrations.[27] "Our Lady's Child" sits naked in the tree, approached by a prince with drawn dagger.[28] Cinderella is shown sleeping in an ashcan, while—inserted into the center of one page—her sister is shown slicing off a section of her toe to fit her foot into the slipper.[29] The moment when the wicked mother decapitates her stepson, full of horror and blood, appears in "The Juniper Tree."[30] Nastiness abounds, and the image of Falada is part and parcel of a violent view of the fairy tale world.

The work of Otto Ubbelohde occupies a special place in the illustration history not only of "The Goosegirl" but of the entire collection of the Grimms' tales. Appearing in 1907 during a resurgence of keen nationalistic historical awareness, his illustrations often evoke the crude woodcuts of German broadsheets in the late fifteenth and early sixteenth centuries. The formal balance of Ubbelohde's style (blank space versus surface detail and black versus white) corresponds to the equilibrium expressed in the content of his images. He depicts the narrative development of "The Goose-

The bold linearity of Ubbelohde's first and last illustrations underscores the relationship of power he depicts.

O WIND, BLOW CONRADS HAT AWAY,
AND MAKE HIM FOLLOW AS IT FLIES,
WHILE I WITH MY GOLD HAIR WILL PLAY
AND BIND IT UP IN SEEMLY WISE !

Crane's frame invites us to read the scene of the goosegirl's power through Falada's gateway, which is inscribed with her lowly station.

girl" with three images: the princess and her maid journeying to court, the goosegirl grieving beneath Falada's severed head, and the goosegirl conjuring the wind, a series of scenes which represent both the power and powerlessness of the goosegirl and which echo the tone set by Ubbelohde's predecessor, Otto Sickert, in a nineteenth-century fairytale broadsheet (undated, probably 1860s or 1870s).[31]

Ubbelohde's chief distinction, however, lies in the fact that the government of the Third Reich officially sanctioned his illustrations and printed and distributed facsimile editions in hundreds of thousands of copies throughout the Reich. Thus his neutral 1907 vision of the tale was revived by Nazi pedagogues in the 1930s and early 1940s, paradoxically providing a temporary visual caesura in the mounting violence of one illustrative tradition for this tale. When Ubbelohde's edition was rejected in Germany immediately after World War II, the two dominant illustrative traditions reemerged, and depictions of the goosegirl/queen in her powerlessness became more violent than ever.

IV

The chief illustrators of the Grimms' tales in Great Britain were George Cruikshank, Walter Crane, Edward Wehnert, and Arthur Rackham. Less important because of more limited distribution were Hester Sainsbury's and Mervyn Peake's illustrations. Although Cruikshank initiated the English tradition with his lively assertion of the goosegirl's powers, an emphasis on the Falada imagery and a corresponding deemphasis of the hair−geese−wind−Conrad−hat imagery emerges from an examination of later English illustrators. There seems to be a clear intention to weaken the image of a strong woman, evident in both the translations and the illustrations.

Walter Crane's 1882 illustrations for "The Goosegirl" (a headpiece, an initial, and a full-page rendering of Conrad chasing his hat as the goosegirl plaits her hair) incorporate reminders of her loss of royal power and prerogative.[32] The headpiece, above the tale's title, shows Conrad and the goosegirl driving the geese out to a day's pasturage, though without the gateway and Falada's head; the initial shows the goosegirl bowed in grief, hiding her face in her hands. He frames the full-page picture of her powers with a *trompe l'oeil* three-dimensional medallion of Falada's severed head between the words "goose" and "girl," linking image and name indissolubly in the reader's mind. Furthermore, the verse evoking the image of the goosegirl's powers,

> O wind, blow Conrad's hat away
> And make him follow as it flies,
> While I with my gold hair will play
> And bind it up in seemly wise

has been stripped of one of its imperatives ("Blow, blow, thou gentle wind"). The translator, Lucy Crane, has also transformed the goosegirl's golden hair into a symbol of self-absorption, while her dependence on social norms is declared by the insertion of the adjective "seemly."

Edward Wehnert, another nineteenth-century English illustrator, significantly diminishes the impression of the goosegirl's strength by reducing the number of elements present.[33] He shows Conrad chasing his hat but with no indication of the ultimate cause for the act, while his full-page illustration is reserved for the goosegirl passing through the gateway with Falada's head. The verse which has given rise to these illustrations also shows subtle shifts. Although the translation retains the three commands, it changes the import of the third to the wind. In the German, the wind directly causes Conrad to run at the goosegirl's command: "Lass ihn sich mitjagen." In this 1861 translation, the wind affects Conrad's actions only by implication:

> Blow Conrad's hat away;
> Its rolling do not stay
> Till I have combed my hair
> And tied it up behind.

Given this verbal separation of the two characters, the artist is justified in omitting the goosegirl combing her hair and the geese from the rendering of Conrad chasing his hat.

The link between translation and image seems to be confirmed by a 1906 edition, in which the verse restores Edgar Taylor's "silvery locks" of 1823 and the goosegirl's conjuration of the wind.

> Blow, breezes, blow!
> Let Curdken's hat go!
> Blow, breezes, blow!
> Let him after it go!
> O'er hills, dales, and rocks,
>   Away be it whirl'd,
> Till the silvery locks,
>   Are all combed and curl'd.[34]

Following this verse, R. Anning Bell's illustration contains all but the geese in the elements of the elaborated image of the goosegirl's strength. Not only is the emblem of her lowly status absent, but her arm is raised towards Conrad's sailing hat, signaling her queenly power over nature. Thus the power of the verse to anchor both text and illustration is once again demonstrated.

Until well into the twentieth century, pirating both text and illustrations figured prominently in the publishing world. Sometimes an illustration was simply lifted for use in another context; sometimes the artist's name bore a certain value in the bookselling business. In 1863, an edition purporting to contain Ludwig Emil Grimm's illustrations appeared on the market in England. This "Goosegirl," as compared with Grimm's, significantly diminishes the power associated with the depicted moment.[35]

The main figure, the goosegirl, surrounded by her geese, remains similar to the original in attitude and in her place in the overall pictorial composition. The background has altered, reducing to one the trees bending in the wind, but most significantly in replacing Conrad, the object of her powers, by the figure of the old king, who will mediate her return to power. This illustration, at first glance an instance of the goosegirl's power, actually carries the opposite message, the goosegirl in need of assistance. Indeed, the old king as helper ambiguously occupies the position of one of the threatening elders in the iconography of Susanna. Conrad is nowhere to be seen chasing his hat; we simply see a girl doing her hair, which she might as well be doing in front of a boudoir mirror, for there is no indication of the conjuring powers accompanying the act. This kind of image reformulates the text rather than summing it up or illustrating it.

Illustration "from design by Ludwig Grimm," *German Fairy Tales and Popular Stories, as told by Gammer Grethel*, trans. Edgar Taylor (London: Bohn, 1863).

With Arthur Rackham's first illustration of "The Goosegirl" (1909) reproduced by the thousands, we remain in the tradition of the goosegirl in her weakness. We see her emerging from the gateway, her innate beauty apparent despite her mean garments, preceded by her geese, while the shadow of a creature whose malevolence is revealed by its angularity, projecting nose, and pointing fingers, falls on the stone wall. Falada's head, necessary to this image, is barely visible. The goosegirl also stands in the shadows, about to step into the sunlight. By its composition, the picture is full of hope. That hope was realized in Rackham's next illustration for the tale, which appeared about ten years later.[36] In a composition of extraordinary grace, in which the goosegirl's hair provides the outlines for both the trees and the clouds, as well as framing Conrad's

Illustrator Arthur Rackham, *Fairy Tales of the Brothers Grimm*, trans. Mrs. Edgar Lucas (London: Constable, 1909).

Illustrator Arthur Rackham, *Snowdrop and Other Tales* (from *Grimm's Fairy Tales*), trans. Mrs. Edgar Lucas (London: Constable, 1920).

chase, Rackham restores to the goosegirl the powers absent so long from the main English illustration tradition for this tale.

Although differing radically in artistic terms—one could best characterize it as socialist realism—Hester Sainsbury's illustration done in a limited edition of 540 in 1930 retains in reduced form the elements of Rackham's jewel-like drawing.[37] Her thick-bodied, heavy-faced goosegirl belongs to no national tradition of beauty, but her powers surface with great clarity.

The passage of another fifteen years, however, and the intervention of a catastrophic war with a consequent reorientation of social values leads us to the final English illustration to be considered, Mervyn Peake's large-eyed, cute Falada, gazing down at a horrified goosegirl, her geese streaming through the gate, her powers apparently dissipated beyond recall.[38] It is hard to take this or any of his other illustrations of the Grimms' tales seriously. Snow White appears with a mane of hair out of all proportion to her actual size, as does Cinderella, the two differentiated only by hair color. And it is this undifferentiated femaleness, either doe-eyed or terrified, which characterizes the vapid powerless creatures he depicts. It represents a radical shift from the drawing that flowed from Cruikshank's pen some hundred and fifty years before to initiate a long and fruitful iconographic tradition in England.

Other European illustrated editions also seem to take their cue from the Cruikshank/Grimm model with some illuminating variations. A widely reproduced Spanish illustration by Angel in 1900 shows the elaborated image of goosegirl – hair – geese – wind – Conrad – hat, but with Conrad in the foreground and the goosegirl barely visible as the cause of the chase; it focuses on the object of the imperative rather than on the giver of the commands:

> "Viento, sal, llevate el sombrero de Conrado
> y hazle correr hasta que me haga la trenza."[39]

A roughly contemporaneous Icelandic version retains the usual foreground with goosegirl.[40]

To an astonishing extent the iconographic continuity of the illustrative tradition of this tale in Germany appears to rest upon the two verses quoted at the beginning of this article, verses which are also responsible for the tale's resistance to change during its oral and literary history. At times, subtle shifts in the English translations of the verses appear to have been sensed and magnified by the illustrators. Thus the verses may account not only for the selection of image but for variations in the treatment of the elaborated imagery of the goosegirl combing hair – wind – geese – Conrad – hat and the gateway – geese – Falada's severed head.

The many illustrators who consistently settled on one of two images have contributed to an iconographic stability for this tale that exactly parallels the two recurring verses in the tale, the basis for its textual stability. Most, if not all, of these illustrators must have been ignorant of the fact that they were illustrating an unusual text, one which preserved intact a positive view of female power over nature. Which image any given artist chose to realize appears to correlate well with his or her view of the fairy tale world and women's role within it, for instance, as active protagonist or as passive subject of other forces. How closely this view matches that of society at large is a question that social historians may wish to ponder.

Notes

1. Translations are taken with permission from the edition published by Pantheon of *The Complete Grimms' Fairy Tales* (New York: Random House, 1972). I have paraphrased the story itself.
2. This point is argued in Ruth B. Bottigheimer, "The Transformed Queen: A Search for the Origins of Negative Female Archetypes in Grimms' Fairy Tales," *Amsterdamer Beiträge* 10 (1980).
3. Although differing in detail from the seventeenth-century French version, these three as recorded by the Grimms owe far more to their French precursors than was generally recognized for much of the nineteenth and twentieth centuries. Heinz Rölleke works out persuasive reasons in *Nebeninschriften* (Bonn: Bouvier Verlag Herbert Grundmann, 1980).
4. Editions examined include those in the Library of Congress, the Widener Library and the Houghton Library at Harvard University, the Brüder Grimm-Archiv and -Museum in Kassel, the Graphic Arts Collection and the general collection at Princeton University, and individual copies from numerous American university collections. The illustrations for this chapter were chosen because they were important for the establishment of an iconographic tradition (Cruikshank, Grimm), because in continuing an iconographic tradition they are particularly beautiful (Vogeler-Worpswede, Rackham), and because they provide characteristic examples of how established patterns are varied (Meyerheim).
5. For an introduction to this methodology, see Erwin Panofsky, *Studies in Iconology* (New York: Oxford University Press, 1939), especially chapter 1.
6. *Kinder- und Hausmärchen* (Berlin: F. Düncker, 1858), opp. 234.
7. *Kinder- und Hausmärchen* (Volksausgabe) (Stuttgart: Deutsche Verlagsanstalt, 1894), 267.
8. *Kinder- und Hausmärchen* (Munich: Braun und Schneider, 1894), 213.
9. *Kinder- und Hausmärchen* (Leipzig: Turm, 1907), (2:137).
10. *Kinder- und Hausmärchen* (Tübingen: Rainer Wunderlich, 1976), drawing from 1920s, 196.
11. *Kinder- und Hausmärchen* (Reutlingen: Ensslin und Laublin, n.d.), 307.
12. *Kinder- und Hausmärchen* (Vienna: Carl Konegan, 1925), 30.
13. *Grimms Märchen: Ein Buch der Deutschen* (Berlin: Buchmeister, 1941), 224.
14. *Kinder- und Hausmärchen* (Vienna: Verlag für Jugend und Volk, 1966), 272–73.
15. *Die Kinder- und Hausmärchen der Brüder Grimm* (Munich: C. H. Beck, 1967), 278–80.
16. Rand J. Spiro, et al., *Theoretical Issues in Reading Comprehension* (Hillsdale, N.J.: Erlbaum, 1980) and Göte Klingberg, *Kinder- und Jugendliteraturforschung*, trans. Erich Pöch (Vienna: Böhlau, 1973).
17. *Kinder- und Hausmärchen* (Berlin: Ferd. Dümmler, 1883), opp. 232.
18. Ibid., 104, 176.
19. *Fünfzig Kinder- und Hausmärchen* (Leipzig: Otto Spamer, 1895), opp. 270.
20. Ibid., opp. 8.

21. Ibid., opp. 184.

22. Ibid., opp. 226.

23. Ibid., opp. 240.

24. *Kinder- und Hausmärchen* (Stuttgart: Franke, n.d.), unpaginated.

25. Ibid.

26. *Märchen der Brüder Grimm* (Zürich: Rascher Verlag, 1927), 273.

27. *Märchen der Brüder Grimm* (F. A. Herbig Verlagsbuchhandlung, 1969), opp. 329.

28. Ibid., opp. 24.

29. Ibid., opp. 99.

30. Ibid., opp. 168.

31. "Die Gänsemagd," no. 87 in a series published by Braun und Schneider in Munich at intervals during the later nineteenth century. It has been (poorly) reproduced in *Märchen Sagen und Abenteuergeschichten auf alten Bilderbogen neu erzählt*, ed. Jochen Jung (Munich: Heinz Moos, 1974), 63.

32. *Household Stories* (New York: Worthington, 1883) (reprint of an English edition), 20–21.

33. *Household Stories Collected by the Brothers Grimm* (London: Routledge, Warne and Routledge, 1861), 263.

34. *Household Tales* (London: J. R. Dent, 1906), 106. The translator bows to contemporary fashion in substituting "curls" for the archaic plaits of the Grimm version.

35. *Gammer Grethel's Fairy Tales* (London: De La More, 1902), 113.

36. *Grimm's Fairy Tales: Snowdrop and Other Tales* (London: Constable, 1920), opp. 96.

37. *Tales from the Brothers Grimm* (London: Etchells and McDonald, 1930), 61.

38. *Household Tales by the Brothers Grimm* (London: Eyre and Spottiswood, 1946), 143.

39. *Cuentos de Grimm* (Madrid: Saturnino, 1914), 14.

40. *Grimms aelinlyri* (Reykjavik: Bokaverzlun Sigurjonsdonssonar, 1922), 55.

Learning from Animals: Natural History for Children in the Eighteenth and Nineteenth Centuries

Harriet Ritvo

The first zoological book intended for English children, *A Description of Three Hundred Animals*, appeared in 1730. Published by Thomas Boreman, it was part of a mid-eighteenth century boom in juvenile literature, created by publishers rushing to cater to a market that had been virtually nonexistent before 1700. Because both the authors and the purchasers of children's books understood them primarily as educational tools, not as instruments of entertainment, it is not surprising that the natural world, especially animate nature, was quickly recognized as a source of useful information and instructive moral precepts.[1] By 1800, according to one bibliographer's count, at least fifty children's books about animals, vegetables, and minerals had been published.[2]

In the middle of the eighteenth century, knowledge about nature was accumulating rapidly. Natural history had become both a prestigious scientific discipline and a popular avocation.[3] An eager adult public awaited the dissemination of information collected by Enlightenment naturalists. Some had the training, patience, and money to appreciate such focused and elaborate treatments as William Borlase's *Natural History of Cornwall* (1758) or Thomas Pennant's *Arctic Zoology* (1784–87). But most awaited the popular distillations of such works. The versatile Oliver Goldsmith provided one of the most successful, an eight-volume compilation entitled *An History of the Earth and Animated Nature* (1774). He was plundered in his turn by several generations of literary naturalists eager to supply the popular demand, including many authors who targeted the growing juvenile audience.

Although natural history was a new literary genre in the eighteenth century, animals were hardly new literary subjects. They

Illustrations reproduced by permission of the Houghton Library, Harvard University.

figured prominently in Aesop's fables, which were frequently used as school texts in the sixteenth and seventeenth centuries. The fables, however, were not really about animals. As Thomas Bewick, a distinguished illustrator and publisher of animal books, explained in the preface to his 1818 edition of *The Fables of Aesop*, they "delineate the characters and passions of men under the semblance of Lions, Tigers, Wolves and Foxes."[4] Nevertheless, because the animals were supposed to bear some temperamental resemblance to the human characters they represented, the fables have always been perceived as animal stories as well as moral tales.

But fables exerted only an oblique influence on natural history writing. The impact of the bestiary tradition, which also had classical roots, was more direct and definitive. Bestiaries were illustrated catalogues or compendia of actual and fabulous animals. They can be regarded as forerunners of natural histories, sharing the same purpose—to describe the animal world—but adumbrating a different point of view. In Latin versions they were widely disseminated across Europe in the Middle Ages.[5]

The fruits of this tradition has been distilled for English readers early in the seventeenth century. Edward Topsell's massive, densely printed *The Historie of Foure-Footed Beastes* (based on Konrad von Gesner's five-volume *Historia Animalium*, which had been published half a century earlier) described each animal emblematically, detailing its "vertues (both naturall and medicinall)" and its "love and hate to Mankind."[6] The information, which was miscellaneously gathered from ancient authorities, modern travelers' tales, and unattributed hearsay, could better be characterized as lore than scientific data. Nevertheless, Topsell's collection exerted a strong influence on at least the form of natural history books well into the eighteenth century.

Like its manuscript predecessors, Topsell's *Historie* was intended for adults, but its bizarre stories and illustrations must also have been attractive to children. Perhaps on this account the authors of the first natural history books for children mined it especially heavily. In so doing, however, they transformed the traditional genre of the bestiary in ways that reflected the concerns of their own age.

Thomas Boreman's *A Description of Three Hundred Animals* has been recognized as the first animal book aimed at children, because the preface announced that it was intended to "introduce Children into a Habit of Reading."[7] Without this clue, it might have been difficult to tell. In many cases, the material presented in animal books written for children in the late eighteenth and early nineteenth centuries did not distinguish them from works designed for an adult audience. Small size often indicated a book intended for small readers. For example, *The Natural History of Four-footed Beasts*, published by Newbery in 1769, measured approximately $2\frac{3}{4}''$ by $4\frac{1}{8}''$ and had a tiny illustration (rather crude and unrealistic, with the animals sporting eerily human expressions) for each entry. T. Teltruth was the pseudonymous author, and the book was clearly meant for children. Yet the text showed no sign of special adaptation. The print was small, and the multipage entries included such oddly selected tidbits as that the flesh of the tiger "is white, tender, and well tasted" and that jackals "howl in a most disagreeable manner, not unlike the cries of many children of different ages mixed together."[8]

Some authors did adapt their material to a juvenile audience. For example, *A Pretty Book of Pictures for Little Masters and Misses, or Tommy Trip's History of Beasts and Birds*, which was first published around 1748 and reprinted through the eighteenth century, offered one-page descriptions of the animals, each introduced by a doggerel quatrain. The anonymous author culled the standard authorities carefully for information that children would find interesting, appealing, and comprehensible. Thus the baboon was evoked in vivid physical detail—rough skin, black hair, large teeth, and bright eyes—and its proclivities for fishing and mimicry illustrated within a brief paragraph.[9] Most authors, however, were more concerned with the baboon's moral than its physical character. Following Boreman, they spent several pages castigating baboons as ugly, surly, and disgusting, describing how troops of baboons attacked people. Throughout the eighteenth century, purchasers of children's books could choose between relatively materialistic and relatively moralistic approaches to the animal kingdom. *A Pretty Book of Pictures* and *The Natural History of Four-footed Beasts* coexisted for decades on the list of Newbery, the leading publisher of children's books.

Even as they catered to a distinctively eighteenth-century thirst for knowledge, these first children's natural history books recalled

Thomas Boreman did not encourage children to distinguish between real animals and imaginary creatures. They were described and illustrated with equal detail and seriousness, side by side.

their medieval roots. Although he claimed that his information was "extracted from the best authors," Boreman crammed *A Description of Three Hundred Animals* with legendary material. Along with the lion, bear, ox, and beaver appeared a host of mythical beasts. The entry on the unicorn acknowledged that it was "doubted of by many Writers," but no skepticism was expressed about the Lamia, with "Face and Breasts like a very beautiful Woman ... hinder Parts like a Goat's, its forelegs like a Bear's; its Body ... scaled all over," or the similarly patchwork "Manticora," "Bear-Ape," and "Fox-Ape."[10] Of the "Weesil," an animal native to Britain and familiar to most country people, Boreman reported that they were "said to ingender at the Ear, and bring forth their Young at the Mouth."[11]

Although Boreman's successors tended to borrow their information from more reliable sources, they nevertheless perpetuated the bestiary format. Animals were catalogued one by one, and each entry was introduced by an illustration, which was at least as important as the text in attracting an audience. In most cases, as in the bestiaries, the entries were randomly ordered, after an initial appearance by the king of beasts. Thomas Bewick's *A General History of Quadrupeds* (1790) was unusual in using, as had Goldsmith, a rough semblance of Linnaean categories—such as the horse kind, the hog kind, and the "sanguinary and unrelenting" cat kind.[12] More typical was *The British Museum; or Elegant Repository of Natural History*, by William Holloway and John Branch, which put wolves next to elephants and peccaries next to opossums.[13] The "guide to the zoo" was a nineteenth-century variation on this theme that presented the animals according to either layout of the zoo in question or the attractiveness of the different exhibits to visitors.[14]

Within this traditional format, however, the kind of information presented had changed significantly. Even Boreman's rather fantastic work appealed to the newly scientific temper of his age. The bestiaries had described animals as figures in human myths or allegories of human concerns. Boreman assumed that his readers were interested in quadrupeds for their own sake, just because they existed as a part of external nature. He asked not "What do they mean?" but "What are they like?" His entries, like those of most of his successors, focused on the animal's mode of life, physical appearance and abilities, temperament, moral character, and possible utility to man.

Because natural history was perceived to be intrinsically interesting to children, books about it were ideal didactic instruments. The educational theories of John Locke, at once more pragmatic and more humane than their predecessors, had redefined the function of early education. Books were to entice children to learn rather than to force them.[15] Thus Boreman suggested his subject matter was preferable to that ordinarily proffered by introductory readers, which was "such as tended rather to cloy than Entertain."[16] Or, as the advertisement for *The Natural History of Beasts* (1793), attributed to Stephen Jones, proclaimed, "The study of Natural History is equally useful and agreeable: entertaining while it instructs, it blends the most pleasing ideas with the most valuable discoveries."[17] This was especially important for middle-class children, who were the main audience for juvenile books, and whose parents, it is safe to assume, were eager for them to succeed in an aggressive commercial society.[18] By seducing children into frequent and careful reading, history books helped instill future habits of energetic and studious application.

If the study of nature in general was instructive, the study of the animal creation was more rewarding still. Quadrupeds or beasts, in particular, frequently received special attention. (Both terms were used in the eighteenth and nineteenth centuries as synonyms for "mammals," which was considered alarmingly pedantic by adults as well as children.)[19] Their greater similarity to man rendered them both more interesting than and intrinsically superior to other animals (Jones, ix). In addition, they were easier to observe and to interact with; unlike birds, fish, and reptiles, they occupied more or less the same space as man and, as one pragmatic author pointed out, "cannot easily avoid us."[20]

A scientific understanding of the animal kingdom was thought to enhance not only studious habits, but also a child's religious feeling; according to Holloway and Branch, "no other [human pursuit] excites such proper sentiments of the being and attributes of God" (1:iii). Two decades later, the anonymous author of *The Natural History of Domestic Animals* was more explicit about the way in which these effects were produced: "Whilst we observe, therefore, so many instances of the Almighty's wisdom and goodness, in these which are his creatures, let us humbly and gratefully acknowledge him as the source of all our happiness."[21] This connection persisted even after Darwin had put the scientific order of creation at odds with the religious one. As late as 1882, Arabella Buckley claimed that the purpose of her strongly evolutionary introduction to vertebrate biology, *The Winners in Life's Race*, was to "awaken in young minds a sense of the wonderful interweaving of life upon the earth, and a desire to trace out the ever-continuous action of the great Creator in the development of living beings."[22]

Understanding the order of creation would also encourage children to treat animals with kindness. Late eighteenth-century moralists were almost obsessively concerned with children's propensity to torture insects, birds, and small domestic animals, as much because it was a prognostication of adult behavior to fellow humans as on account of the animal suffering it caused. The main crusaders against this kind of cruelty were sentimental fabulists like Sarah Kirby Trimmer and Samuel Pratt.[23] Natural history writers shared the concern of the fabulist, but they addressed their readers' heads as well as their hearts. Thus in *The Rational Dame*, Eleanor Frere Fenn used the results of scientific observation to demonstrate that although inferior in rank to man, animals shared his ability to feel—that "man is the *lord*, but ought not to be the *tyrant* of the world."[24]

Thus the study of natural history was morally improving. But it did not separate children from more practical considerations. If benevolence and piety were intrinsically laudable, they were also associated with more tangible rewards. God's order itself was understood to be good because it benefited man. Fenn found in the animal world "the most evident appearances of the Divine Wisdom, Power, and Goodness," one example of which was "how wisely and mercifully it is ordained, that those creatures that afford us wholesome nourishment, are disposed to live with us, that we may live on them" (19, 22). The author of *The Animal Museum* appealed first to the highest moral authority in urging children to treat animals "as the property of our common Creator and Benefactor, with all the kindness their nature is capable of receiving." Then he suggested an additional motive: "This conduct is not only our duty, but our incentive; for all the animals domesticated by man or that come within the sphere of his operations are sensible of kindness, and but few are incapable of some return."[25]

In addition to direct moral lessons, children's books about animals were crammed with information that might also have desirable moral consequences. Thomas Varty's *Graphic Illustrations of Animals* consisted of a series of enormous colored cartoons, each devoted to a single animal or group of animals. That which displayed "The Bear and Fur Animals," for example, featured a central illustration of bears, beaver, lynx, and mink in a northern pine forest, flanked by smaller pictures of the animals transformed into such useful objects as winter coats, soldiers' hats, royal regalia, perfume, paintbrushes, and food (bears' tongues and hams were considered delicacies). Understanding how useful animals were—that they constituted "the

"The Bear and Fur Animals" in Thomas Varty's *Graphic Illustrations of Animals.*

life of trade and commerce, and the source of national wealth . . . the cement of human society"—would impress the mind of a child reader with the improving emotions of "gratitude, admiration, and love."[26]

While being uplifted, however, he would also be edified. According to Varty, the "graphic illustrations" would allow the child to form a just estimate of the "intrinsic value of each creature," independent of sentimental considerations such as beauty or amiability. The practical value of compilations that surveyed only the domestic animals, "which human perseverance has reclaimed from wildness and made subservient to the most useful purposes" (often the same compilations that stressed the importance of humane treatment most heavily), was considered so obvious as to require no further explanation. And even information about more exotic animals might come in handy. Thus the camel could substitute for the horse in a desert, as the goat could replace the sheep in harsh climates.[27]

Wild animals too might serve practical human purposes. They could be killed for their skins and horns, or for their flesh; they could be tamed as pets or as performers. A shrewd eye could recognize which wild animals were likely candidates for domestication. The zebra, for example, recommended itself as a carriage animal by its beauty and its similarity to the horse; in the view of one naturalist, "it seems formed to gratify the pride of man, and render him service." That it had not yet been tamed by the human inhabitants of its native savanna was ascribed to their lack of information and enterprise: they had "no other idea of the value of animals of the horse kind, but as they are good for food" (Holloway and Branch, 2:45–48). Well-instructed adventurers would neglect no such opportunity. Thus, leaning about animals could help children be good, and it could help them do well.

The most important lesson taught by animal books was less directly acknowledged by their authors. This was a lesson about the proper structure of human society. Quadrupeds occupied a special position in relation to man, a position symbolized but not completely described by their biological closeness. (This closeness, which was recognized long before Darwin, did not imply any evolutionary connection.) Both religion and experience taught that they had been created for human use; some kinds even seemed to seek, or at least to accept without protest, human companionship and exploitation. The attraction was reciprocal; as Mary Trimmer put it, quadrupeds were unlike "birds, fishes, serpents, reptiles, and insects" in the greater extent to which "their sagacity and constancy of affection excite our observation and regard." People and quadrupeds seemed to understand each other. In all, "their circumstances bear some analogy to our own" (4).

By learning about animals children could also learn about mankind. The animal kingdom, with man in his divinely ordained position at its apex, offered a compelling metaphor for the hierarchical human social order, in which the animals represented subordinate human groups. Embodying the lower classes as sheep and cattle validated the authority and responsibility exercised by their social superiors. Embodying the lower classes or alien groups as dangerous wild animals emphasized the need for their masters to exercise strict discipline and to defend against their depredations. These identifications were nowhere explicitly stated, but they constantly informed the language used to describe the various animals. In addition, they were implicit in the system of values that determined the moral judgment pronounced upon each beast.

What was explicitly stated was the inferiority of animals to man. For this reason the metaphorical hierarchy remained incomplete; animals never exemplified the best human types. But the sense of human dignity that barred animals from realizing, even figuratively, the highest human possibilities made them particularly appropriate representatives of the less admired ranks and propensities. If animals carried the message—if it were not completely clear where natural history ended and social history began—it might be easier to teach children unpalatable truths about the society they lived in.

The dividing line was reason, "the privilege of man." Although the behavior of some animals "often approaches to reason," according to the author of *Animal Sagacity*, it never crossed the impenetrable boundary; "men weigh consequences . . . animals perform their instinctive habits without foreseeing the result."[28] This distinction justified man's domination of animals, both pragmatically and in principal. According to Mary Trimmer, "While man is excelled in strength, courage, and almost every physical excellence, by some one or other of the animal creation, he is yet able, aided by intellect, to subject to his own uses the very powers, which, properly directed, might greatly injure, if not destroy him." And in this case, at least, might made right. The "subserviency" of quadrupeds "to our comforts and wants" was therefore "manifest" (M. Trimmer, 4, 9).

Even the sentimental fabulists were firm about the line separating man and beasts, a line which placed certain ineluctable limits on the obligation to be kind to them. It was, for example, permissible to exploit them economically in all the usual ways.[29] In no case, according to these earnest didacticists, should concern for animals eclipse concern for other human beings. Although during most of Sarah Kirby Trimmer's *Fabulous Histories*, the virtuous Mrs. Benson concentrated on teaching her children to be kind to rather humanized animals, she also included a salutary lesson on the dangers of excessive fondness. The foolish Mrs. Addis neglected her children while doting on her birds, squirrel, monkey, dog, and cat. Eventually the animals died, and her children turned out badly, leaving her to an old age of loneliness and regret.

The need to distinguish appeared most clearly when the resemblance was most striking. Descriptions of apes and monkeys often vacillated between admiring recital of their resemblances to man and firm denials of their closeness. Orangutans were said to walk erect, to build huts, to attack elephants with clubs, and to cover the bodies of their dead with leaves and branches. One status-conscious ape, bound for England by ship, expressed his sense of kinship with mankind by embracing the human passengers whenever possible and snubbing some monkeys who were also aboard. But, as the author of *The Animal Museum* noted, these similarities were "productive of . . . few advantages": orangutans could not talk or think (204–07).[30]

Monkeys illustrated the dissociation of physical and intellectual qualities still more satisfactorily. Despite occasional reports of their extraordinary sagacity—one Father Carli, a missionary, found the monkeys more tractable than the human residents of Angola—they were usually characterized as "mischievous" at best, "filthy" and "obscene" at worst.[31] Yet as T. Teltruth detailed in *The Natural History of Four-footed Beasts*, they resembled humans closely in the face, nostrils, ears, teeth, eyelashes, nipples, arms, hands, fingers, and fingernails. This similarity, however, turned out to be completely superficial. Teltruth reassured his readers that monkeys "if compared to some quadrupeds of the lower orders, will be found less cunning, and endowed with a smaller share of useful instinct" (72–73).

In the case of quadrupeds, zoology was destiny. Their inferior mental capacities dictated their subordination to man. As with people, subordination was routinely expressed in terms of servitude; natural history writers urged children to wonder what use the various beasts could be to them. Although some wild animals could be harvested, the most useful species were those that "man has subjected to his will and service" (*Animal Museum*, 1). So domestic animals, described in terms that suggested human domestics, provided the model by which other animals were judged: "They seem to have few other desires but such as man is willing to allow them. Humble, patient, resigned, and attentive, they fill up the duties of their station, ready for labour, and satisfied with subsistence" (Jones, ix). By a somewhat circular calculation, animal intelligence or sagacity was equated with virtue. Like the best human servants, the best animals understood their obligations and undertook them willingly; the worst were those that not only declined to serve but dared to challenge human supremacy.

For this reason, the most appreciated domestic animals were not the sheep, "the most useful of the smaller quadrupeds," or even the ox (the term used generically for cattle), whose "services to mankind are greater than those of sheep, for . . . they are employed . . . as beasts of draught and burden."[32] Occasionally these beasts might show some understanding of their special bond with mankind—for example, a ewe that led a girl to a stream where her lamb was drowning or a bull that showed gratitude to a man who saved him from lightning (*Animal Sagacity*, 28–30, 130–32). And it was pleasant (especially in contrast to "the savage monsters of the desert") "to contemplate an animal designed by providence for the peculiar benefit and advantage of mankind" (Holloway and Branch, 2:181). Nevertheless, cows, on the whole, were merely "gentle," "harmless," and "easily governed by Men," and sheep, though "affectionate," were "stupid";[33] both kinds were the equivalent of mindless drudges.

The services of animals able to understand their subordinate position and accept its implications were valued more highly. The horse was repeatedly acclaimed as "noble." In part this accolade reflected its physical magnificence, "more perfect and beautiful in its figure than any other animal" and "adapted by its form and size for strength and swiftness."[34] Even more worthy of admiration, however, was the fact that, although "in his carriage, he seems desirous of raising himself above the humble station assigned him in the creation," the horse willingly accepted human authority (Holloway and Branch, 1:145). "With kind treatment," according to one appreciative writer, it would "work till it is ready to die with fatigue."[35] Horses were affectionate creatures—there were many stories of their attachment to stablemates and farmyard animals of different species, as well as to people—and their understanding was, at least in the opinion of some admirers, "superior to that of any other animal."[36] This perspicuity produced "a fear of the human race, together with a certain consciousness of the services we can render them" (Jones, 7).

Even more eager and aware in accepting the bonds of servitude was the dog, the favorite species of almost all the writers who described the animal kingdom for children. Like the horse, its only competitor for the highest appreciation, the dog was said to combine extreme sagacity (the term regularly employed by those reluctant to assign "intelligence" to animals) with affection and obedience. According to The Natural History of Beasts, the dog was characterized by "affectionate humility . . . His only aim is to be serviceable; his only terror to displease" (Jones, 79). Stories of dogs who had preserved their masters' lives and property were so routine that it was worthwhile recounting only those in which the animal had displayed unusual devotion or shrewdnesss, such as when a ship's dog saved the whole crew by warning them that the hold was filling with water or an alert watchdog caught a human fellow servant stealing corn (Animal Sagacity, 55–56, 97–98). Such demonstrations made the dog "the most intelligent of all known quadrupeds"; in addition it was "the most capable of education."[37] It was "the only animal who always knows his master, and the friends of the family" (Fenn, 41). The dog's mental powers were such that "in the rude and uncultivated parts of the earth, he might, in point of intellect . . . be placed almost upon a footing with his master," yet it never showed dissatisfaction with its subordinate rank. It wanted nothing more than to be "the friend and humble companion of man" (Holloway and Branch, 1:31).

Some domestic animals had trouble meeting even the minimal standards of obedience set by sheep and cattle, let alone the high standards of cooperation set by the dog and the horse. Like disrespectful underlings, they did not adequately acknowledge the dominion of their superiors. The pig, for example, despite its incontestable value as a food animal—"ample recompense . . . for the care and expense bestowed on him"—was routinely castigated as stupid, filthy, and sordid, seeming "to delight in what is most offensive to other animals."[38] Pigs were defective in morality as well as in taste. Sows were accused of devouring their own young, which in turn scarcely recognized their mother (Fenn, 36). Naturally, they did not recognize their human caretakers. Even physically, they had been less responsive to the guiding hand of man; according to one writer, "The hog seems to be more imperfectly formed than the other animals we have rendered domestic around us" (Jones, 50).

Although the cat could not have been more different from the pig in its beauty and cleanliness, it had similarly resisted human efforts to mold it physically. Nor did it seem disposed to accept other forms of domination. It served man by hunting and thus did not depend on people for sustenance. It was suspected of having "only the appearance of attachment to its master," really either "dreading" him or "distrusting his kindness"; people feared that "their affection is more to the house, than to the persons who inhabit it."[39] It was considered faithless, deceitful, destructive, and cruel; it had "much less sense" than the dog, with which it was inevitably compared; and, in all, it was only "half tamed."[40] Its diminutive resemblance to the lioness and the tiger provoked many uneasy remarks.

If domestic animals symbolized appropriate and inappropriate relations between human masters and servants, the lessons to be drawn from wild animals were more limited. This may explain the surprising extent to which zoological popularizers neglected exotic wild animals in favor of familiar domestic beasts. For example, in Bewick's *General History of Quadrupeds*, which appealed to both children and adults, the briefest entries were less than a page long and the standard entry for a significant wild animal (one that was reason-

THE LONG-HORNED OR LANCASHIRE BREED   THE ORAN-OUTANG, OR WILD-
                                         MAN OF THE WOODS,

Thomas Bewick's *General History of Quadrupeds* was distinguished from many other
popular natural history books by its detailed and lifelike illustrations. As in the
text, Bewick lavished a disproportionate amount of attention on familiar domestic
animals.

ably well-known and about which some information was available)
was from five to nine pages. Yet thirteen pages were devoted to the
horse, fourteen to the ox, seventeen to the sheep, eleven to the goat,
eleven to the hog, and thirty-nine to the dog. The only wild animals
to receive comparable attention were the elephant and the squirrel,
which could be measured by the standards set by domestic animals.
The elephant had been semidomesticated in India. Although it did
not breed in captivity, it was easily tamed, in which condition it was
docile, mild, and an "important auxilliary to man" (*Animal Museum*,
162). As a result, it was also characterized as noble, friendly, cour-
teous, and sagacious.[41] Like elephants, squirrels were easily tamed.
Unlike elephants, they were frequently kept as pets by English
children, who might learn from them to be "neat, lively . . . and
provident" (Fenn, 53). In any case, their willingness to abandon
their "wild nature" for domesticity had made them "fine" animals,
"universally admired."[42]

The descriptions of many other wild animals were neutral in tone.
Writers were unable to muster much enthusiasm about the fact that

exotic animals like the raccoon and the capybara (an enormous rodent) were tameable or that the endless variety of deer and antelope encountered in every newly explored territory could all be eaten.[43] Some speculations showed a limited sympathy for strange creatures; for example, the author of *The Natural History of Animals* remarked of the sloth that "though one of the most unsightly of animals, it is, perhaps, far from being miserable."[44] For the most part, however, animals were not even important enough to merit a moral judgment unless they somehow influenced human experience. Thus the rhinoceros, the giraffe, the hippopotamus, the badger, and the camel were often dismissed as simply inoffensive.[45]

Beasts of prey were seldom dismissed in this way. Their carnivorous way of life disposed them to challenge man rather than to serve or flee him; they were rebels who refused to accept his divinely ordained dominance. Natural history books for children therefore tended to present them as both dangerous and depraved, like socially excluded or alien human groups who would not acknowledge the authority of their superiors. (Sometimes this analogy was made explicit, as when the author of *The Natural History of Beasts* noted that "in all countries where men are most barbarous, the animals are most cruel and fierce," meaning Africa) (Jones, xi). Even small creatures that could not directly defy human power were castigated for their predatory propensities. The weasel, for example, was "cruel, cowardly, and voracious" (Jones, 117). If such animals could not be controlled, they might have to be exterminated. "However much we detest all cruelty to the brute creation," intoned the author of *The Animal Museum*, the fox "is so destructive to the property of the farmer . . that his destruction is absolutely necessary" (93).

Large, powerful animals were, naturally enough, even more threatening, and, with one exception, they were described as unmitigatedly wicked. The exception was the lion, whose prestige as the king of beasts (lingering from the medieval bestiaries) was enhanced by its contemporary function as the emblem of British power. Although it was acknowledged to be dangerous and powerful, it was praised for its generosity and magnanimity in using its strength.[46] It attacked bravely, from the front, and never killed unless it was hungry. Most important, the lion respected man. It had learned to fear human power, and according to the African explorer Mungo

Park, whose travels were available in a special children's edition, it would "not offer violence to a human being, unless in a state of absolute starvation."[47] (At least not to Europeans—another naturalist, perhaps more learned but with less hands-on experience, opined that "the Lion prefers the flesh of a Hottentot to any other food.")[48]

The tiger was the reverse of the lion in every way, the epitome of what man had to fear from the animal kingdom. If the lion was the judicious king of beasts, the tiger was the evil, usurping despot. Its beauty cloaked "a ferocious and truly malignant disposition" (M. Trimmer, 17). Indeed, the tiger's appearance so misrepresented its character that Holloway and Branch warned their young audience that "providence bestows beauty upon so despicable an animal to prove, that when it is not attached to merit, it neither deserves to be estimated or prized" (29). It was cruel and greedy, interrupting a meal of one carcass to kill another animal or slaughtering an entire flock and leaving them dead in the field (*Animal Museum*, 173). Like the wolf and some other big cats, it was often called "cowardly," which apparently meant unwilling to face men with guns.[49] Nevertheless, it did not fear man and refused to respect him. The authors of *The British Museum* used the language of redemption to lament that "no discipline can correct the savage nature of the tiger, not any degree of kind treatment reclaim him" (Holloway and Branch, 1:22).

The ultimate index of the tiger's unregeneracy was its fondness for human flesh. Not only was it "ready to attack the human species," but it seemed actually "to prefer preying on the human race rather than on any other animals."[50] Tigers were deemed not to be alone in this predilection. They shared it with several other contemptible animals: wolves, who were characterized as "noxious," "savage," and "cruel" (also as afflicted with bad breath),[51] and the "ferocious," "insatiable," and "uncouth" polar bear.[52] Not so dangerous, but equally presumptuous, jackals and hyenas scavenged for human corpses.[53] But in a way the message was the same. Dead or alive, human flesh was forbidden fruit. These creatures were supposed to serve man's purposes, not appropriate him to theirs. To reverse this relationship was to rebel against the divine order, to commit sacrilege.

The writers of natural history books for children in the late eighteenth and early nineteenth centuries liked to dwell on man-eating. It loomed far larger in texts than its frequency as a behavior among those species really capable of it or its likelihood as a fate for members of their audience would have justified. But if reading about the animal kingdom was also a way for children to lean how their own society was organized, then man-eating offered a serious lesson as well as an armchair thrill. It provided a graphic and extreme illustration of the consequences that might follow any weakening of the social hierarchy, any diminution of respect and obedience on one side and of firmness and authority on the other.

This kind of juvenile natural history, in which the animals, presented one by one, provided an implicit commentary on human social norms, was frequently reformulated and republished until the middle of the nineteenth century. And it did not vanish completely even then. Occasionally, subsequent scientific description of animals served a double function by instructing children about the rules governing the human world. Between the lines of Arabella B. Buckley's *The Winners in Life's Race*, for example, lurked the sternest social Darwinism, although she attempted to mitigate it by declaring that "the struggle is not entirely one of cruelty or ferocity, but . . . the higher the animal life becomes, the more important is family love and the sense of affection for others" (351–52).

On the whole, however, moralizing dropped out of juvenile natural history literature in the middle of the nineteenth century. As science became more sophisticated, the very term *natural history*, which had an aura of amateurism and speculation, gave way to soberer, more precise rubrics. Buckley's book itself exemplified this trend. The introduction and conclusion provided a didactic context for a text that was otherwise stuffed with Latinate taxonomical terms, paleontological evidence, and an unremitting concern with adaptation to function. As the title of one of Buckley's other works, *The Fairyland of Science*, suggests, she wished to introduce children to accurate zoological ideas. The moral dimension was a kind of sugar coating, not an integral part of her demonstration.

As well as changing the tone of juvenile nonfiction about animals, the Victorian advance of science undermined the metaphor equating subordinate human groups with animals in a more profound way. If Darwinian evolution were acknowledged, man had to be included among the animals; the once-impassible gulf of reason ceased to matter. Although Buckley did not go so far as to treat man in her survey of vertebrates (organized by functional and developmental groups, rather than creature by creature), she did include him in her "Birds-eye View of the Rise and Progress of Backboned Life" as "the last and greatest winner in life's race." He was not intrinsically separate from "large wild animals" but was their competitor for "possession of the earth" (343–45).

In earlier natural history literature for children, the metaphorical equation of inferior humans and inferior animals derived much of its appeal from the implicit assumption that the human social world was somehow nicer as well as more civilized than that of even domestic animals. Understood in the context of an unbridgeable gap between human beings and even the most advanced and sympathetic quadrupeds, the similarities between animals and people made it possible to teach children lessons about hierarchy and power that might have been unpleasant, even frightening, if expressed directly. As zoology brought animals and people closer together, real animals became inappropriate carriers of moral lessons. Only animals that had been humanized and sentimentalized could be admitted into Victorian nurseries as teachers. Learning about themselves from animals became the exclusive prerogative of readers of the other, fictional branch of animal literature for children, where it continued to flourish, producing such sentimental favorites as Black Beauty, Toad of Toad Hall, and the Cowardly Lion.

Notes

1. F. J. Harvey Darton, *Children's Books in England: Five Centuries of Social Life*, 3rd ed. rev. by Brian Alderson (1932; rpt. Cambridge: Cambridge Univ. Press, 1982), 1; J. H. Plumb, "The First Flourishing of Children's Books" in *Early Children's Books and Their Illustration* (New York: Pierpont Morgan Library, and Boston: David R. Godine, 1975), xviii–xix, xxiv; for a general discussion of edifying children's literature in the eighteenth century, see Samuel F. Pickering, *John Locke and Children's Books in Eighteenth-Century England* (Knoxville: Univ. of Tennessee Press, 1981).

2. R. B. Freeman, "Children's Natural History Books before Queen Victoria," *History of Education Society Bulletin* 17 (Spring 1976): 8, 11. The second installment of Freeman's article, subtitled "A Handlist of Texts," appeared in *History of Education Society Bulletin* 18 (Autumn 1976): 6–34. See also Eric Quayle, *The Collector's Book of Children's Books* (New York: Clarkson N. Potter, 1971), 28.

3. See David Elliston Allen, *The Naturalist in Britain: A Social History* (1976; rpt. Harmondsworth, Middlesex: Penguin Books, 1978), chapters 2 and 3, for a discussion of how natural history became a fashionable pastime. Keith Thomas's *Man and the Natural World: A History of the Modern Sensibility* (New York: Pantheon, 1983) includes a survey of attitudes to nature in early modern Britain. For a survey of the history of Western attitudes to animals, see John Passmore, "The Treatment of Animals," *Journal of the History of Ideas* 36 (1975): 195–218.

4. Darton, 10–12; Plumb, 4; *The Fables of Aesop, and others, with Designs on Wood* (1818; rpt. Newcastle: T. Bewick and Co., 1823), iii. Eugene Francis Provenzo offers a history of the fable, with special attention to its didactic function, in "Education and the Aesopic Tradition," Ph.D. diss., Washington University, 1976, chapter 2.

5. Montague Rhodes James, *The Bestiary, being a Reproduction in Full of the Manuscript Ii.4.26 in the University Library, Cambridge . . . and a Preliminary Study of the Latin Bestiary as Current in England* (Oxford: Roxburghe Club, 1928), 2–3, 7, 22; T. J. Elliott, trans., *A Medieval Bestiary* (Boston: David R. Godine, 1971), n.p.

6. *The Historie of Foure-Footed Beastes* (London: William Iaggard, 1607), title page.

7. *A Description of Three Hundred Animals, viz. Beasts, Birds, Fishes, Serpents, and Insects*, 3rd ed. (1730; rpt. London: R. Ware, 1736), "Preface," n.p.

8. T. Teltruth, *The Natural History of Four-footed Beasts*, 3rd ed. (1769; rpt. London: E. Newbery, 1781), 11, 62. Further references to Teltruth will be given in the text. Modern bibliographers are usually generous in their classification, including as juvenile literature any work that might conceivably have attracted children. See Freeman, "Children's Natural History Books," 9–10, and his practice in "A Handlist of Texts."

9. *A Pretty Book of Pictures for Little Masters and Misses, or Tommy Trip's History of Beasts and Birds*, 15th ed. (1748; rpt. London: Edwin Pearson, 1867), 21.

10. Boreman, 6, 22, 19, 27. Boreman was not alone in either his credulity or his skepticism. Topsell had doubted the existence of the unicorn over a century earlier (711–21); on the other hand, the author of *The Natural History of Four-footed Beasts* included it in his compendium.

11. Boreman, 67.

12. *A General History of Quadrupeds* (1790; rpt. Newcastle upon Tyne: Beilby and Bewick, 1822), 178.

13. William Holloway and John Branch, *The British Museum; or Elegant Repository of Natural History*, 2 vols. (London: John Badcock, 1803). Further references to Holloway and Branch will be given in the text.

14. Examples of this genre include Edward Turner Bennett, *The Tower Menagerie: Comprising the natural history of the animals in that establishment; with anecdotes of their characters and history* (London: Robert F. Jennings, 1829) and Frederica Graham, *Visits to the Zoological Gardens* (London: George Routledge and Sons, 1853).

15. Pickering, 70–71; Plumb, xvii–xviii.

16. Boreman, "Preface," n.p.

17. [Stephen Jones], *The Natural History of Beasts, Compiled from the Best Authorities* (London: E. Newbery, 1793), iii. Further references to Jones will be given in the text.

18. Darton, 5; Plumb, xviii; Isaac Kramnick, "Children's Literature and Bourgeois Ideology: Observations on Culture and Industrial Capitalism in the Later Eighteenth Century" in *Culture and Politics from Puritanism to the Enlightenment*, ed. Perez Zagorin (Berkeley and Los Angeles: Univ. of California Press, 1980), 211–12. Sylvia Patterson dissents from the scholarly consensus that identifies the middle classes as the primary producers and consumers of children's literature in the eighteenth

century, claiming that upper-class children were the primary targets in "Eighteenth-Century Children's Literature in England: A Mirror of Its Culture," *Journal of Popular Culture* 13 (1979): 38–39.

19. James Rennie, *Alphabet of Zoology, for the Use of Beginners* (London: Orr, 1833), 5–6.

20. Mary Trimmer, *A Natural History of the Most Remarkable Quadrupeds, Birds, Fishes, Serpents, Reptiles, and Insects* (1825; rpt., abridged, Boston: S. G. Goodrich, 1829), 4. Further references to M. Trimmer will be given in the text.

21. *The Natural History of Domestic Animals: Containing an Account of their Habits and Instincts and of the Services They Render to Man* (Dublin: J. Jones, 1821), vi.

22. Buckley, *The Winners in Life's Race, or the Great Backboned Family* (1882; rpt. New York: D. Appleton, 1883), viii. Further references to Buckley will be given in the text.

23. See, for example, Samuel Jackson Pratt, *Pity's Gift: A Collection of Interesting Tales to Excite the Compassion of Youth for the Animal Creation* (1798; rpt. Philadelphia: J. Johnson, 1808) and Sarah Kirby Trimmer, *Fabulous Histories: Designed for the Instruction of Children, Respecting Their Treatment of Animals* (1786; rpt. London: Whittingham and Arliss, 1815).

24. [Eleanor Frere Fenn], *The Rational Dame: Or, Hints Towards Supplying Prattle for Children*, 4th ed. (1790?; rpt. London: John Marshall, c. 1800), vi. Further references to Fenn will be given in the text.

25. *The Animal Museum; or, Picture Gallery of Quadrupeds* (London: J. Harris, 1825), iii–iv. Further references to *Animal Museum* will be given in the text.

26. Thomas Varty, *Graphic Illustrations of Animals, Showing Their Utility to Man, in their Services During Life, and Uses After Death* (London: Thomas Varty, n.d.), n.p.

27. *Natural History of Domestic Animals*, v, 92; *A Pretty Book of Pictures*, 30.

28. *Animal Sagacity, exemplified by facts showing the force of instinct in beasts, birds, & c.* (Dublin: W. Espy, 1824), 3, 5, 8. Further references to *Animal Sagacity* will be given in the text.

29. Pickering, 25–33; Darton, 3.

30. See also Jones, 65, and *The Natural History of Animals: Beasts, Birds, Fishes, and Insects* (1818; rpt. Dublin: Smith and Son, 1822), 46–47.

31. Jones, 73; *Tom Trip's Museum: or, a Peep at the Quadruped Race* (London: John Harris, n.d.), pt. 2, 11; Boreman, 26; William Bingley, *Animal Biography: or, Authentic Anecdotes of the Lives, Manners, and Economy of the Animal Creation, arranged according to the system of Linnaeus* 3 vols. (1802; rpt. London: Richard Phillips, 1804), 1:36.

32. *Natural History of Domestic Animals*, 84, 106.

33. *Tom Trip's Museum*, pt. 1, 6; Boreman, 11; Thomas Bingley, *Stories Illustrative of the Instincts of Animals, Their Characters and Habits* (London: Charles Tilt, 1840), 65.

34. *Tom Trip's Museum*, pt 1, 3; *Animal Museum*, 1.

35. *Tom Trip's Museum*, pt 1, 3.

36. T. Bingley, 15; *Animal Museum*, 1.

37. *Natural History of Domestic Animals*, 9; *Rational Dame*, 41.

38. *Natural History of Domestic Animals*, 78–82.

39. M. Trimmer, 25–26; Fenn, 38.

40. Jones, 93; *Natural History of Domestic Animals*, 64–67; Fenn, 23.

41. Jones, 62; *Natural History of Animals*, 13; Holloway and Branch, 44; M. Trimmer, 39.

42. M. Trimmer, 81; Holloway and Branch, 2:136.

43. *Tom Trip's Museum*, pt. 3, 13; Jones, 55.

44. *Natural History of Animals*, 53.

45. M. Trimmer, 41; Jones, 34, 59, 115; *A Pretty Book of Pictures*, 30−31.

46. *Tom Trip's Museum*, pt 2, 2; *Animal Museum*, 168−71.

47. *Travels in the Interior of Africa* (Dublin: P. Hayes, 1825), 113.

48. W. Bingley, 1:268.

49. Jones, 106; *Tom Trip's Museum*, pt. 2, 8; Holloway and Branch, 2:25.

50. *Natural History of Animals*, 11; Jones, 101.

51. *Natural History of Animals*, 35; Fenn, 44; Jones, 86; Holloway and Branch, 1:54.

52. M. Trimmer, 43; Frederic Shoberl, *Natural History of Quadrupeds*, 2 vols. (London: John Harris, 1834), 2:169; Holloway and Branch, 1:222.

53. Holloway and Branch, 2:245; Shoberl, 2:72−73.

Tintin and the Family Romance

Jean-Marie Apostolides

In 1929 a Belgian illustrator, Georges Remi (1907–83), published under the acronymic pseudonym of Hergé (R. G.) his first large album of comic strips recounting the adventures of a newspaper reporter, *Tintin au pays des Soviets*. The childlike hero stumbled in this and subsequent volumes into civil wars, mysteries, and criminal conspiracies (bootleggers, counterfeiters, drug rings). He was, of course, always able to escape or solve the difficulties he encountered. Since the 1930s, Hergé's twenty-three colorful albums have captured French imaginations and persuaded *la grande nation* that Belgian culture goes beyond *pommes frites*. In the last decades they have become readily available in English translations that do remarkable justice to Hergé's puns (the one objection American readers might raise is that the translated names and jokes are so *very* English).[1]

John Rodenbeck in volume 1 of *Children's Literature* argued that Hergé's series offered an almost unique conjunction of high artistic quality with genuine mass popularity.[2] Devotees including Henri Peyre and André Malraux have admired the beauty and brimming life of the books,[3] as did the reviewer in the *Times Literary Supplement*. An Aristotelian would note the pleasures of recognition: everywhere Tintin goes, he is accompanied by his devoted little dog Snowy (Milou in French) and runs into many of the same characters. This central cast of warmly comic figures engenders both slapstick and verbal play: two bumbling policemen reminiscent of the Keystone Kops, a happily drunken sailor prone to polysyllabic invectives such as "bashi-bazouk! diplodocus!," a gentle inventor whose deafness leads to comic misunderstandings, and a generously endowed diva whose piercing voice takes her to a variety of political hotbeds. The artistic quality of these comic strips derives in part from the ethnographic accuracy, dramatic composition, and refined color values of each frame. Adventures set in Egypt thus provide splendid images of pyramids, mummies, and cartouches whose visual puns are charged with an "aesthetic overplus." The narrative too balances suspense against physical farce in a comic, episodic mode reminiscent of a Fielding.

Yet the appeal of the books seems strangely linked to the character and moral vision of Tintin. As Rodenbeck put it, "Tintin is absolutely and almost mysteriously autonomous" (95). Jean-Marie Apostolides here pursues that mystery in depth, focusing on certain recurrent structures: doubles, scenes of regression, disguises, and above all the insistently ambivalent relationships among the characters. He turns to Freud to explain the connections among these narrative patterns, in the process enhancing our understanding and our pleasure in the series.[4]

M. H.

The Foundling

The first seven albums by Hergé depicting the adventures of Tintin present a childhood myth that Freud called the "family romance of neurotics." During his (or her) first years, according to Freud, a child finds security by idealizing his parents as divine or royal beings whose commands and values seem absolute. In time, the child compares his procreators to other living or imaginary beings and discovers that they share the human condition of fallibility, far from the omnipotence of his narcissistic revery. To overcome his disappointment, the child concludes he is simply a foundling adopted by these parents. He traces an imaginary genealogy and imitates invented, more prestigious parents, represented as monarchs whose omnipotence helps the child to deify himself.[5]

Marthe Robert has shown that part of Western literature—fairy tales, romantic literature, and pathbreaking works such as *Don Quixote* and *Robinson Crusoe*—emerged directly from this fantasy of the "family romance," common to many individuals and not just to neurotics.[6] The theme produces a common literary stance: the foundling turns his back on real life; dominated by an exigent ideal, he refuses women and sexuality, for he aims directly at the infinite. He can be content with revery, but if he fights, it is to impose his values on the world, though he sometimes does so only in his imagination.

In this theory there is a key that permits us to understand several traits of Tintin. In effect, we do not know his parents or his kin. When asked if Tintin were an orphan, Hergé answered with a joke or a rationalization that concealed his hero's aggressiveness toward his parents.[7] Yet this nonexistent family can in the long run be found everywhere, especially in the many paternal figures Tintin encounters and helps.

The parental figures closest to Tintin, the two policemen named Thomson and Thompson (Dupond and Dupont), who recur in all seven of the first episodes, are constantly ridiculed. Like automatons, they mirror each other in looks, gesture, and errors; as Tintin becomes involved in the cases they wish to investigate, he unsettles their plans, then helps them. His own omnipotence compensates for their slapstick incompetence. The hero's relationship to the two policemen also betrays his unconscious guilt and need for

The Thompsons double up to misapprehend a suspect: Tintin framed as a cocaine dealer. Authority is always double.

punishment. Tintin never stands up to the father but refuses the combat that would make of him an oedipal rival. In the albums up to *King Ottokar's Sceptre* (1938), the Thompsons pursue the hero and condemn him (on false appearances). They arrest him three or four times, taking him for a bandit, and Tintin submits to their decision with an astonishing docility for so bold a hero. Behind his nonconformism lies a conformism that, like (or even better than) that of the indistinguishable police, ultimately restores order.

Tintin cannot stand the ambivalence of the paternal figure, and to escape it he makes use of a typically preoedipal strategy.[8] He rarely confronts a single image (at once positive and negative): the father substitutes he encounters usually come in pairs. Thus on a hunt for big game during his tour of Africa, Tintin encounters twin white-frocked fathers, one good, who saves him several times from death, the other evil (the bandit Tom in disguise), who tries to kill him (*Tintin au Congo*, 1930).

If the father figures are not doubled, Tintin misinterprets their attitude, denying their hostility. In *Tintin in America* (1931) the bootlegging gangster Bobby Smiles at first appears as police chief,

Illustrations from *The Adventures of Tintin & Milou* by Hergé. Art © by Casterman. Text © by Methuen/Little Brown.

until his twinship with Al Capone is uncovered (the United States is a country of evil, just like the Soviet Union). Tintin's difficulty in interpreting the father emerges most clearly in the original version of *The Cigars of the Pharaohs* (1932), when he stumbles onto a conspiracy to smuggle opiates hidden in cigars. Tintin first suspects the scholar Siclone of complicity, but this innocent addict does not know the consequences of his acts when he tries to stab Tintin or shoots pointblank at him. Senor Olivcira de Figueira undergoes the same transformation: apparently criminal, he eventually will save the life of the hero. The businessman Rastapopoulos presents an inverse difficulty; not until the very end does the hero unmask his bandit's face. Most important, the maharajah who rescues Tintin from Siclone occasions the "romance" triumph of the hero: it is Tintin who will return power to his weakened father. (His relationship to the threatened monarch Muskar XII is similar in *King Ottokar's Sceptre*.) Tintin thus inverts the normal process of creation; it is not the father who engenders the son but the latter who permits the father to exist and to declare the law. By this imaginary inversion of the relationship of power, the hero escapes from conflict, that is, can at once exist beyond the law and preserve the structure of order.

Tintin's anguish before the paternal figure is perceptible in an early page of *The Cigars* showing a narcotic-inspired dream sequence. Tintin has just penetrated the pyramid of Kih-oskh, the forbidden place par excellence, since it is there that the father hides the arsenal of his power (the cigars). The hero approaches oedipal knowledge when he picks up a "cigar of the pharaoh"—which we learn later is untouchable (*The Cigars*, 61). He will not have time to break the object and discover its secret until the end of the adventure, under the approving eye of the maharajah. Just when he could resolve the enigma of the father, Tintin is overcome by a narcotic. Before he falls unconscious, his hallucinations reveal to him part of the truth, the secret of his relationship to the father (*The Cigars*, 9).

In the first image on this dream page, Tintin imagines himself embalmed with Snowy; he realizes his transgression has provoked the father's menace—there are things the child should not know, scenes he cannot see without punishment. The second image shows the seeping green vapors of the narcotic (emblematic color of rebirth in Egyptian religion). Tintin on all fours (regressing to an

Overcome by narcotic fumes in the pyramid of Kih-Oskh, Tintin regresses to infancy and glimpses a primal scene.

anterior phase) sees two figures: the Pharaoh, about to capture him, and Anubis, the jackal-god, who presides over funerals and embalmings. He holds an umbrella, a polysemic object which condenses cultural and individual meanings: it evokes both the hook Osiris carries at judgment and the phallic instrument of Professor Siclone.

In the third image, Tintin discovers the forbidden scene: the Thompsons, archaic parents, faintly differentiated as male and female.[9] Thompson, on the left, smokes a cigar and wears a phallic serpent on his hat and masculine toga. On the right, Thomson, more feminized, lights the cigar of his colleague in a gesture of submission and wears the toga of a queen. Retreating, Philemon

Siclone doubles the image of the father by bringing a box of cigars, symbol of power and sexuality. We interpret this scene as a substitute, acceptable through its censorship, of the primal scene; the Thompsons are rolling their eyes, like the severe parents of infantile fantasies; their menacing looks address Tintin, voyeur of the scene. The voyeurism of the hero immediately entails his punishment in the next image; judgment is held, the sentence executed. A box of cigars floats above the scene as a reminder of the law. In the first half of the scene Tintin is carried to his tomb (or in the first version to a green sea) by Rastapopoulos, dressed as an Egyptian, and by Snowy-Anubis. The balance of forces has been inverted, the animal dominates man, though keeping his human characteristics. In the second part of the scene the hero returns to his origins, shrunken into a baby crying in anguish in a sarcophagus-cradle and swaddled in the wraps of a mummy.

After *The Cigars* Tintin will always confront doubled paternal figures, one good and the other evil, with the exception of General Alcazar in *The Broken Ear* (1935). The Latin American revolutionary Alcazar is an ambivalent father, who honors the hero, then condemns him to death. One can consider him as Hergé's first attempt to stage a realist image of the father. But at contact with such a father, Tintin sees his imaginary superhuman power melt because the two are linked: the ambivalent father corresponds to a son deprived of magic power, who must confront the world with more realistic arms. Hergé chooses to go backwards to the principle of twins, which permits him an economy of guilt.

Whereas the "evil" double allows us to exculpate the father of the murderous desires that the son projects onto him, the strategy equally applies to the son. Tintin constantly encounters brothers filled with desires that he does not recognize in himself, a strategy which permits the hero to keep his mask of innocence. The young boys with whom he keeps company are generally foundlings, but Tintin must always disrupt the situation of twinship in order to avoid recognizing himself, to remain unique. Thus he must constantly reintegrate his young friends into a family. For some, such as the son of the maharajah in *The Cigars*, it is their own family, for others it is adoptive—Chang in *Tintin in Tibet* (1960) and Zorrino in *The Prisoners of the Sun* (1949). The most complex of these is Didi, almost the twin of Tintin. He is the closest to the oedipal situation and threatens to castrate the father to avenge his own castration. Tintin succeeds, however, in silencing this double, whose madness is too visible, and he has him "cured" by a paternal figure traditional in Hergé, the scholar: Professor Fang Se-Yang, friend of Mr. Wang, who finds the cure for the terrible *radjaijah*, the poison that makes its victims go mad (*The Blue Lotus*, 1934).

The rejection of overt rivalry and constant regression into a safer preoedipal zone explain certain special characteristics of our hero. Like the characters in a fairy tale, Tintin has neither personal life nor individualized name. His "infantile" nickname, which may have come from a poem by Benjamin Rabier, "Tintin lutin," may also be taken as a pun.[10] For the exploits of Tintin resemble the titanesque labors of mythology and tales. Always leaping from the grandiose to the ludicrous, he draws these albums toward the epic mode as long as he remains the principal figure in the adventure. The hero's remarkable powers, and more particularly his capacity for metamorphosis, permit him to escape the constraints of reality. Pursued by the Thompsons (themselves endowed with ubiquity), Tintin becomes an aged lady or the old man of the village, a monkey, a giraffe, a black, a Japanese general, a Chicago kid, and so on. Naturally, we never see how the change came about.

Just as imaginary as his omnipotence, of course, is the evil he combats. He simply projects on to the the external world the double structure of his parental image, the only efficacious means of escaping ambivalence and relativity, that is to say, from an adult conception of the familial and social universe. Tintin, the little boy who does not want to grow up, understands the world as a single family. That is why, in the first episodes, he overlooks the differences between people and between cultures. He has in common with the hero of romance a pessimistic vision of the world, onto which he projects narrow-mindedness, lovelessness, and incoherence—effects of his own immaturity. As Marthe Robert writes, "Romantic desire is always divided between truly promethean ambition and that mystic communion with the world soul which is the other side of megalomania."[11] The Herculean labors of Tintin, who aims at nothing less than imposing on the world his obsession with the good and his ignorance of sexuality, are as impressive as they are imaginary.

The hero can do everything because he is the incarnation of a dream of an impotent child who never accepts adult exchange. Tintin will not marry, any more than we see him accept money. Lost in the symbolic universe of the exchange of persons and consumer goods, he seeks magically to reestablish on earth the age of paradisal innocence which was his before he gained knowledge of reality. For lack of power to find the lost paradise (except for those rare moments when Tintin finds someone like Chang who shares his vision of the world), the hero flees the degraded world to return to mother nature. There, like Mowgli, he is on an even footing with animals, speaks their language, cares for them, becomes their master, and makes use of their power. In short, he takes the place of Snowy and regresses to a state anterior to all distinction. Nature then is not hostile to him, because his soul is in union with that of the world. At other times Tintin flees into Robinsonades. He seeks a deserted island where he can restore the lost paradise. But the father, whom he can of course never eliminate, always precedes him and establishes his kingdom of exchange and death. For Tintin, every island becomes a black island.

He must always start again from zero, repeating the same exploits, for the villains he fights (for example, Rastapopolous) are not creatures of flesh and blood; they are fantasms that incarnate evil and disappear with daylight. The first seven episodes do not engage the hero personally because he refuses all situations of conflict. He accumulates nothing, learns nothing, possesses none of the characteristics that would make him like an ordinary human. Experience leaves no trace on him. His first adventures present themselves as a cyclic epic. All he could learn is cast onto the doubles who disappear as soon as Hergé creates them; that is why Tintin never ages. The apartment he occupies on Labrador Street is revealing. Despite his wanderings around the world, nothing of the external universe penetrates Tintin's home. We never see any personal souvenir, any trace that would indicate a private existence or even a human sentiment. His lodgings are cold by contrast with the chateau of Marlinspike (Moulinsart) where he finally agrees to live.

The lack of any personal life, linked to the humanly unexplained birth of Tintin, makes of him a soteriological hero.[12] Like Christ, he is the savior of a world given to sin. Miracles are the daily bread of the young man. He has neither love nor hatred, simply an obsession with the good which he believes he incarnates. The spiritual salvation that he tries to impose on the world is exercised first on Snowy. This canine companion is constantly victim of the exorbitant demands of his master. As soon as he hopes for some rest or simply tries to profit from the goods of life (to drink, to gnaw a fine bone), Tintin arrives to keep him from satisfying his desire. Pleasure does not count in the face of the only task worthy of the superman: bringing the world back to its primal innocence.

Probably at the outset Hergé projected much of himself onto Tintin (who resembles him physically) and associated the good with the rightwing thought which then seemed to him absolute: Tintin flees from Soviet Russia. Gradually, the concrete experience of the world separated the author from his character. Tintin prevents the anschluss of Syldavia by Borduria in *King Ottokar's Sceptre*; Hergé knew perfectly well that Hitler was preparing for war and that fascism was only a caricature of his own ideas. After *King Ottokar's Sceptre* (which marks the apogee of Tintin as world savior, irrealism in his adventures, and the reconciliation of the foundling with his parents) the author retreats in his relationship to his hero. Facing Tintin there will now be the figure of Captain Haddock.

The Bastard

The passage from a theological universe to a psychological one in Hergé's work is accompanied by a recentering of the point of view. Starting with *The Crab with the Golden Claws* (1941), when Tintin meets Captain Haddock, the limelight falls to a greater extent on his inebriated friend. Haddock, like Tintin, can be attached to the family romance, of which he too is an avatar. But with Haddock, Hergé develops the theme at a later stage.

Freud notes that as soon as the (male) child acquires some knowledge of human sexuality, he modifies the myth of his family origin. He discovers that maternity is certain, but not paternity. This discovery permits an alternate way of inventing his paternal filiation. After having thought of himself as a foundling, he now imagines that his mother has had sexual relations with prestigious men other than his father and that he is a bastard born from one of these encounters.[13] Such degradation of the maternal image at the moment of the oedipal crisis reverses the prior tendency to idealize her. To consider the mother as a woman desired by men other than the father permits the child to satisfy in good conscience the oedipal drives that push him toward her at the same time.

According to Marthe Robert, the image of the bastard dominates nineteenth-century literature, and she analyzes its principal traits starting with portraits of adventurers in the novels of Stendahl and Balzac. Opposed to the introverted foundling, the bastard profits from his precise knowledge of the world to conquer society and carve out an empire, the model of all bastards—from Vautrin to Julien Sorel—being Napoleon. He wants all the signs of success: women, money, power, honors. He acts in the world as if on a battlefield. Rather than try to transform the world by imposing his own values, as the foundling does, the bastard wants to avenge himself and profit from everything that he can offer to his appetite for conquest. In a more recent essay, Marthe Robert has shown how an author like Flaubert can be divided between the attitude of the foundling and that of the bastard.[14]

The same duality is at work in the universe of Hergé and perhaps in his existence. Besides the Hergé sensitive to success, brilliantly worldly, and fond of the pleasures of existence that some of his friends have presented to us,[15] there was Hergé the rigorous artist, harnessed more than fifty years to the same task, who complained of being bound to Tintin as a criminal is chained to his ball. The maniacal perfection of Hergé's albums was legendary. Sometimes he spent five or six years in completing an adventure. Unlike Flaubert, the readability of his style aimed not at eternity but at becoming the most precise witness of his epoch, another way of escaping time. The albums constitute a first-class digest of material civilization, since the author surrounded himself with specialists responsible for reproducing with the greatest possible fidelity the objects, places, and people to be depicted.

This fundamental duality is already perceptible in the first two albums in which Hergé attributes to Snowy or Tintin the characteristics of both the foundling and the bastard. Already in Hergé's first comic strip, his earliest protagonist, Totor, who prefigured Tintin, had entered into oedipal rivalry, taking on the father to conquer the woman.[16] It was Tintin who in the USSR had a fondness for alcohol and cursed with words found later in his friend's mouth. It was he who in the first version of *Congo* lounged in a luxury hotel dressed elegantly in the fashion of the 1930s. From *Tintin in America* onward, Hergé tends to attribute each tendency to a different person, and from *The Crab* onward Haddock naturally replaces the fox terrier and his master in the role of the impenitent hedonist. Since the pursuit of mundane values was incompatible with the rigorous ideal of the later Tintin, Hergé chose in later albums to limit Tintin's personality primarily to the traits of the foundling, though permitting him to keep a few of the bastard.

The way in which the early Tintin prefigures Haddock can perhaps best be observed in *The Broken Ear*, in which Tintin seeks a fetish stolen from the Brussels Museum, encountering Latin American Indian tribes and becoming involved in a war between two countries modeled on Bolivia and Paraguay. In this album, the only adventure before 1940 in which the light style cuts across the imperturbable seriousness of the others, Tintin clearly reveals his resemblance to the bastard. Tintin cannot resist the prestige of a uniform; he accepts the grade of colonel that his friend General Alcazar offers him and the title of aide-de-camp of the new head of state. In this album, too, he faces up for the first time to ambivalent paternal figures. We see him fight Alcazar, first in a game (he beats him at chess), then really in politics, making decisions that the general refuses to carry through (rupture with the General American Oil Company). Tintin is also the rival of Ridgewell, who tries to chase him from the forest where he wants to rule among the Arumbayas. But in subsequent albums, especially *King Ottokar's Sceptre*, Hergé tries to recoup, for he must have realized that in following a penchant for worldly vanity, Tintin loses not only his soul but the omnipotence that makes him so different a hero. *The Broken Ear* is also the adventure in which the hero loses his imaginary power: he is borne in triumph by the partisans of Alcazar, but he has done nothing more than offer some puns under the influence of alcohol, at the moment when he was to be shot.

This episode is so clearly appropriate to the character of the bastard that Hergé did not hesitate to reuse it to describe Haddock in *The Crab with the Golden Claws*, the album in which Tintin meets him during an inquiry into drug traffic that leads him to Morocco and the Sahara. When Haddock's last bottle of aperitif has been broken, the captain, half-drunk, leaves his protected position to leap to an attack on the Berber bandits, yelling curses. He thinks that his cries alone sufficed to put the enemy to flight but discovers later that he is but a cardboard hero—the men sent by Lieutenant Delcourt with their rifles have done the job (*The Crab*, 37−38).

The arrival of Haddock permits Hergé to oppose the two tendencies without risking Tintin's heroic personality. Unlike the hero, who defines himself an orphan, the captain immediately invokes his mother. Tintin's comment when he finds the captain of the ship drunk ("What would your old mother say if she saw you in this state?") releases a crisis and the tearful cries of the drunkard: "Boo.. . hoo . . . *Mummy!* . . . *mummy!*" (*The Crab*, 16, dramatized even more in the first version by bold letters). While the maternal figure is evoked here in a clearly oedipal fashion, the biological father of Haddock is never mentioned. Having suppressed him, the captain feels freer to invent a prestigious filiation. In *The Secret of the Unicorn* (1943) he will discover a glorious ancestor, rich and titled, the chevalier François de Hadoque, who will compensate for the modesty of his real origins. (The different spelling of the names is a tip that this kinship is imaginary.) Of course, it is only little by little that one discovers in Haddock the principle traits of the bastard. In *The Crab*, the claim of infantile love is still too pronounced for him to use the world to his profit. Moreover, in this—their first—encounter, the moral demands of the foundling weigh too heavily on the captain for him to expresss freely the bastard's penchant for pleasure. It exists nonetheless, manifest in a primitive fashion in his immoderate taste for drink, with all the ambiguous aspects that one can read in such a penchant.

The distinction between Tintin, as foundling, and Haddock, as bastard, is clearly delineated in their relationship to the main woman of the series, Bianca Castafiore. Both male characters repress sexual desire, but with a difference. The infantile, preoedipal foundling Tintin flees whenever he meets her from her repetitions of the

"Jewel Song" from Gounod's *Faust*, the only means by which she attempts to seduce the young hero. He thus negates the difference between the sexes.

The oedipal bastard Haddock likewise flees "Catastrophe," hiding behind a pillar or evading her through poses of sleep and impotence. But he is more seriously threatened than Tintin by Bianca's universal flirtation with potential admirers, her wordplay and significant gestures. Indeed, Castafiore's advances to him are all symbolically castrating: her arrival at Marlinspike precipitates his sprained ankle, the parrot she offers him as a house gift bites his nose, and a wasp hidden in the rose she holds out repeats the insult—she actually *removes* the "sting" from this appendage (*The Castafiore Emerald*, 1963). Yet Haddock sits through fifteen performances of the "Jewel Song" (*The Seven Crystal Balls*, 1946) and slips when he introduces himself in *The Calculus Affair* (1956) as "Haddada," which can be read in French as "*a dada*," that is, "on horseback," a playful sexual invitation. Even if he is sincere in fleeing her, we can see from his behavior that she nonetheless secretly attracts him. Her invasions rationalize his flight and permit him to avoid thinking about his feelings. The flirtatious singer threatens him with castration in the name of the father, precisely because the son runs the risk of violating the incest tabu.[17]

The sequence of Tintin's adventures finds its dynamic in the rivalry between foundling and bastard. The first will continue his vagabond travels around the world, searching everywhere for a place where he can impose his ideas of the good and of justice. But under the influence of his friend, he will soon find that this ideal is literally a utopia, that it can be embodied nowhere (*u-topos*). As for the bastard Haddock, he takes on greater and greater importance, dominating at first Tintin and then the albums, in which he becomes the central figure, even though he does not figure in any title. The first stage of his rise fixes him in a corner of the world: the "secret of the unicorn" is merely the secret of his birth, of his bastardy. When the captain invents the chevalier François de Hadoque, whose worthy heir he hopes to prove himself, he installs himself in the chateau of this mythic ancestor at Marlinspike, living in leisure and served by a Nestor as zealous as he is discreet.

The bastard's penchant for honors and earthly goods, however, is always balanced by the presence beside him of the foundling. For Tintin, though he soon renounces the conversion of the world, does not despair of improving his friend, of imposing on him his exigent ideal. One might believe, because of the omnipotence Hergé gives his hero, that Tintin would be the winner in this combat. No such thing. It is the drunken Haddock who will end by sobering the foundling. Gradually he brings him to a more realistic and more cynical vision of the world, as one can see in comparing *The Broken Ear* with the last volume, *Tintin and the Picaros* (1976). Captain Haddock, Professor Calculus (Tournesol), and Bianca Castafiore will ultimately compose at Marlinspike the family that the foundling claims never to have had. In these last episodes, Tintin becomes a normal little boy: beneath the mask of an adolescent, he finally has the soul of a sobered adult who accepts the world as it is.

Notes

1. The original comic strips published in newspapers were revised and collected in the form of large albums. The date of first publication in album format is given in the text; most of the albums were rewritten and redrawn to adapt them to postwar ideological conditions, so that dates of current copyright differ. The following two English translations will be cited in the text: *The Cigars of the Pharaoh*, trans. L. Lonsdale-Cooper and Michael Turner (London: Methuen, 1971) and *The Crab with the Golden Claws*, trans. L. Lonsdale-Cooper and Michael Turner (London: Methuen, 1958). French names will be given in parentheses on first mention and French titles for albums not yet translated. The pagination of the French and English fascicles is identical.

2. "The Tin-Tin Series: Children's Literature and Popular Appeal," *Children's Literature* 1 (1972): 93–97.

3. "The Epic Strip: Tintin Crosses the Channel," *Times Literary Supplement*, December 5, 1958, 698.

4. Margaret Higonnet has translated and adapted this article from several chapters of *Les Métamorphoses de Tintin* (Paris: Laffont, 1984) in collaboration with the author, Jean-Marie Apostolides.

5. Sigmund Freud, "Family Romances," *The Standard Edition of the Complete Psychological Works*, ed. James Strachey et al., 24 vols. (London: Hogarth, 1953–74), 9:235–41. Hergé confessed, "I am always interested in psychoanalysis. Moreover, I have read a good part of the works of Jung." "Entretien avec Hergé," *Minuit* 25 (September 1977): 26.

6. Robert, *Roman des origines et origines du roman* (Paris: Grasset, 1972). See also Bruno Bettelheim, *The Uses of Enchantment: The Meaning and Importance of Fairy Tale* (New York: Knopf, 1976).

7. "He never had parents, they are too burdensome. He would have had to ask permission each time he went out, we would never get over it." Interview of Hergé by Pierre Ajamé, *Les nouvelles littéraires*, 27 June 1963, 10.

8. Bettelheim explores this technique of splitting the parental figure in *The Uses of Enchantment*.

9. Freud observed that little boys suppose possession of a penis by members of both sexes and commented, "A knowledge of infantile sexual theories . . . can be of interest in various ways—even, surprisingly enough, for the elucidation of myths and fairy tales." "On the Sexual Theories of Children," *Standard Edition*, 9:211.

10. Rabier is cited in Numa Sadoul, *Entretiens avec Hergé* (Paris: Casterman, 1983), 82–83.

11. Robert, *Roman*, 115.

12. Otto Rank, *The Myth of the Birth of the Hero*, trans. F. Robbins and Smith Ely Jelliffe (New York: Journal of Nervous and Mental Disease Publishing Co., 1914).

13. The child's "curious curtailment" of the earlier version of the family romance expresses "his desire to bring his mother . . . into situations of secret infidelity" (Freud, *Standard Edition*, 9:239).

14. Robert, *En Haine du roman* (Paris: Balland, 1982).

15. See Robert Poulet, "Adieu, Georges," *Rivarol*, 18 March 1983, p. 11.

16. *Archives Hergé I* (Paris: Casterman, 1973), 37.

17. For a totally different explanation of *The Castafiore Emerald*, see the fine article by Michel Serres, "Les Bijoux distraits ou la cantatrice sauve," *Critique* no. 277 (June 1970):485–97.

Text as Teacher: The Beginning of Charlotte's Web

Perry Nodelman

Most recent narrative theories assume that the ability to understand fiction depends upon a reader's prior knowledge of the codes and conventions that any narrative inevitably evokes and depends on. The assumption seems justified; consider how incomplete and pointless unadulterated versions of North American folk tales appear when approached in terms of our usual European ideas about what makes a story a story. In fact, even the simplest of stories imply and seem to demand prior knowledge. Jonathan Culler speaks of the presuppositions of the beginnings of stories—the way they imply a context:

> Logically the opening sentence with the fewest presuppositions would be something like *Once upon a time the king had a daughter*. Poor in logical presuppositions, this sentence is extremely rich in literary and pragmatic presuppositions. It relates the story to a series of other stories, identifies it with the conventions of a genre, asks us to take certain attitudes towards it (guaranteeing, or at least strongly implying, that the story will have a point to it, a moral which will govern the organization of detail and incident.) The presuppositionless sentence is a powerful intertextual operator. [115]

Such sentences inevitably evoke the vast body of literature they are a part of—perhaps, even, the vast body of all literature. What seems simple is in fact ineffably complex—not a discrete entity, but the small twig of a vast tree. In order to properly comprehend that small twig, we must know something of the vast tree.

But even very young children understand and enjoy stories, and many four- or five- or six-year-olds take much pleasure from the longer and more complex novels their parents or teachers read to them. One such novel is E. B. White's *Charlotte's Web*, a favorite choice of many adults as a first extended narrative to read to young children. How is that possible, when their previous literary experience is likely to have consisted only of television cartoons and the simple stories in picture books?

One possible answer is that the skills required to understand narrative structures are inherent, preexisting in all human beings. In his influential study of the patterns of Russian folk tales, Vladimir Propp implies that they might be; he says that "fairy tales possess a quite particular structure which is immediately felt and which determines their category even though we may not be aware of it" (6). But it seems likely that Propp had such feelings because of his own involvement with the culture these stories emerged from; other cultures have produced quite different bodies of stories with quite different systems of narrative structuring, and, as Seymour Chatman suggests, "What constitutes 'reality' or 'likelihood' is a strictly cultural phenomenon. . . . The 'natural' changes from one society to another" (49). That we have the sort of "feelings" about narrative structures Propp describes only because we learn them is indicated even in the introduction to the English translation of Propp's study, in which Alan Dundes asks, "And how precisely is fairy tale structure learned? Does the child unconsciously extrapolate fairy tale structure from hearing many individual fairy tales . . .? This kind of question must be investigated by field and laboratory experiments" (x).

As it happens, such investigations have been carried out in recent years—not by folklorists or even by child psychologists, but by specialists in children's literature. While their conclusions are still vague, they almost always confirm that children must *learn* how to understand stories. In a recent article in *Children's Literature in Education*, for instance, Robert Protherough concludes that "children learn from experience the kinds of reading they have to give to different texts" (14).

But while Protherough says that happens, he doesn't describe how it happens. Narrative theorists don't provide much explanation either. They usually just assume that such knowledge does already exist, in anyone capable of understanding narratives. "Narrative evokes a world," says Seymour Chatman, "and since it is no more than an evocation, we are left free to enrich it with whatever real or fictive experience we acquire" (120); but he offers no explanation of how we acquire that experience. Similarly, Louise Rosenblatt insists that "the reader of any text must actively draw upon past experience" (22), "on the resources of his own fund of experiences" (43); in regard to verbal symbols in the text, "these the reader has presumably assimilated in past experiences with language in life situations and in reading" (53). Jonathan Culler agrees: "One's notions of how to read and what is involved in interpretation are acquired in commerce with others" (55).

There can be little doubt that the mere act of living teaches us the societal conventions we need to understand literature—at least the literature of our own time and place. It may even teach us something about language. But many of the conventions by means of which literature communicates, such as the patterns of narrative structure, are exclusive to literature, not learnable from other linguistic experience. Furthermore, communication with other people is different from our involvement with language in literature in at least one important way; Wolfgang Iser says in his discussion of "Interaction between Text and Reader" that a text cannot adapt itself to each reader with whom it comes into contact. Since a text never addresses any one of us specifically, never responds to us, never clarifies matters for us in terms of our own particular problems with it, learning to read and understand a text is quite different from nonliterary forms of linguistic experience. Experience may well be the best teacher; but experience of life cannot teach us how to understand literature to the extent that literature is different from life.

As well as calling upon linguistic experience in general, Culler also suggests that we learn to interpret literature from our specific experiences with literature. "Learning to read is an interpersonal activity: one sees how others respond, grasps intuitively or through explicit demonstration what kinds of questions and operations they deploy" (124). That may well be true of students in university classrooms and of literary theorists; but children with no previous experience of extended narrative can "read"—that is, understand—*Charlotte's Web* as they have it read to them, and few parents or teachers accompany the reading with a running commentary on the "kinds of questions and operations they deploy." The fact is, children usually learn to handle such narratives, not by being told how to handle them, but unconsciously, and in the process of handling them.

The significance of their doing so becomes especially apparent in terms of Walter Ong's analysis of the distance between orality and literature. While Ong is interested in how cultures based on oral communication vary from those which have printed texts, we should not forget that the young listeners who respond so positively to *Charlotte's Web*, a print-based text, are themselves in the process of emerging from the oral culture of childhood. And as Ong says,

> Little has thus far been done . . . to understand reader re-sponse in terms of what is now known of the evolution of noetic processes from primary orality to high literacy. Readers whose norms and expectancies for formal discourse are governed by a residual oral mindset relate to a text quite differently from readers whose sense of style is radically textual. [171]

The process by which children have oral access to written texts is obviously a part of this evolution. While Ong doesn't explain how the transition occurs, his analysis implies that such an evolution must take place in the life of every child in a literate culture.

Furthermore, it is something like that transition from orality to literacy that causes literary theorists to make distinctions between naive readers and sophisticated ones. Karlheinz Stierle suggests that "every fictional text is open to a naive reading—an elementary form of reception that has been learned in everyday communication" (85). Stierle describes such reading as the matter of identifying with or becoming immersed in what one reads, an accurate description of the reading not only of many children but also of too many adults. Not surprisingly, Ong suggests that one of the distinctive qualities of oral stories is the demand they make that listeners immerse themselves in them; they are "empathetic and participatory rather than objectively distanced" (45), and listeners ideally identify with the characters they hear about. But sophisticated reading requires distance; we perceive the satisfying completeness of a narrative structure only when we do not involve ourselves in it. Presumably, Stierle's naive readers are treating literary texts as if they were oral stories—novels as if they were folk tales. While Stierle also offers no explanation of how one makes the transition from naive reading to literate reading, from identification to maintaining a proper distance from a text, his distinction does make one thing clear: if adults can be naive readers, then ceasing to be a naive reader is not natural and inevitable.

But that merely restates the problem: one must learn how to read stories, but one cannot learn it from anything but stories, for stories are significantly different from the rest of life. Once cannot understand stories without understanding the codes and conventions that underly them; and one cannot learn those codes and conventions except by experiencing the stories that contain them and presumably require prior knowledge of them. Apparently, we need to know what we have to learn before we can have access to the thing that will teach it to us.

Fortunately, the developmental psychologist Jean Piaget takes something like that as the central issue in his discussion of structuralism: how can we learn the structures necessary for explaining our world to ourselves if we don't know them already? His answer is that we *don't* know them already; we construct them, make them up ourselves in response to experience. But even though the structures we construct are different, each an individual response to individual experience, the process by which we construct them is not individual; Piaget insists that "this construction is governed by special laws" (10). The laws remain the same, even though the structures are different. Consequently,

> Whereas other animals cannot alter themselves except by changing their species, man can transform himself by transforming the world and can structure himself by constructing structures; and these structures are his own, for they are not eternally predestined either from within or without. [118–19]

For Piaget, the basic law of construction is assimilation—the process by which one changes the structures one has already created in response to less complex situations, in order to comprehend new complexities. Cognitive psychologists use the metaphor of mapping to describe this process; we comprehend new, uncharted experience by using our old experiences as a map, noticing what does not fit the map, and then composing a new map, a more complex structure of explanation. This process by which the old experience becomes the structure of the new experience is of great importance in understanding how it is that young children who know only simple stories can understand certain complex literary narratives.

Unfortunately, too many educators distort the findings of developmental and cognitive psychologists by assuming that the movement from simpler structures to more complex ones is automatic and inevitable, a magic transformation that should not be meddled with. This sort of misunderstanding leads parents or teachers first to deprive children of books that are at the wrong "level," and then to be surprised when the children reach the "right" level and cannot cope with those books. As Stanley Fish asserts in discussing how sophisticated readers move from one interpretation of a text to another, "The change from one structure of understanding to another is not a rupture but a modification of the interests and concerns that are already in place" (316). If we acknowledge that no such rupture occurs, that there are no discrete levels and no magical jumps between them, but only a constant process of transformations to ever more intricate structuring of experience, then we might be more willing to help children to make such transformations—or to choose texts that will help them to make them. Transformations aren't likely to happen if we simply assume that they will.

We always start with one way of understanding, one structure of assumption—a cognitive map. Even young children must possess such structures, for as Fish so acutely points out in his discussion of how adults read literature, "There is never a moment when one believes nothing, when consciousness is innocent of any and all categories of thought, and whatever categories of thought are operative at a given moment will serve as an undoubted ground" (319). Or in Iser's words, again in a description of the reading of adults, "The acquisition of experience is not a matter of adding on—it is a restructuring of what we already possess" (*The Act of Reading*, 132). We bring our expectations of stories to any given story; then the way the story diverges from our expectations alters our expectations. Presumably, then, children first respond to all the stories they hear with the expectations created by their actual lived experience and then respond to more complex stories by means of the expectations created by their experience of simple stories.

If that happens every time children hear another story, then it must happen in the complex novels that young children enjoy. In fact, it must happen in such novels in an extreme form, for such novels do not merely introduce readers to a form of reading experience different from but equal to the one they already possess; rather, they allow, to use Piaget's term, a genuine act of assimilation to take place. They must be constructed so as to allow those young readers who know only simple fictions to comprehend their greater complexity. I believe that *Charlotte's Web* does that. How it does so is the subject of the rest of this essay.

II

According to Louise Rosenblatt,

> As one decodes the opening lines or sentences and pages of a text, one begins to develop a tentative sense of a framework within which to place what will follow. . . . One evolves certain expectations about the diction, the subject, the ideas, the themes, the kind of text that will be forthcoming. [54]

But the opening pages of *Charlotte's Web* do not seem to have much to do with the novel that follows them. After reading only the first two chapters, someone with no prior knowledge from other people or from the cover could only be surprised that the book deals with the friendship of a pig and a spider who can talk to each other. There is no spider at all in those two chapters, and the pig in them doesn't talk. He likes being picked up and doesn't like cold water; but those are human feelings of the sort we often attribute to pets, without necessarily implying that they have the personalities of human beings. The most likely novel to follow this quite naturalistic description of how a young girl saves a runt pig and then plays with it would be a naturalistic description of how she continues to play with it—and, perhaps, gets into trouble with her friends or family because of it. There is no suggestion of the fantasy to follow. If the opening of a book has the purpose of allowing readers to develop a set of expectations that will help them come to grips with the book that follows, then White seems to be creating the wrong expectations here.

Furthermore, the book contains a passage that seems to be a far more appropriate opening; and it occurs just after the first two—

apparently inappropriate—chapters. The justly famous description that opens chapter 3 poetically evokes the setting of the rest of the novel:

> The barn was very large. It was very old. It smelled of hay and it smelled of manure. It smelled of the perspiration of tired horses and the wonderful sweet breath of patient cows. It often had a sort of peaceful smell—as though nothing bad could ever happen again in the world. It smelled of grain and of harness dressing and of axle grease and of rubber boots and of new rope.

And so on, for another whole page. Not only does this passage set the scene for the rest of the novel; it also introduces its central images, its central structural patterns, and its central themes.

White has said that he wanted to write "a paean of life, a hymn to the barn" (quoted in Neumeyer, 493). He has done both, the barn being a symbol of the larger life outside it. *Charlotte's Web* is a book about the acceptance and celebration of all aspects of existence, the good along with the bad; in its own phrase, it celebrates "the glory of everything" (183). Such an acceptance depends upon an acknowledgment that the good and the bad are inextricably intertwined, that creatures or events we think of as bad often allow good things to happen, and that, given the impermanence that makes life beautifully various, good often turns to bad. Consequently, when Wilbur first meets his friend Charlotte, he is disturbed that she is so bloodthirsty and that she kills for a living; but not only does she turn out to be a loyal friend, this death-dealing creature saves his life. She does so by using her web, an instrument of death that can keep both Charlotte and, as it turns out, Wilbur alive. Furthermore, while Wilbur can be saved, Charlotte herself must die. Wilbur's life can be saved only because Templeton, the rat, acts like a rat, and because people are stupidly gullible. Good ends always emerge from bad qualities. At one point, Wilbur points out that "it was that rotten goose egg that saved Charlotte's life" (73); at every point, White insists on the ambivalence of life as it is, and the glory of its ambivalence.

The basic structural pattern of *Charlotte's Web* is the list. The book is full of lists, lists that suggest both the glorious multitudinousness and the glorious variety of everything. After he meets her, Wilbur lists Charlotte's qualities; later, Charlotte provides him with a list of the parts of a spider's leg. Templeton, who lists his activities as "eating, gnawing, spying and hiding" (29), later says to Wilbur, "I don't want to be stepped on, or kicked in the face, or pummelled, or crushed in any way, or squashed, or buffeted about, or bruised, or lacerated, or scarred, or biffed" (125). When it rains, White lists all the things the rain falls on; when Charlotte kills flies, he lists all the creatures who dislike flies, and when people come to see the word in her web, he lists the different kinds of cars they come in. White even provides a list of the "astonishing pile" (97) of things one can find at the garbage dump. He lists the sounds made by birds in early summer and all the people who hear the cricket's song in autumn. He provides Charlotte with a list of things that will happen in spring: "Winter will pass, the days will lengthen, the ice will melt in the pasture pond. The song sparrow will return and sing, the frogs will awake, the warm wind will blow again" (164). Above all, there are lists of what various creatures eat, from Charlotte's "flies, bugs, grasshoppers, tasty cockroaches, gnats, midges, daddy longlegs, centipedes, mosquitoes, crickets" (39) to what Templeton will find at the fair: "a veritable treasure of popcorn fragments, frozen custard dribblings, candied apples abandoned by tired children, sugar fluff crystals, salted almonds, popsicles, partially gnawed ice cream cones, and the wooden sticks of lollypops" (123). There are no less than three lists that exult over the disgusting contents of Wilbur's food trough.

Even the action of *Charlotte's Web* often proceeds by means of lists—lists of activities. The first part of chapter 4 is a list of the boring events of Wilbur's day. White's description of the rope swing in the barn lists the sequence of events that constitute swinging on it. At one point, Charlotte calls the roll of the animals in the barn, and at another she lists the actions she performed while writing in the web.

The lists of *Charlotte's Web* often end with a phrase that sums them up. Charlotte's list of her food supply ends with "anything that is careless enough to get caught in my web," and her list of the events of spring with the phrase "all these sights and sounds and smells." The list of the contents of the garbage dump ends with "useless junk of all kinds, including a wrong-sized crank for a broken ice-cream freezer." The old sheep's list of the food a rat can find at a fair ends with "enough disgusting leftover food to satisfy a whole army of rats" (123). These summary phrases reinforce the idea that "all" or "everything" is glorious simply because it is so various.

The description of the barn that begins chapter 3 is itself a list, first of the smells of a barn, and then of "all sorts of things that you find in barns" (14). It too ends with a statement that sums it up: "And the whole thing was owned by Fern's uncle, Mr. Homer L. Zuckerman" (14). In the second-last paragraph of the last chapter, there is a final list. This one again evokes the barn, but it also acts as a summary of all the other lists that have occurred throughout the novel; and it ends with the phrase that sums it up, sums up all the previous lists, and sums up the novel in its entirety:

> It was the best place to be, thought Wilbur, this warm delicious cellar, with the garrulous geese, the changing seasons, the heat of the sun, the passage of swallows, the nearness of rats, the sameness of sheep, the love of spiders, the smell of manure, and the glory of everything. [183]

Both the events of the novel and the lists that suggest their significance are suspended between these two passages, which not only evoke the qualities of barns but also imply the glorious wholeness of existence. They are paeans to life, hymns to the barn.

But the first two chapters, which are not set in the barn, contain only two short lists. White tells us that the kitchen smells of "coffee, bacon, damp plaster, and woodsmoke from the stove" (3), and that Wilbur likes mud that is "warm and moist and delightfully sticky and oozy" (11). These evocations of sensuous detail don't draw attention to themselves *as* lists until one has read the rest of the novel; if the book is indeed "a paean of life, a hymn to the barn," it doesn't start being that until the third chapter. The opening seems inappropriate not just because it contains no fantasy, but also because it does not share the structure or the imagery of the rest of the novel.

In his discussion of the drafts of *Charlotte's Web*, now housed at Cornell University, Peter Neumeyer reports that White had trouble with the beginning of *Charlotte's Web*; White said he "had as much difficulty getting off the ground as did the Wright brothers" (491).

Neumeyer describes twelve different attempts at openings that represent five quite different ways of getting off the ground:

> Introducing the main character Charlotte; introducing the main character Wilbur; beginning with a song of praise to the barn; beginning with John Arable pulling on his boots to go out in the night to find the new piglet; and —finally—beginning dramatically *in media res* with the originally quite incidental little girl Fern, who asks where her father is going with that ax. [623]

While not quite totally incidental in the finished novel, Fern does cease to be of any real significance after Wilbur moves to the barn; after the first two chapters, she merely sits and watches the animals, and while she can understand them, she never talks with them or takes part in their plans. Then, toward the end, she deserts Wilbur for the human boy, Henry Fussy, an aspect of the book that disconcerts many readers. White uses this incident to suggest one more version of the glorious intertwining of everything; Fern could not grow up if she did not stop being childlike. But the fact that White so cleverly makes use of this eventually insignificant character doesn't explain why he felt called upon to introduce her at all, or to focus so much attention on her at the beginning.

Furthermore, and most significant, eight of the twelve openings that Neumeyer reports finding in the drafts are versions of the barn passage. White clearly knew that this was the *real* beginning of the novel he wanted to write; and he just as clearly knew that it was the wrong way to begin, for he fussed over it endlessly and eventually added those two apparently inappropriate chapters. Why?

A closer look at the first two chapters shows that they do have one curious thing in common with the book that follows; in many ways, the story they tell is a shorter but nevertheless complete version of the story the rest of the book tells. Both in the first two chapters and in the rest of the novel, a pig is saved from death by a female of a different species with whom he actually has nothing in common. She saves him because his death is unjust. She saves him by using words and by appealing to theoretically undesirable qualities in human beings. Those qualities are undesirable because they get in the way of practical considerations. As well as saving the pig, the female also mothers him; the mother-child relationship is satisfying to both and offers them both comfort. It is threatened by an aggressive, warlike male, a real rat. But not seriously; for the real threat is time itself, which eventually changes both the female and the pig enough to separate them from each other. In both versions of this story, the pig is Wilbur; but the female of another species is first Fern and then Charlotte, and the aggressive rat is first Avery and then Templeton.

There are large differences between the two stories. Templeton is a real rat, Avery only a metaphorical one. The first two chapters tell of these events naturalistically, without recourse to fantasy; the rest of the novel is a fantasy story involving animals that act like humans rather than humans that sometimes act like animals. A second important difference is the absence of those thematically significant lists; the meaning of the naturalistic story of the first two chapters is much less subtle, much less complex, much less ambiguous than the meaning of the rest of the novel.

The major difference is signalled by the different means by which Fern and Charlotte keep Wilbur alive. Charlotte, who knows the way of the world, saves Wilbur by using her knowledge; Fern saves Wilbur because she has *no* knowledge of the world, and because her father wants to keep her that way. She tells Mr. Arable that the pig's death is unjust; creatures ought not to die just because they are weak and in need of protection. Mr. Arable knows that such "injustice" is indeed the way of the world, on pig farms and elsewhere; but it is not the way of the world for small children, for Mr. Arable also knows that he protects his own weak, vulnerable daughter from that world, and does so because she is vulnerable enough to need protecting—as she proves by her innocence about pigs. Knowing that, and loving her for her innocence, he sentimentally defers the end of that innocence by not killing the pig. Fern not only gets what she wants; she is also able to keep on believing that the world is a place where one does get what one wants.

Mr. Arable says that Fern is trying "to rid the world of injustice," and magically, she does: she saves the pig. Fern then thinks "what a blissful world it was" (7). The world of the first two chapters is indeed blissful; despite the absence of fantasy in these two chapters, the story they tell has the wish-fulfilling qualities of the most widely known fairy tales—the tales most young children become familiar with at very young ages. Like Cinderella or Snow-White or Sleeping

Beauty, Fern is rewarded for being weak, vulnerable, and in need of protection. She need do nothing but appeal to a strong male's admiration for her weakness, and she triumphs not by becoming strong or by being wise, but because she is charmingly weak and ignorant.

Mr. Arable twice tells Fern about things she must learn in order to be more mature; in the first two chapters she learns neither of them. He first tells her, "You will have to learn to control yourself" (2) and then responds to her lack of control by controlling things for her. After he gives her the pig, he says, "Then you'll see what trouble a pig can be" (3). But she doesn't. In the first two chapters, her relationship with Wilbur continues to be blissful and to be described in superlatives: "Every day was a happy day, and every night was peaceful" (11). Until Wilbur leaves for the barn, there is no trouble. The first two chapters describe a prelapsarian world, a paradise of innocence.

In this perfect world of no trouble, the troublesome facts of life are not troublesome because they have been turned into games. Ferns plays at being a mother, Wilbur plays at being a human baby, and Avery, who is "heavily armed," plays with the weapons of war. Transformed into games, motherhood and violence not only lose their potential for troublesomeness, they come to seem a little silly. White's phrasing suggests that he wants us to laugh at Avery's toy weapons. He points out the silliness of Fern's adoration for Wilbur when he has her call the capital of Pennsylvania "Wilbur," and the silliness of Wilbur acting like a human baby when he describes Wilbur in a doll carriage beside a doll. Later, Wilbur will become a pig with a human personality; now he is just a pig ridiculously aping human behavior.

But readers need not be disturbed by that, for they do not yet have the later Wilbur with which to compare this one. Eventually, the novel makes the inadequacies of Avery's and Fern's play versions of adult behavior clear by placing them beside more genuine versions of the same thing. But at the start, readers can enjoy these descriptions of play for the same reason that Fern and Avery enjoy playing: the pleasure of the real thing without any of the dangers or difficulties. Avery can shoot without danger of being shot at. Fern can mother without having to deal with colic or worry about her child's future. Even Wilbur can have the pleasure of being adored without, apparently, feeling suffocated by it. This is not "the glory of every-thing"; it is the glory of one side of things that ignores the other side altogether.

For young readers, I suspect, all of this is both easily understand-able and very enjoyable. It is enjoyable because it describes a pleasur-able fulfillment of common wishes: to have a real live doll to play with, to get your own way with your parents and feel the satisfaction of saving another creature's life in the bargain, always to be happy. It is understandable, not just because it describes play, a recogniz-able activity described in an easily recognizable way, but also because it demands a minimal literary competence from young readers. The descriptions of play and its pleasures could be understood by young readers in terms of their own actual experience; the wish-fulfillment patterns and the simple moral statements about injustice could be understood by anyone familiar with a few fairy tales. Furthermore, wish-fulfillment, the description of how a character in a story gets what one would like to have oneself, demands identification. One must see oneself in the characters whose wishes are fulfilled in order to feel fulfilled oneself. As I suggested earlier, identification is a habit of naive readers. So the first two chapters of *Charlotte's Web* should involve young readers on two paradoxical counts: they de-scribe a familiar and recognizably real world, and they do so in unrealistic terms that young children are both likely to understand and likely to be familiar with.

According to Iser, in more sophisticated texts, a reader

> is given a role to which he must then adapt and so "modify" himself, if the meaning is to be conditioned by the text and not by his own disposition. Ultimately, the whole purpose of the text is to exert a modifying influence upon that disposition and so clearly, the text cannot and will not reproduce it. [*The Act of Reading*, 53]

Beginning with chapter 3, the text of *Charlotte's Web* cannot and will not reproduce the reader's own disposition. Significantly, the self-indulgent, troublefree, wish-fulfilling paradise of the first two chap-ters comes to an end when Wilbur moves to the barn—White's symbol of the complex variety of life.

White's description of the barn is a signal that a different attitude will be required. The many details in it prevent self-indulgence; absorbing them requires that we keep some distance from the events described. In fairy tales and other wish-fulfillments—and for that matter, in the first two chapter of *Charlotte's Web*—setting is vague enough to allow us to imagine our own details and, therefore, to become more immediately involved; in more realistic fiction, greater detail forces us to acknowledge a place different from the one we might have imagined for ourselves and therefore controls our self-indulgence.

Yet it is in this densely evoked and quite realistic setting that Wilbur suddenly stops being a piglike pig who is merely treated like a human and develops a real human personality and the human ability to communicate with other creatures by means of speech. Children who have had even limited access to children's literature are not likely to be surprised by the idea of talking animals. But the strangeness of Wilbur talking after two chapters in which he is merely a conversationless pig is unsettling enough to distance readers. Even more distancing is the paradoxical fact of Wilbur's new existence as a real animal in a real barn. Children who could identify with Fern turning Wilbur into a living doll will have trouble identifying with that doll when it turns into a real pig. They might be inclined to do what Lewis Carroll's Alice did when a baby turned into a pig—drop it altogether.

But White doesn't allow that. He quickly establishes a new involvement, this time with Wilbur in terms of the human personality he now reveals. Because he is a pig, readers will be bound to keep some distance from him; in fact, it seems obvious that children's writers often write about animals who act like people so that they can tell children things about people that their parents or teachers would not let them hear if the characters those things happened to were not disguised as animals—how many young children would be allowed to read about Wilbur's death problem if he were a human being? Yet his problems are in fact those of human beings and are presented in human terms: and for that reason, young readers will certainly feel some sympathy for him.

Ironically, the first thing Wilbur learns after it is revealed that he can talk and think is that he is bored—bored by a barn that White has just finished describing as a blissful paradise. Once Wilbur develops consciousness, he becomes conscious of the constraints and limitations that he did nothing but enjoy in his troublefree days with Fern. In a sense, then, chapter 3 repeats the events we have just read about, the life of a protected creature; but now we see their dark underside. Protected from harm and provided with all the food a pig could want, Wilbur begins to think of paradise as a prison.

In Wilbur's wish to escape the barn almost as soon as he enters it, White shows that the world is not as purely "blissful" as the innocent Fern thought it was in the first two chapters. Wilbur thinks he wants to go out into "the big world" outside his pen; but despite his longing, he is forced to realize that he is "really too young to go out into the world alone." The world is not simple, and one's feelings about it are bound to be mixed up.

Fern never realized that—or at least White never told us that she did. But White has transferred the focus of our attention from Fern to Wilbur, which allows him to consider numerous aspects of the world's complexity. The new friend Wilbur makes is not as purely adorable as Fern found Wilbur to be; Charlotte has bad qualities as well as good ones, and she makes demands of Wilbur as well as offering him solace. Furthermore, Wilbur also has to put up with Templeton and negotiate with him, as Fern did not have to do with Avery, whose access to pigs was simply prevented by Mr. Arable. All the games that were played earlier are no longer games. Templeton is *really* vicious, *really* dangerous, those characteristics which Avery merely played at earlier. For that matter, Avery himself turns out to be dangerous also, as he nearly captures Charlotte. Earlier, we could dismiss Avery's violence because we could share his point of view; he was just playing. But distanced from our usual human perspective and forced to take the point of view of animals and insects, we see the real violence of the presumed game. Similarly, Fern's game of motherhood now seems shallow in relation to the more complex relationship of Wilbur and Charlotte—instead of mere adoration, Charlotte yells at Wilbur when he is hysterical, and instead of merely being adorable, Wilbur is hard work for Charlotte; she spends most of her life saving his.

Earlier, Fern had treated Wilbur as a "pretend" human being, a doll; in the process, she ignored his piglike qualities. In the light of the new information White now provides, that comes to seem less cute than ingenuous. Wilbur has human feelings: he *is* a person, so it was silly indeed to treat him like a pretend person.

But the greatest import of the transference of our attention from Fern to Wilbur is that the problem of Wilbur's death takes on far more significance. In saving Wilbur, Fern's worries about herself as a vulnerable human being were deflected; she was able to keep on believing that the world was indeed a place in which such injustices did not need to happen and that one could be weak and vulnerable and still count on other, less weak people to protect oneself. Now that we see the situation from the victim's viewpoint, we must acknowledge our own involvement in the human condition: we too are vulnerable; more powerful people do not always protect those weaker than themselves; sometimes weaklings may have to look after themselves; the world may well be unjust. In all these ways, the pleasures of *Charlotte's Web* after the first two chapters point out the limitations of the pleasures offered by those chapters.

Understanding *Charlotte's Web* depends upon two things: a perception of its subtlety, of the complex intertwinings of good and bad, acceptable and controllable, in its reading of reality; and in order to perceive that, distance. Rather than the simple confirmation of previous expectations offered by wish-fulfillment, readers need enough distance from this novel to contemplate the unexpected relationships between its characters—and enough distance, also, to be conscious of how the novel's language informs one about those relationships. After the first two chapters, White achieves that distance by focussing our attention on descriptive passages, and by constantly making us conscious of the animal-like nature of his characters, of the ways in which they are not like us.

But the first two chapters are different. They do not demand distance. In them, White prepares readers for the complexities that follow by presenting a simpler, more easily identified with, more wish-fulfilling version of the same story. These chapters will satisfy the narrative competence of naive readers. But because they do tell of events similar to those that follow, they act as a cognitive map, a pattern to be changed and enriched by what follows. Without the first two chapters, I am sure young readers would find *Charlotte's Web* harder to understand. With them, even readers with the most primitive of narrative competences have the opportunity to make a transition and cope with the complexities of the rest of the novel. In telling his story twice, once from the viewpoint of innocence and in terms of naive literary skills, and then from the viewpoint of experience and in terms of sophisticated literary skills, White gives young readers the experience they need to transcend their own innocence as readers.

Many of the novels young children first experience have similar two-part structures. In A. A. Milne's *Pooh* books, the proportions are reversed; there are numerous episodes in which innocent creatures play at having adventures without ever acknowledging or experiencing real pain, and then one final chapter in which Christopher Robin, having experienced the real adventure of going to school, reveals that he has moved beyond mere blissfulness. Kenneth Grahame's *The Wind in the Willows* begins with Mole leaving home and finding the delightful life of the river bank; but after that, every time one of the animals leaves home, or is even tempted to leave, he must face the cruel implications of life in the real world. As in *Charlotte's Web*, the first sequence is paradisal, the later ones show the implications of life beyond paradise.

Perhaps surprisingly, many of the novels older children read themselves also have two-part structures, in which characters first innocently play at adventures and then must face real-life versions of what they first played at. Jim Hawkins has delightful dreams of pirates and treasure before he experiences the horror of the real thing. In L. M. Montgomery's *Anne of Green Gables*, Anne plays at romantic fantasies involving deep, painful emotions; but then she must face pain and death in her own real life, as her stepfather dies and she must give up her plans for the future. And in Louise Fitzhugh's *Harriet the Spy*, Harriet spends more than half the book playing at being a spy and then must face the painful implications of her game.

There are two possible reasons why so many popular children's novels present the same events first in terms of innocence and then in terms of experience. The first is that children, being new in their fictional competences, need reassurance about them; having learned sophisticated reading techniques from books with two-part structures, they continue to find pleasure in similar books. The second is simply that a two-part structure of this sort is an established pattern of children's fiction, and children's novelists may be drawn to such structures from their conscious or unconscious knowledge of other children's novels. In either case, a two-part structure of this sort does allow readers the possibility of making the transition between two quite different ways of understanding stories; all these texts may act as teachers of narrative competences.

References

Chatman, Seymour. *Story and Discourse: Narrative Structure in Fiction and Film.* Ithaca: Cornell Univ. Press, 1978.

Culler, Jonathan. *The Pursuit of Signs.* Ithaca: Cornell Univ. Press, 1982.

Fish, Stanley. *Is There a Text in This Class? The Authority of Interpretive Communities.* Cambridge: Harvard Univ. Press, 1982.

Iser, Wolfgang. "Interaction between Text and Reader," *The Reader in the Text: Essays on Audience and Interpretation*, ed. Susan R. Suleiman and Inge Crosman. Princeton: Princeton Univ. Press, 1980.

Iser, Wolfgang. *The Act of Reading: A Theory of Aesthetic Response.* Baltimore: Johns Hopkins Univ. Press, 1978.

Neumeyer, Peter F. "The Creation of *Charlotte's Web*: From Drafts to Book," *The Horn Book* (Oct. 1982) 489−97 and (Dec. 1982) 617−25.

Ong, Walter J. *Orality and Literacy: The Technologizing of the Word.* London and New York: Methuen, 1982.

Piaget, Jean. *Structuralism*, trans. and ed. Chaninah Maschler. New York: Basic, 1970.

Protherough, Robert. "How Children Judge Stories," *Children's Literature in Education* 14 (Spring 1983): 3−13.

Propp, V. *Morphology of the Folktale*, trans. Laurence Scott, rev. Louis A. Wagner. Austin: Univ. of Texas Press, 1968.

Rosenblatt, Louise M. *The Reader, the Text, the Poem: The Transactional Theory of the Literary Work.* Carbondale and Edwardsville: Southern Illinois Univ. Press, 1978.

Stierle, Karlheinz. "The Reading of Fictional Texts," *The Reader in the Text: Essays on Audience and Interpretation*, ed. Susan R. Suleiman and Inge Crosman. Princeton: Princeton Univ. Press, 1980.

White, E. B. *Charlotte's Web.* New York: Harper Trophy, 1952, 1973.

The Mystery of Figgs & phantoms

Constance B. Hieatt

Ellen Raskin won the 1979 Newbery Medal and the *Boston Globe–Horn Book* fiction award for *The Westing Game*, a book which has won a good deal of lavish praise.[1] Although her earlier *Figgs & phantoms* has slipped by with much less notice (two relatively minor awards), it is, in fact, a work of considerably greater depth and resonance.[2]

Raskin generally describes her books as mysteries, and *Figgs & phantoms* is so subtitled. But a Raskin mystery is not of the common or garden variety. All of them offer more than the simple appeal of what Graham Greene calls "an entertainment." While *Figgs & phantoms* indeed has many elements of the "puzzle mystery," the term Raskin used for *The Westing Game*, those readers are misled who think that the "mystery" lies in whether certain events described as taking place in "Capri" (the Figg family's eccentric version of heaven) really happened or are to be understood as a sort of dream sequence. In fact, the central mysteries of this book are of a different and more serious nature.

At first glance, it may seem preposterous to consider a book "serious" when its characters bear names such as Mona Lisa Newton, Florence Italy Figg, and Sissie Figg Newton. Sissie's tap-dancing classes hardly seem meant to suggest eternal verities: how can we do anything but laugh at the high school ball team tapping to the sound of "Take Me Out to the Ballgame," the sanitation department practicing a highland fling, and the Horticultural Society tiptoeing through the tulips? Reason tells us that a used-car dealer like Newt Newton could not support a wife and child (even in a house where the sofa has broken springs) if he is so impractical as to trade a blue Buick for a raspberry-red Edsel and a black Cadillac for a sky-blue Studebaker. This slapstick comedy appears to undercut the "realism" of Raskin's characters. And typographical jokes abound throughout the book: there is always something wrong in the signs which punctuate the story (except for the old, presumably genuine, theatrical posters), as we note advertisements for out-ofprin*k* books, 2*r*d-hand cars, and lessons in baton-twir*p*ing. Even the signpainter's own name is mislettered (Tru*nam*) in one of them. In fact, though, these "errors" challenge the reader, establish a cadre of initiates, and actually advertise the importance of rereading and revising interpretations.

While Raskin certainly enjoys buffoonery, those who assume her subject matter therefore has no genuine significance are making the mistake of the book's heroine. Mona, daughter of the manically cheerful Newt and Sissie and niece of such eccentrics as Gracie Jo and Kadota Figg (who have named their only child after a favorite bull terrier), is acutely aware of the ridiculousness of it all and rejects her family as too absurd to be borne. Overweight and resentful of what "the people" of her hometown, Pineapple, may be saying of her unattractive appearance, she rudely cuts off an uncle who inquires about her diet. All but the most superficial readers ought to be able to see that Mona is not doing herself any good by wallowing in self-pity, and when a real crisis occurs, her very life is at stake. That is, when the one member of the family she respects, her uncle Florence, dies and passes on to "Capri," Mona is determined to follow him—ostensibly to share his "dream," but logically she must also share his death. "Capri" is not really very funny after all.

A truer estimate of Raskin's intentions may be gained by seeing *Figgs & phantoms* in the light of serious traditions of literary burlesque—as in the works of Charles Dickens or in books for children such as those by Louise Fitzhugh. *Harriet the Spy*, in fact, provides a number of illuminating parallels and contrasts to *Figgs & phantoms*.[3] It is also a novel about a young girl's development and need for understanding of social relationships. Both books center on very bright but not exactly likeable little girls, each of whom is dependent on an adult who is removed from the scene fairly early in the action. In both cases, the little girl's imperceptiveness leads her to near disaster before she learns to understand others well enough to get along in the world on her own.

But an apparent difference between these two novels may be perceived in the degree to which each is presented from the central character's point of view. *Harriet the Spy* is absolutely limited to Harriet's point of view: nothing whatsoever is divulged to the reader that is not known to Harriet. The few brief instances in which we

hear remarks made by Harriet's parents not intended for her ears
actually occur at moments when Harriet is at the edge of the scene
and is clearly stated to be eavesdropping (for example, 88, 126,
246−47). *Figgs & phantoms*, on the other hand, has a few scenes in
which Mona is not present at all (notably 27−31), others in which
we presume she is out of earshot (10), and a number of instances in
which we are told what another character is actually thinking (for
example, Newt, 23, and Florence, 30). Thus the third-person narrator here is a good deal more omniscient than in *Harriet the Spy*.
Raskin's narrator also appears to be more detached than the
narrator of *Harriet the Spy*, whose remarks often actually convey
Harriet's viewpoint: for instance, in regard to the school paper,
"There was a page reserved for every grade in the Middle School
and every grade in the Upper School. The Lower School were such
idiots they didn't need a page" (88).

Since the narrator of *Figgs & phantoms* is not limited to Mona's
point of view, are we to take as objective reporting the italicized
passages set off by stars which tell us "what the people of Pineapple
said"? This technical issue is pertinent not only to the scope of the
narrator's vision but also to the problem of Mona's development. As
astute a critic as Jean Stafford, who found this book "excellent" and
well worth rereading, interpreted the italics as a chorus.[4] She said,
"From the sidelines, the people of Pineapple judge and denounce
the Figgs. . . . In time, however, after a series of most wondrous
adventures and tragedies, the family is accepted by the citizenry."
Confirmation and/or denial that Pineapple holds such a general
view of the Figgs may be found in remarks made by some of the
other characters. We may dismiss Newt Newton's disbelief that the
people of Pineapple are saying such things (45) as yet another
instance of Newt's sunny optimism (and total lack of astute observation). But at the same time, we may ask ourselves whether Mona,
who prompts Newt's protest by telling him what "people are saying"
about her uncle Truman, is any more qualified to know exactly what
is said and thought by others. To resolve this question, we should
examine the passages in italics reporting "public opinion" to determine their objectivity and narrative status.

In the first half of the book, every one of these passages is inserted
at a moment in which Mona is feeling acute embarrassment or

resentment, and the chorus of "the people of Pineapple" can be seen to mirror accurately her own concerns. The first, suggesting Pineapple's low opinion of Mona herself, comes when she has been roundly scolded by Mrs. Lumpholz, the only other person present. The italicized passage reads, *"Just look at her balancing up there like Truman the Human Pretzel"* (4). In fact, there is no one but Mrs. Lumpholz there to look at her. A comment about her uncle Florence reflects Mona's own feeling that he is "the best of the lot, by far" and comes directly after we have heard, "That's all the people of Pineapple did these days was laugh and gossip about Figgs, she thought" (10). The third of these passages criticizes her mother as "that tap-dancing Sister Figg" and Mona herself as a "misfit" (14). Immediately following Mona's arrival home, this passage mirrors her "inner fury" at being greeted by Sissie's "tap-tappity-tap-tap" (13).

The other passages of this type are all equally tied to Mona's preoccupations of the moment. Like Mona, the italicized voice appreciates her uncle as "a real star." But when Sissie has just explained that she has been teaching the volunteer fire department a double-time step for the Founders' Day parade, we hear that "the people of Pineapple said" Sissie was "making a fool of herself and the volunteer fire department to boot" (36). Oddly, though, almost everyone in town seems to be taking those tap-dancing lessons, including the Chamber of Commerce ("tapping to 'There's No Business like Show Business' "). In fact, the only remarks critical of Figgs that we actually hear, aside from the italicized passages on pages 4–88, are exclamations from Mrs. Lumpholz—with whom we may well sympathize.

Mrs. Lumpholz may offer the key to the puzzle of objectivity. It is obvious that Mona misinterprets Mrs. Lumpholz's motives all along. While she presumes Mrs. Lumpholz is being mean and vindictive in the first episode, we can gather that the protest was, at least in part, generated by concern for aging, ailing Florence, staggering under the weight of the plump niece perched on his shoulders to constitute the "Figg-Newton giant": Mona has indeed grown to be too heavy a burden. The next time we see Mrs. Lumpholz (Mona is conspicuously absent from the scene), she is concerned to see Florence walking in the car lot in the early morning in his bathrobe and with bare feet (29). The bare feet prepare the reader for the contents of

the shoebox Mrs. Lumpholz later tries to present to Florence; tell-
ingly, however, Mona thinks it must contain a bomb: " 'It's probably
a bomb,' Mona said. Newt and Sissie laughed, but she had not meant
to be clever" (57). She still apparently harbors such paranoiac suspi-
cions when Mrs. Lumpholz brings the same box to her hospital room
(142–43). Mrs. Lumpholz may be something of a busybody, but she
is clearly harmless—in everyone's eyes but Mona's.

Bump Popham, another person whose perfectly normal jesting
greeting is interpreted as an insult by Mona, has also been shown to
be friendly and concerned about Florence's well-being in the scene
which leads up to Florence's going into Bargain's bookshop to
"dicker over the price of a book he just happened to find on the third
shelf" (10). Florence's relationship with Eb Bargain is another matter about which Mona is profoundly mistaken. She thinks Bargain
does not know about the Figg-Newton giant's inspections of the
upper shelves of the bookshop, and she therefore is alarmed when
an item about the "giant" appears in the local newspaper (31). In
the end, it is obvious that Bargain knew about the giant all along.
At a later point, when Fido loses his balance in the bookshop and
leaves Mona hanging from the top shelf, we hear that "old man
Bargain had raised his head and was waving a notebook at her
threateningly" (93). This threat is not the objective observation of an
omniscient narrator, but another instance of Mona's fears, in this
case blending into the third-person (nonitalicized) narration.

Of course, the fact that Mona *is* quite mistaken does not become
clear until the last section of the book, in which we observe the entire
population of Pineapple enjoying Sissie's Founders' Day extrava-
ganza, either as participants or on the sidelines. Does this mean the
town has finally accepted the Figgs, after much denunciation, as
Jean Stafford thinks? I have already noted that the only suggestion
of such general denunciation comes in the italicized passages in
the first half of the book. There are no italicized passages in the
"Capri" sequence, in which Pineapple is almost entirely absent from
Mona's consciousness, and the italicized passages in the final section
(142–51) are of an entirely different nature. These recount what
Mona actually sees and hears for herself: and that is a scene which is,
as she finally realizes, a "happy scene" (152).

Typographical distinctions are part of Raskin's strategy, not mere jokes or the invention of a publisher's book designer. In the final argument between the author and Truman at the end of the book, our attention is called to the fact that the book ends with an ampersand. If we then turn back to the beginning, we can see that it also *begins* with an ampersand. As in *Finnegans Wake*, where the first sentence finishes the incomplete last sentence, this device symbolizes the cyclical or continuous nature of human life. But if typography is so important to Raskin, we must ask why the early italicized passages are set off by a single introductory star, whereas the final section uses rows of stars, both for italicized and nonitalicized passages.

The answer appears to be that the early italicized passages signalled by a single star and usually placed in the midst of a continuing scene (that is, not divided from what precedes or follows by a chapter break or a spaced row of five stars) represent what Mona *imagines* others may be saying about her family and herself. We cannot assume that Mona is right when one such passage (58) echoes Mona's own earlier words in calling her uncle Truman "a double-jointed idiot" (45).[5] When Mona is recovering, the "hearsay" passages cease in favor of objective reporting, set off by the rows of stars used throughout to indicate normal narrative divisions. Those earlier "one-star" passages, then, function like the excerpts from Harriet's notebook in *Harriet the Spy*: that is, they give us more direct information about what is going on in the mind of the central figure, in her *own* words, than is possible for the third-person narration, no matter how centered the point of view is on what Harriet (or Mona) observes. Thus the italicized passages in the first half of the book form the central "mystery" of *Figgs & phantoms*. To grasp what is going on in the mind of the central character fully, we must (like Mona) sharpen our perceptions and look below the surface, weighing all sorts of evidence—including what appears to be merely comic typesetting.

If we do not do this, we are in danger of sympathizing with Mona for all the wrong reasons and likely to miss one of the book's most significant concerns. To see why this is so, let us consider the first statement on the back cover of the paperback edition: "If the Figgs in *your* family were a Tap Dancing Mother, a cousin named Fido the Second, and Nine Performing Canines, you'd be miserable, too."[6] Perhaps so. Most of us live through times when we find our families embarrassing—especially, although by no means exclusively, at about Mona's age. And no doubt there is more to find embarrassing in this family than in a more "average" one. But rejection of one's own family is a serious matter. To reject one's background is to reject an important part of oneself, as Alan Garner suggests through the character of Gwyn in *The Owl Service*.[7]

Mona's descent into deepening alienation and her eventual recovery are shown both literally and symbolically in Raskin's splendid illustrations, which, like the typographical eccentricities, provide keys to the structure and meaning of the book.[8] The frontispiece shows us a "phantom": a panther in a palm tree, an image which contributes to the nightmare quality of the dream sequence in which Mona finds herself in someone else's dream. The illustrations to parts 1 through 4 show Mona's face: scowling, sulky, distraught, and associated with a progression of images of figs and pineapples. These pictures trace Mona's worsening state, and in the same way the last one indicates her restoration to physical and mental health as a result of the salutory shocks she has received in the dream world of "Capri."

To look at the sequence more closely, we first see her enclosed in a fig-shaped space—but dropping from the fig tree, not firmly attached, which points to her wish to disassociate herself from her family. Then we see the fig planted within a pineapple: Mona feels hemmed in, not only by her family but by the town of Pineapple, which she sees as scorning her as one of the ridiculous Figgs. Next we see the pineapple expand and become vacant space itself, at the same time that it begins to show an expansion of wildly growing foliage, at the beginning of the chapter in which we hear about the Figg family "Capri" ritual—an exotic growth which has nothing to do with the other residents of Pineapple.[9] At the beginning of part 4, which takes up events after Florence's death, a vacant, not fully materialized palm tree sprouts from the vacant (except for Mona's face) pineapple. This is appropriate because in this section Mona's thoughts turn from "the people of Pineapple" almost completely and there is only a single "one-star" italicized passage (the last in the book). At this stage, Mona is searching for clues to lead her to her uncle's "Capri," and one of the most important of these is a picture of a pink palm tree. Part 5, the dream sequence, is linked to the earlier sequence *only* by the palm tree, now with the head of the would-be pirate materializing in it and dominating the scene: as indeed it should, for this particular "Capri" is the pirate's own dream.

The last section, part 6, begins with an illustration which carries over none of the fig–pineapple–palm images. In fact, we see there nothing that has been seen before at all except the decorative and exuberant foliage, a vacant space, and Mona's head, all three of which are as transformed as the Mona we read about in this section. Mona is smiling and clear-eyed for the first time, looking out rather than into herself, and the foliage trained about a window bears flowers. Mona, now come into "bloom," is able to look outward because the pirate has helped to heal her by telling her the painful truth: that she is "a selfish, stubborn, self-centered child" (128). He has revealed her ignorance—both of other people, including her beloved uncle, and of books. One of many instances which prove the former is her encounter on "Capri" with the woman with the head of a pig (117), whose picture she had seen in a book that she "quickly decided . . . had found its way into [Florence's] trunk by accident" (86). And her ignorance of books, despite her "professional" expertise, is depicted with splendid symbolism when she is unable to conjure up the contents of Conrad's *Typhoon*: as the pirate says, to her a book is a package.

The connection between Mona's inability to recognize her uncle's separate existence and needs and her ignorance of Conrad's words is an important one. While not the only author alluded to or echoed in this book,[10] Conrad is a vital key for a full understanding of the "mysteries" involved. A first quotation, from *Heart of Darkness*, frightens Mona: "We live, as we dream—alone" (94). Mona "refused to believe it had anything to do with Capri": but of course it is exactly the lesson she has to learn in her invasion of "Capri," someone else's dream. It is only through books that we can live in the dreams of others. The other quotations from Conrad are one-word summaries which are likely to be puzzling to readers who do not know Conrad's works. Fido's summary of *Lord Jim*—"Jump" (97)—is potentially hilarious to those familiar with Conrad. Whatever Fido may think it means, Mona takes the message literally in a sense central to the great disaster of Lord Jim's life: "Abandon ship." Even readers who do not know this should be able to see that "Jump" might be disastrous advice for Mona, suggesting suicide. Fido appears to sense the danger and returns with another one-word summary of a work by Conrad just as Mona slips into a coma: "Wait" (101). Wait is the name of a principal character in *The Nigger of the Narcissus* and conveys a message Fido rightly sees as appropriate for Mona.

Mona is not only trying to invade someone else's dream, she has been trying to read by proxy, through Fido. If she had finished *Heart of Darkness*, she might eventually have realized that it had some interesting parallels to her own experience. Albert J. Guerard remarks that both *Heart of Darkness* and *The Secret Sharer* are "in fact the same story, and have the same mythical theme—the theme of initiation and moral education, the theme of progress through temporary reversion and achieved self-knowledge, the theme of man's exploratory descent into the primitive sources of being."[11] They also share the motif of the double, the other human being with whom the narrator identifies, but who he must learn is actually other.

Something like this is also Mona's experience: she has regarded her uncle as part of herself, the other half of the Figg-Newton giant. She must learn that he is himself and leave him to his own identity before she is finally released to find her own. And as it happens, her progress towards common humanity is signified in a gesture which comes right out of *Heart of Darkness*. Readers of that work will recall that the narrator, Marlow, has identified himself with the terrible Kurtz, who represents what he, or any of us, could, at our worst, become. After the death of Kurtz, Marlow returns to Europe and, in an act of kindness, tells Kurtz's fiancée what she wants to hear: that the last words Kurtz had spoken were her name. This is a lie, but one necessary to preserve the woman's peace of mind. In exactly the same way, Mona, comforting the tormented Fido, gives him a posthumous message from Florence which is a lie pure and simple, but just what Fido needs to hear.

Mona may not have finished her reading, but she behaves like a Conrad character. The great themes of Conrad's novels are isolation and alienation, and their opposites and remedies, fidelity and human solidarity. What Conrad called the "true lie," as in Marlow's lie to Kurtz's fiancée, is part of the remedy for isolation and alienation. Mona, like Marlow, tells a lie which is "true" in the sense that it affirms the values people must or should live by. As Conrad put it in an essay, "For the great mass of mankind the only saving grace that is needed is steady fidelity to what is nearest to hand and heart in the short moment of each human effort."[12] Fido, and his need, are what are nearest to Mona in her particular moment.

Conrad, then, is a vital clue to those who would read *Figgs & phantoms* as a mystery—or as a puzzle, as the cover illustration for the paperback edition suggests, aptly showing some volumes of Conrad as bits in a jigsaw puzzle.[13] But everything else in the book also fits in as neatly as pieces of a jigsaw puzzle, including the details of names and language, which I am tempted to relate to a crossword puzzle. I cannot help wondering whether it is not likely that Raskin came across *caprifig* in such a puzzle—or, more likely, *caprification*, "to ripen figs by the stinging of a gall insect."[14] The word makes an apt metaphor for Mona's ripening: she is green, immature, bitter, and has to be thoroughly stung before she shows signs of mellowing and sweetening.

Raskin reminds us that buffoonery may camouflage matters which are deadly serious by also interweaving references to *The Yeoman of the Guard*, the only Gilbert and Sullivan operetta which ends tragically for a character with whom we feel real sympathy. The jester Jack Point is not mentioned by name in *Figgs & phantoms*, but a song primarily associated with him is quoted at the crucial moment after Mona slams shut *Heart of Darkness* (95). And anyone who knows *The Yeoman* (a group likely to loom larger among the readers of Ellen Raskin than do Conrad readers) is likely to recall Jack Point's two songs about the bitter lot of the "private buffoon." The one which seems most appropriate to bear in mind in relation to the art of Ellen Raskin is the song which ends,

> He who'd make his fellow, fellow, fellow
> creatures wise
> Must always gild the philosophic pill.

Notes

1. (New York: E. P. Dutton, 1978; Avon Camelot edition, 1980.) For typical reviews of the book, see those of Virginia Haviland in *Horn Book* 54 (August 1978): 404, and Georgess McHargue in the *New York Times Book Review*, June 25, 1978, 36–37.

2. (Dutton, 1974; Avon Camelot, 1981.) Page references herein will be to the latter, a paperback edition. *Figgs & phantoms* was a Newbery Honor book and an ALA notable book. Jean Stafford's review in the *New Yorker* (50:41, December 2, 1974, 188–90) appears to have been the only review of more than one paragraph. I have not capitalized the title's "*phantoms*" because of evidence that all the peculiarities of typography in this book are authorial and intentional.

3. (New York: Harper & Row, 1964.) Page numbers cited herein refer to the Dell paperback edition. For critical discussion of *Harriet the Spy*, see especially Virginia L. Wolf, "*Harriet the Spy*: Milestone, Masterpiece?," *Children's Literature* 4 (1975):120–26.

4. For other more or less favorable views of the book, see the reviews of Marilyn R. Singer in *Library Journal* 99 (May 1974): 1475, and those appearing in *Book List* 71 (September 1, 1974):46 and (March 15, 1975): 767. A more puzzled reaction is that of Ethel L. Heins in *Horn Book* 50 (October 1974):138.

5. It is barely possible, by the way, that the remark by "the people of Pineapple" on page 58 suggesting that Truman was named after the president of the United States involves a youthful misunderstanding on Mona's part: chronology sketched elsewhere suggests Truman must have been born before Harry S Truman became president.

6. Note that this is a misquotation: Kadota has *K*anines, not mere *c*anines.

7. (London: Collins, 1967.) This aspect of the characterization of Gwyn seems to have been insufficiently grasped by those who find the ending of *The Owl Service* upsetting.

8. Another parallel between Raskin and Fitzhugh is their enrichment of these books with their own illustrations. Fitzhugh's are not, of course, symbolic in the same way that Raskin's are here, but they are very much worth attention.

9. It is worth noting that Mona has also failed to grasp the true meaning of the family ritual: central to it is "the tree that grows wild and free," which is "the key to the perfect dream." But, in the words of Noah Figg, "there are many trees—each must find his own Capri." In other words, "Capri" is each individual's private (free, not cultivated) dream, and each must find his own. Her uncle has found his in books.

10. Among the others is Milton; the passage the pirate quotes on p. 113 is from *Paradise Lost* 2:624–68 (describing hell).

11. Introduction to *Heart of Darkness* and *The Secret Sharer* (Signet Classic, 1950), 15.

12. "Well Done," quoted by Robert Penn Warren in his introduction to *Nostromo* (New York: Random House Modern Library, 1951), xvi.

13. The cover is not Raskin's own work; it is credited to Little Apple Art.

14. *Oxford English Dictionary*, s.v. "caprification."

Reading Outside Over There

Michael Steig

Living testimony of the artist's view of the picture book as a "beautiful, poetic form." . . . The more it is enjoyed, the more the book yields up its secrets.

—Ethel L. Heins[1]

Drearily nostalgic and sentimental.

—Donnarae MacCann and Olga Richard[2]

Every serious reader . . . must bring to the book his own interpretation. . . . The pictures are quite simply magnificent.

—Elaine Moss[3]

Too much is left unexplained.

—Susan Hankla[4]

I had waited a long time to be taken out of kiddy-book land and allowed to join the artists of America.

—Maurice Sendak[5]

The range of reactions to *Outside Over There*[6] represented in the first four epigraphs suggests that readers have found themselves presented with problems of affective content, aesthetic value, meaning, and, in Sendak's own comment, the status of this work as a children's book. My own experience in coming to terms with Sendak's most difficult text (by which I shall throughout mean both words and pictures) indicates to me that there is some value in beginning a study of it from the premise that such "problems" are in readers as much as in author or text. Such a study can become in part a "story of reading,"[7] but such an account of one's reading experience does not deny that a text has a separate existence. It is, rather, a deliberate choice to concentrate on the process of reading, partly in order to understand the basis of difficulties with the text, and partly to make possible a meaningful comparison with other readers' reactions. Such an approach seems especially appropriate to children's literature, which so often appeals to adults, as to children, by evoking strong emotions and associations—especially with childhood. It is also a means of discovering and communicating the way a reader—

not "the reader"—comes to terms with the difficulties in a complex text found to be disturbing.[8]

My own approach to literary works originated in the classroom, in the process of a shift from a fairly conventional new-critical teaching style with a Freudian slant to a reader-response approach which requires from the students—and from myself as a classroom participant—written and shared analyses of individual experiences of reading, with special attention to the affects and associations which give some insight into what David Bleich (following the psychotherapist Leon Levy) calls individual "language systems."[9] According to Bleich's model, when we read we translate the author's language system into our own, a process which is then objectified in the attempt to interpret—whether or not we are explicit about the subjective aspect, our feelings and associations. (Bleich's terms for what I am calling translation and objectification are *symbolization* and *resymbolization*.)

Such a double process, I suggest, takes place in all literary interpretation and evaluation, usually without direct acknowledgment. Although David Bleich has probably been accused of "eliminating the text" and equating one interpretation with any other more often than have Stanley Fish and Norman Holland, paradoxically it is Bleich who pays the most attention to traditional aspects of literary criticism: evaluation, exegesis, biographical interpretation, and genre-study.[10] The twist Bleich gives in his model of reading is that these areas of study are approached through an individual's "language system" which is dependent upon his or her entire life experience up to the moment of "resymbolization." The author becomes a symbolic and affect-laden entity whom many readers naturally construct as they read; and Bleich insists that the construction of an author is not fundamentally different from the documentation of that author's life in order to support an interpretation. Such documentation is "sought in order to validate one's conception of the author," and "there is no final way to decide that a particular biographical formulation of an author's life is objectively true" (*SC*, 259). Thus biographical data are always in the service of the reader's subjective motivation, as are all approaches to understanding a text.

Unfortunately for those who might like to have a ready-made method for doing literary criticism according to this model of reading, Bleich's own published work is really metacriticism, dealing primarily with theory and pedagogy. And the application of his theory only to his students' and his own written responses, with greatest emphasis on developing knowledge of the self, creates difficulties for one who feels motivated also to understand the text as other. Nonetheless, I am convinced that a reader can "find" meaning and coherence only by remaining alive to the way his or her motives and responses determine his interpretation. In practice a reader-response approach to interpretation must oscillate between the text as self and the text experienced as other, between "subjective" and "objective" considerations (though these may only be the names we give to different states of mind).

Although Elaine Moss sounds rather like a subjective critic in asserting that "every serious reader" must bring to *Outside Over There* "his own interpretation," she also insists that if one wants the book to "live"—and, presumably, to make sense—Sendak's life and emotional conflicts had better be ignored. Teaching *Outside Over There* in a children's literature course, I would probably ask students to write individual responses before I talked about Sendak himself; yet having absorbed various kinds of information I shall never be able to perform a "pure" reading, untainted, so to speak, by extrinsic knowledge. Such knowledge, once acquired, becomes part of the reading process, which is not to say, for example, that Sendak's explanations of his work must control another reader's understanding.

Though my reading is "subjective," it also incorporates knowledge of the responses of other critics, in the context of the five-year build-up of the book. It was, we were told, going to be the capstone of his work, most impressive artistically and most important emotionally for Sendak, completing what he had begun in the first two volumes of his "trilogy," *Where the Wild Things Are* (1963) and *In the Night Kitchen* (1970).[11] With such a long period of waiting, readers were likely either to be coerced into uncritical admiration when the work appeared or to suffer various degrees of disappointment. Ethel Heins's praise unaccompanied by any interpretation was at one extreme. At the other extreme, Donnarae MacCann and Olga Richard not only label *Outside Over There* "vacuous," but claim that it, like much of Sendak's other work, has a major weakness in its adaptation of earlier artists' styles, which do not fuse into original form. They identify this eclecticism as a quality of "popular art"— art which takes few risks and relies upon "collective 20th century experience which elicit[s] a loyal following" (13). Further, they take Sendak's description of the process of creation as a response to "unbidden feelings" and his conjecture that "children read the internal meanings of *everything*" to be an abdication of the responsibility to achieve original form and coherent meaning (16).

It might be argued that MacCann's and Richard's judgments are based on a narrow, elitist view of fine art in relation to popular art, a view they apply to Sendak without real discussion. But Susan Hankla's *cri de coeur* in reply to Ethel Heins's review makes a much more serious charge, for Hankla finds *Outside Over There* a "paranoid vision" and a "shallow, icy surrogate for a literature which will benefit humanity." I do not know whether Sendak's book will benefit humanity, but Hankla's response has to be taken seriously, if only to be countered. And my fascination with the book cannot be separated from my own strong initial revulsion, from the controversy over Sendak's eclecticism, or from what I believe I have detected about a key literary source of the book. Because that discovery was what enabled me to begin to come to terms with *Outside Over There*, I shall treat it first in presenting my story of reading.

According to Selma Lanes, Sendak derived the "bare-bones plot" of *Outside Over There* from the brief Grimms' tale, "The Goblins," which he had illustrated in 1973 (228).[12] The connection with a story about a baby stolen by goblins is clear enough, and the artist seems to allude to his earlier illustration by providing the hooded goblins of *Outside Over There* with the same kind of staff.[13] But so far as I know, no critic has identified what seems to be a more fundamental and complex source for Sendak's text, George MacDonald's *The Princess and the Goblin*, and to a lesser extent Arthur Hughes's illustrations for that book and for MacDonald's *At the Back of the North Wind*.[14] Nor has Sendak mentioned these in published interviews as influences on the third volume of his trilogy.

Sendak has, however, in most of those interviews mentioned MacDonald as a "model . . . someone I try to copy in many ways."[15] He has spoken of "ripping off" MacDonald, whose "fairytales . . . are for me the source book of much of my work."[16] In a 1970 interview

Sendak refers specifically to *The Princess and the Goblin*, and to Princess "Irene's travels through the cave with the goblins" as being so strange that "they can only come out of the deepest dream stuff" (Haviland, 247). The greatest interest of the latter statement is the fact that eleven years before the publication of *Outside Over There* Sendak has already in his memory transformed MacDonald's novel into something more like his as yet unwritten book than it really is: for although there is a goblin plot to kidnap Irene "to be a nasty goblin's bride" (Sendak's words in *Outside Over There*), and she does travel through their caves, she never actually comes into direct contact with the goblins, as Sendak's Ida is to do.

In *Outside Over There* Sendak was further to transform a kidnapping plot into an actual kidnapping, and the victim from a young girl into a baby sister in such a girl's charge. But the initial circumstances and even setting are similar. Irene lives in a great house halfway up a hill, her parents absent—father traveling throughout his kingdom and mother elsewhere because of a serious illness. Ida, who also lives on a hill, must take the place of an absent-minded, preoccupied mother in caring for her little sister, while her father is "away at sea." The hill in Sendak's first two-page spread is similar to Hughes's first cut for *The Princess and the Goblin*, which also depicts a stone bridge like that over which Sendak's goblins carry the baby.

But perhaps the most revealing evidence of Sendak's debt to MacDonald is a remark in his 1976 interview with Jonathan Cott: "The only way to find something is to lose oneself: that's what George MacDonald teaches us in his stories" (Cott 1977, 201). Although in the immediate context Sendak is referring to Mahler's "losing himself" in his *Waldhütte*, the MacDonald reference would seem to be to Irene's earliest adventure, when she must lose herself in order to find the protective (and strangely erotic) figure of her "great-great-grandmother" at the top of the mansion. MacDonald remarks that "it doesn't follow that she *was* lost, because she had lost herself" (ch. 2, p. 17); and Irene's failure in the next attempt to find this mysterious figure whose love she so greatly needs, when she *is* described as being "lost," seems to stem from her failure to lose herself, her self-consciousness, her waking rationality (ch. 5, p. 32). This matter of losing oneself fits the pattern of all three works in Sendak's trilogy (as well as many of MacDonald's works, such as

"The Golden Key" and the adult fantasy, *Lilith*): the journey into the dream and back of *Where the Wild Things Are* and *In the Night Kitchen*, where the dream is a losing of oneself that effects a new reconciliation to one's life; and what I see as the more ambiguous experience of Ida and her sister's being lost and restored.

The forms of the recurrence of fictional situations from MacDonald to Sendak suggest that Sendak is not merely imitating, or "ripping off," but transforming source elements. And as I read and reread, I find that I internalize those elements, which come to form a level of intertextual meaning in Sendak's text. Thus, Sendak's double-page spread, "If Ida backwards in the rain . . . ," where Ida's floating on her back in the air trailing the yellow raincoat resembles Arthur Hughes's engraving of the North Wind floating in the air as she prepares to take Little Diamond to his final rest, assumes for me a special resonance because the North Wind is "saving" Diamond as Ida is saving her sister (*At the Back of the North Wind*, ch. 37, p. 285). Hughes's surprisingly erotic drawing and MacDonald's text associate the beautiful North Wind, like Irene's great-great-grandmother, with physical maternal love, spiritual goodness, and a vaguely defined afterlife. Though there is no exact resemblance—apart from that of saving a small child—between the functions of the North Wind and of Sendak's Ida, identifying this apparent influence helped to clarify my feelings about aspects of Sendak's text: feelings of loneliness, loss, and anxiety in childhood about sexuality and death.

The connections between *Outside Over There* and the work of MacDonald and his illustrator Hughes seem too obvious to be doubted.[17] From *The Princess and the Goblin* in particular come the neglect of a child; actual or intended kidnapping by goblins for the purpose of a wedding; and the necessity of losing oneself. Perhaps even more fundamental is the way in which, in both texts, danger comes from *outside*, and from the depths of the earth. One answer to Susan Hankla's question as to where "outside over there" really is would seem to be (for MacDonald as well as Sendak) anywhere primal dangers might lurk, outside one's own comfortable bedroom, home, and family. Yet "outside over there" is also "inside in here,"[18] the domestic world where all the child's guilty feelings of oedipal desire, aggression, and jealousy originate; and Sendak's tale

One of several illustrations in which Arthur Hughes depicts the North Wind floating on her back.

could almost be taken as a paradigm of how the *heimlich* (domestic, private, secret, forbidden) becomes the *unheimlich* (alien, threatening, strange, but also eerily familiar).[19]

Elaine Moss brings a knowledge of psychoanalysis—remarks about which pervade Sendak's statements about his own work—to her reading but warns against taking account of Sendak himself. She finds Ida to be threatened by "malign forces which may shatter the eggshell protection of childhood" and to be projecting her fears upon her baby sister, who in fantasy becomes the victim in place of the nearly adolescent Ida; Ida can then save her sister, in a resolution as "reassuring as is Max's hot supper." And Sendak has commented on what ties the parts of his trilogy together: "They are all variations on the same theme: how children master various feelings—anger, boredom, fear, frustration, jealousy—and manage to come to grips with the realities of their lives" (Lanes, 227). Such a scenario nicely describes the first two books, but for *Outside Over There* it seems less adequate, failing (like Moss's reading) to account for the ambiguity of the ending and the more complex and disturbing symbolism.

My own reading now starts from the premise that Sendak's creative process is autobiographical and eclectic. This allows me to integrate what I see as his main sources and what I have learned about his life into my total understanding. But this is a point arrived at only with difficulty, after an initially negative response to the apparent obscurity and didacticism and the new graphic style of *Outside Over There*. That response was provoked, and the possibility of empathy was blocked, first of all, by a feeling of betrayal in Sendak's change of style. The flat, comic-book style of *In the Night Kitchen*, which recalled the tokens of love given to me especially when I was ill as a child, and the cross-hatching of *Higglety-Pigglety-Pop*, so reminiscent of my favorite, Cruikshank, had been replaced by a mode which, especially in its modeling of figures, recalled the despised *Saturday Evening Post* commercial art of my childhood.[20] This experience is undoubtedly related to some literary critics' tendency to denigrate works by a favorite author which seem to deviate from an expected norm, as in the supposed failure of irony in Austen's *Mansfield Park*. But worse than the shock at Sendak's new style was my feeling about the apparently didactic implications of the story: girls, if they want to be happy and content, must take care of their baby sisters *and* their mothers. What I sensed as an attempt to provide reassurance for the reader just didn't work.

Discovering what I thought to be Sendak's main source in Mac-Donald provided a framework within which I could reconsider my response. If a single aspect of *The Princess and the Goblin* is dominant for me it is the combination of Irene's virtually orphaned state with her strong and determined sense of self, a combination which allows her both to find her succoring great-great-grandmother *and* to make the "mistake" (Sendak's word about Ida) of staying outside too long with her maid, thus putting herself in danger from the goblins (ch. 6). Of course it is this mistake that leads to her meeting Curdie, whom she later saves from the goblins in the mine, and who in turn saves her from a "goblin wedding" (again, Sendak's expression).

Because my identification is strongest with the lonely but self-possessed child, and secondarily with the older male child, Curdie, I find especially appealing MacDonald's notion that being a princess depends on inner rather than contingent (hereditary) qualities. And the narrative structure recalls childhood fantasies about the foundling who attains love, power, and acceptance.

The goblins' threat to Irene has affective significance for me in three ways. There is a guilty identification with the goblins in their desire to treat sadistically and possess sexually the pure young girl. Insofar as I identify with the princess as child, however, I also feel a fear of physical violation. And for my adult consciousness, an ongoing pleasure is provided by the extraordinary way MacDonald presents a pre-Freudian model of the human psyche, corresponding roughly to the id (the savage goblins in their deep caverns), the developing ego (Irene), the integrated ego (the miners, and especially Curdie, who can work in the mines but also functions rationally above ground), and, in the great-great-grandmother, a female ego-ideal which is given clear preference over the machismo of the super-ego King-Papa (as Irene calls him).[21] Thus *The Princess and the Goblin* provided some insight into Sendak's creative process and an external framework which seemed to make *Outside Over There* more coherent.

The available information about Sendak's childhood memories also helped to unblock empathy with the fantasies behind his most difficult book. Like Sendak, I spent long periods sick in bed; I adored comic-book art, especially the Disney comics of the early 1940s—and this was related to illness, as I would receive extra comic-books to keep me occupied. What is probably common to such childhood memories is a feeling of illness as something special, something that makes one the focus of attention for a while, and brings both extra affection and extra freedom to be alone with one's thoughts. Although I was an only child, I did have a surrogate sister, an older girl with whom I spent much time, and when she entered puberty and became less interested in her "little brother" I suffered a feeling of great loss. Although there is nothing like this in Sendak's accounts of his sister, who was twelve rather than two years older than he, I am inferring that he had similar experiences from the way he depicts Ida's neglect of her little sister.

These connections, which are really constructs, as Sendak and I in most ways had very different childhoods, further opened up the possibility that *Outside Over There* might not be impossibly alien after all. Upon reflection, it occurs to me that many of the greatest children's books, seemingly based on bizarre personal fantasies, have their incoherences and their hints of what Leon Edel has called the "tristimania" of great art, the feeling, beginning in childhood, of a fundamental sadness in life.[22] Given my experiences with students who, not having read *Alice's Adventures in Wonderland* as children, find it both disturbing and incoherent, I should not be surprised at my own resistance to recognizing the emotional coherence of *Outside Over There*.

Probably the most seriously unresponsive aspect of my early readings of Sendak's tale was that I saw not only the conclusion, but also the initial situation, as approved by the narrator: "When Papa was away at sea, / and Mama in the arbor . . ." I can now see that both the initial two-page spreads include disturbing elements, not only the ominously lurking hooded goblins, but the evident ignoring of Ida and her screaming baby sister by their mother, and the frustrated look on Ida's face. Her sister's bonnet has just fallen on the ground and Ida is looking down at it as if hoping her mother will turn around and pick it up for her. Given this opening, where things are emotionally wrong, "Ida played her wonder horn to rock the baby still—but never watched" has connotations of deliberate and hostile neglect, emphasized by the visual parallel with the previous illustration, where Ida's mother's back is turned just as Ida's is here.

Sendak told Selma Lanes that he identified as much with Ida as with the baby, although it was he who was cared for as a child by his older sister; and it is Ida, rather than the baby, who is given strong emotions (though the baby's face is more expressive), the fear and jealousy. Ida's unawareness of the kidnapping seems to be due to her almost hypnotic fascination with the horn, roses, and sunflowers (which combine male sexual force in their tumescence with phallic and vaginal shapes in their leaves), just as her failure to see the ice changeling is due to her own icy feelings toward her burdensome sister. To say, as Susan Hankla does, that Sendak's is a "strikingly paranoid vision" which implies that without constant vigilance "the world as you know it can be replaced by one in which repulsive

goblins steal real babies," apart from taking a symbolic (or, as Geraldine DeLuca argues, allegorical) tale too literally, denies a particu-
larity to Ida's experience and overlooks the possibility that Ida
herself is in conflict. That is, the kidnapping and saving of the baby,
as manifestations of Ida's fantasies, represent a conflict between
hostility and love.

The idea of psychological projection is borne out by the fact that
Sendak (at least as I understand his use of MacDonald) changes the
object of the goblins' lust and cruelty in MacDonald from the "I"
(Irene, Ida) to the baby.[23] That Ida symbolically tries to take on her
mother's role by donning her raincoat seems clear, but why is it a
"serious mistake" to climb "backwards out the window into outside
over there"? Backwards may have various implications, including
regression, but in the context of the previously turned backs of Ida
and her mother, it suggests to me a continuation of unconscious
neglect (since Ida is, after all, trying to save her sister). It is the voice
of the father (psychologically the introjected father or super-ego)
that provides Ida with the right kind of magic: in effect, the command, "Turn around and look!" This seems to be stressed in
the double-page spread in which she is hearing her father's voice,
through the inclusion of a portrayal of the neglectful (and, it should
be remembered, maritally neglected) mother in her seat in the
arbor, with the baby's bonnet still not picked up, and separated by
many caves from her baby, the mother looking quite unaware that
anything is happening.

The revelation to Ida that the goblins are "just babies like her
sister!" has at least a double edge. While it can be seen as a defense
against the threats that seem to loom in puberty, it also implies that
for Ida her sister is indeed something of a goblin—screaming and
making ugly faces when Ida wants to talk to her mother or play her
horn. Of additional interest is the ambiguous gender of the goblin
babies; all are naked, but the only sex (in two of the goblins) revealed
is female, which suggests again that Ida's sister is as much of a
"goblin" threat as the onset of her own sexual maturity. There is also
a telling phrase which connects the scene to what Sendak has called
his "individualized" childhood (Stott, 37): "We're dancing sick and
must to bed." Does this mean that Maurice himself is one of those
troublemaking goblins in his fantasies about his childhood? (Sendak

told Cott that everyone in the book is female, including the five goblins, though I see no way of telling about three of them; and further, two unquestionably male sailors and a male shepherd are depicted in the two-page spread, "If Ida backwards . . . ").[24] Again, in the "dancing sick" scene, the reference to the hornpipe making "sailors wild" recalls Ida's father the sailor, and a girl's ambivalence about her father's sexuality. In this same connection the eggshell in which Ida finds her sister seems to be a symbol of both the protective shell of childhood mentioned by Moss and a child's belief that chickens come from eggs and babies from mothers without any role for the father—although here it could also be a fantasy-denial of the mother's role. Indeed, it is only after being (apparently) born from the egg that Ida's sister is "crooning and clapping as a baby should," quite different behavior from that at the book's opening, when the mother is present.[25]

A problem for some readers, and one of the main obstacles to my taking *Outside Over There* seriously, is the apparent didacticism of the conclusion. Returning with her sister to their mother, Ida finds that a letter has come from her father which instructs her to "watch the baby and her Mama for her Papa, who loves her always." Sendak reports that a friend found this disturbing, in the way it "dumps everything on Ida," but he refuses to commit himself to a definite meaning for this conclusion (Cott 1983, 77). Elaine Moss, apparently feeling a need of closure, construes the ending as reassuring, and I think my own reaction and that of Sendak's friend indicated a similar wish for closure but an inability to find it.[26] It now seems more satisfying to take a clue from Sendak's demurral and consider that ending as a step reached in a process of emotional development for Ida (and perhaps her mother as well). One may venture a nonreductive Freudian reading at this point. The symbolic meaning of the father's absence and his letter, for Ida, is that the female child must come to recognize that she cannot have her father for herself and need not regard her mother as a rival. But because of the double configuration of the oedipus complex experienced by girls, the conclusion can also signify that the *mother* is not exclusively one's own—especially in the context of a sibling rivalry. Ida is, surely, accepting some of the functions of a mother in relation to her baby sister.[27] Yet it is a *step*, not a completed process. And if my earlier resistance to this ending was obtuse, this was perhaps because I, like Elaine Moss and Sendak's friend, was expecting a certain kind of resolution, in part because of unexamined assumptions about what a children's book should accomplish, and at a deeper level because of anxieties stemming from childhood, about loss and the fear of growing up.

At this point in the account of my story of reading, it seems relevant to turn again to *The Princess and the Goblin*, in order to stress the intertextual component of my response (and one might note that Sendak's view of his work is also intertextual, though so far he has cited texts other than the one I find most important). Irene's losses are greater than Ida's, for not only is her father mostly absent, but it is clear toward the end of the novel that her mother is dead. Yet Irene too has moved at least one step in her development: by taking the initiative to enter the mine and rescue Curdie, she has made possible the eventual routing of the goblins, symbols of male sexuality as dirty, violent, and demeaning. She thus clears the way for a mature relationship with Curdie, who will eventually (in *The Princess and Curdie*) replace Ida's King-Papa as her main love-object, after he goes through his own process of testing.

The Princess and the Goblin, *Outside Over There*, and *The Magic Flute*, one of Sendak's avowed sources, are all fantasies of the testing and development of individuals. It is evident from Sendak's published statements that at the time of writing *Outside Over There* he was consciously creating a tribute to Mozart (and the Grimms) rather than to MacDonald; I can only guess that if one of his interviewers had raised the question of MacDonald's influence on *Outside Over There* we might have a different set of statements. But this is relatively unimportant for what has been the telling of a story of reading. Both MacDonald and Sendak have shown me the danger of reading their fantasies either too literally or too much as strict allegories. My experience of *Outside Over There* has also shown me the need to let one's response and thus understanding flow from a contact with one's (inevitably reconstructed) child-self. Neither *The Princess and the Goblin* nor *Outside Over There* should be defined as "children's" or "adult's" books; rather, they are works which demonstrate just how fine the line is between being a child and being an adult.

Notes

1. Review of Maurice Sendak, *Outside Over There, Horn Book* 57 (June 1981): 288.

2. Review of Selma G. Lanes, *The Art of Maurice Sendak, Children's Literature Association Quarterly* 6 (Winter 1981/1982): 13. Subsequent references are given in the text.

3. Review of Maurice Sendak, *Outside Over There, Times Literary Supplement*, July 24 1981, 841.

4. Letter to *Horn Book* 58 (June 1982): 347.

5. As quoted by Selma G. Lanes, *The Art of Maurice Sendak* (New York: Abrams, 1980), 235. Subsequent references are given in the text.

6. Maurice Sendak, *Outside Over There* (New York: Harper and Row, 1981).

7. The term is Jonathan Culler's. See *On Deconstruction: Theory and Criticism after Structuralism* (Ithaca, Cornell Univ. Press, 1982), 64–83. I should mention that Culler has little respect for "stories of reading."

8. Only at the time of final revision did Geraldine DeLuca's excellent article become available. Since our methods and aims are quite different I shall cite only instances of clear overlap. See "Exploring the Levels of Childhood: The Allegorical Sensibility of Maurice Sendak," *Children's Literature* 12 (1984): 3–24.

9. *Subjective Criticism* (Baltimore: Johns Hopkins Univ. Press, 1978), 84–85 et passim. Subsequent references (to *SC*) are given in the text.

10. The titles of chapters 7–10 of *SC*, which cover the areas I have listed, are "Acts of Taste and Changes of Taste," "The Construction of Literary Meaning," "The Conception and Documentation of the Author," and "Collective Interests and Literary Regularities."

11. The prepublication publicity began as early as Jonathan Cott's 1976 *Rolling Stone* interview (reprinted in Cott, *Forever Young* [New York: Random House/Rolling Stone, 1977], 189–219; subsequent references are given in the text), and extended to Selma Lanes's coffee-table volume, published nearly a year before *Outside Over There*.

12. It appeared as the frontispiece to the first volume of *The Juniper Tree and Other Tales from Grimm*, translated by Lore Segal and Randall Jarrell, 2 vols. (New York: Farrar, Straus, Giroux, 1973).

13. In Jonathan Cott's expansion of his 1976 interview of Sendak, the importance and significance of both "The Goblins" and *The Magic Flute* are more fully explained. These accounts do not change the direction of my argument. See Jonathan Cott, *Pipers at the Gates of Dawn* (New York: Random House, 1983), especially 70–75.

14. *At the Back of the North Wind* was published in 1870, *The Princess and the Goblin* in 1871. My texts are, for the first, the Octopus Books edition of *At the Back of the North Wind* (with the Princess novels) (London, 1979), and the second, the Puffin Books edition (Harmondsworth: Penguin, 1964).

15. 1970 interview of Sendak by Virginia Haviland, reprinted in *The Cool Web: The Pattern of Children's Reading*, ed. Margaret Meek, Aidan Warlow, and Griselda Barton (London: Bodley Head, 1977), 247. Subsequent references are given in the text.

16. "The Nature of Fantasy: A Conversation with Ruth Nichols, Cooper, and Maurice Sendak" (interviewer, Jon Stott), *The World of Children's Books* 3 (Fall 1978): 34. Subsequent references (to Stott) are given in the text.

17. Curiously, in his introduction to *Pipers at the Gates of Dawn*, Cott, in referring to MacDonald, mentions as his works for children only *At the Back of the North Wind, The Princess and Curdie*, and *Sir Gibbie*. *Sir Gibbie* is not generally considered a children's

book, and it is strange to refer to the sequel of *The Princess and the Goblin* only. (My sense of Cott's reliability—and perhaps that of any interview—was further shaken by the chapter following that on Sendak, "William Steig and His Path," which includes interviews with several members of my family and initially led me to consider writing a personal essay with the title, "On Seeing One's Family Myths in Print.")

18. I came to this conclusion as a way of answering Susan Hankla's puzzlement at where "outside over there" *is*, before I saw Cott's 1983 book (75), in which Sendak is quoted as making precisely the same statement.

19 The classic account of the paradoxical connection between *heimlich* and *unheimlich* is Sigmund Freud, "The 'Uncanny' " (1919), in *The Complete Psychological Works of Sigmund Freud*, translated by James and Alix Strachey, 24 vols. (London: Hogarth Press, 1955) 17: 219–52.

20. Sendak has made it clear that the primary influence on his new style is the work of the German Romantic, Philipp Otto Runge.

21. See Richard H. Reis, *George MacDonald* (New York: Twayne, 1972), especially the section, "Psychology: Freudian before Freud," 41–45.

22. See Leon Edel, *Stuff of Sleep and Dreams: Experiments in Literary Psychology* (New York: Harper and Row, 1982).

23. Lanes (232–34) reports that Sendak was delighted to find that Ida included 'Id," and that the three letters were also contained, backwards (cf. "Ida backwards"), in his mother's name (Sadie). But given the connections with *The Princess and Goblin*, it seems as likely that the unconscious source is the resemblance between Irene, Ida, and "I," which is also the literal translation of Freud's *"Ich"* (ego).

24. Critics thus far seem unable to cope with (or acknowledge) the sexual ambiguity in some of Sendak's works. Thus, because she is based on a photograph of Sendak as an infant, both DeLuca (9) and Lanes (162) refer to Baby in *Higglety-Pigglety-Pop* as "he," although Sendak's text uses feminine pronouns.

25. Sendak told Cott (1983, 72) that "the reason the eggshells appear in *Outside Over There* is mostly in homage to the original source," that is, the Grimms' "The Goblins," where eggshells are used to test whether a baby is a changeling or not. But the use of eggshells in Sendak's illustrations seems to go beyond this "homage."

26. DeLuca comments on the lack of "release," and remarks that "we—particularly children—are left at the end of this work with too much pain" (22).

27. DeLuca (15) expresses gratitude to Sendak for recognizing the conflict in young girls between self-achievement and serving others.

Michel Tournier's Texts for Children

Joseph H. McMahon

I think that a child's readings constitute for him an intangible mine, an unattackable base on which are built, more than his literary culture and judgments, his personal sensitivity and mythology.

—Le Vent Paraclet

The texts Michel Tournier—who is thought by some to be France's outstanding living novelist—has written for children are for the most part strikingly different from those he has written for adults.[1] In the latter, he has purposefully played with his readers in an effort to force them to ask themselves questions about the attitudes they bring to reading. He has found other ways of being provocative by enunciating in *Le Vent Paraclet*, where he writes mainly about his own works, elaborate defenses of forms of human behavior which many believe to be aberrant.[2] It is as though he wants, through strident notes, to force his readers to hear a subtler tone.

The same is not true of the works he has written for children, where his purposes are, on the whole, clear; there he often defends the kinds of values he ridicules in the works he has addressed to an adult audience, in which, as he himself has said, "I find myself pawing the ground of taboos."[3] The different narrative stances produce a situation in which the texts for children can be used to illuminate those written for grownups. The stances may also be related to some sharp distinctions he draws in *Le Vent Paraclet* about the intentions which lurk behind particular literary forms. Literature has power to influence the ways in which individuals see the world about them. They never shake off the influence of those works which have shaped their views at an early age. That assertion is of great pertinence to his interest in writing for children; it sheds light on the way in which he writes for adults. Implicit in his discussion of reading is a contradiction. On the one hand, he seems to be saying that there comes a moment when one no longer reads as a child does, for various kinds of distances are eventually created between texts and readers, who become wary. On the other hand, much of what Tournier writes seems to suggest his belief that today's readers are willing to look at and even believe almost anything; and, in that sense, they have never ceased being children.

That apparent contradiction may help to explain Tournier's two manners of writing and suggests that, whatever it is he is trying to do in writing for children, what he is doing when he writes for adults is trying to make them read as grownups. He would not put it that way, for he claims, "I never deliberately write children's books but sometimes I write so well that what I've written can also be read by children. When I'm less lucky, what I come up with is only good enough for adults."[4] Earlier, in 1979, he had told an interviewer from *Le Monde* that "a work can be addressed to a young public only when it is perfect. Every weakness reduces it to the level of adults alone. The writer who takes up his pen with that high aim in mind is obeying an immeasurable ambition."[5]

Those sentiments, as we shall see in one case, do not conform to Tournier's own practice. His first work for children was a revision of a novel published for adults; he has announced his intention of rewriting for a younger public, when he finds the time, two of his other novels. What Tournier seems to espy is a complex situation: children, up to a certain time, bring to their reading a limited amount of experience and many look upon reading as a way of understanding *and adding to* that experience. What adults bring to reading is an indefinable attitude which in many cases may make reading an act *adjacent* to their experience, with the consequence that it may or may not become part of their experience. Those different degrees of susceptibility may demand the use of deliberate, alternate strategies on the part of the writer, strategies designed to give him the chance of having the greatest amount of impact on each of the two audiences he addresses.[6]

Obviously, when he is writing for children, Tournier is under several influences. One is the memory of his own childhood, which he says was miserable, and that may perhaps help to determine the subjects he chooses to explore. Another is his appreciation of what he sees as the needs of today's young reader in the industrialized world. In a number of articles and interviews, he has discussed the rebelliousness and boredom of today's youth and its historical causes.[7]

If the child is the favorite prey of that gloomy void, of that bleak anguish, of that nothingness colored in dust, it is doubtless the result of a lack of roots in the course of things, the result of an excess of availability. It is in the nature of his age to await the unexpected arrival of something or someone extraordinary who is going to renew everything, overturn everything, even if that entails a planetary catastrophe.[8]

Complicating that condition is the absence, in the life of the adolescent, of clearly identified, permissible ways of orienting his affectivity and sexuality. Today, Tournier says,

they continue, in official circles at least, to consider that the absolute evil for the child is his sexuality. . . . If I say that eroticism has never done any harm to anyone, and especially not to children, and that there is no reason why one shouldn't show pornographic films on television on Wednesday afternoons, I am expressing something that is evident; but it runs up against a wall.[9]

A third influence on Tournier's intentions is a desire to get away from his own solitude through contact with readers.[10]

A final influence on his intentions is his own experience with children. Though he has never married and has no children, Tournier has been intimately involved in the rearing of at least two youngsters. He told Theodore Zeldin:

The ideal companion for me is a boy because I can do things with him that I cannot do alone: go to the zoo, walk in the woods, light a fire, read books with him, rediscover literature: we are both initiators and initiated to each other. It could equally be a girl, except parents don't trust little girls with bachelors. I do not have sexual relations with my boys. But I like to hold a child in my arms, I like to serve a child, to give him food, to wash him, to put him to bed. It's my maternal side. . . .

When I look at a man of 20, and think of the boy of 10 he used to be, I feel a lump in my throat: it's like a death. I prefer to have not my own children, but all the children of the world.[11]

In the context of the intentions I am discussing, those final observations, which recall some of the judgments made by the narrator of
André Gide's *L'Immoraliste* as well as many made by the narrator of
Le Roi des Aulnes, [12] cause problems mainly because they suggest a
futile exploitation of children: one takes them through initiatory
procedures over the years only to produce, it seems, a condition of
being one does not like. A further suggestion is that there is no
remedy; accession to adulthood can only be calibrated in losses; to
become an adult is to live as a defeated child, unless one associates
with youngsters in order to repeat with them the games and other
adventures of one's own disappeared childhood. That is the situation which confronts Robinson Crusoe at the conclusion of *Vendredi
ou la vie sauvage*.[13]

Initially, the children's version follows closely the story of the
adult version, as its story follows closely the story-line of Defoe's
novel. Robinson is shipwrecked and finds himself alone on a deserted, verdant island. Gradually, he overcomes his desolation, resists
his temptation to wallow in the parental comfort he claims to find in
the mud; he makes a commitment to work and eventually recreates
on his island a solid bourgeois world. He names it Speranza and
writes a constitution for its governance. After the first intrusion on
what he considers his space by Indians, who use the island for their
sacrificial rites, he begins to fortify it. All these events, and the
pattern of life they create, reinforce in the child who reads about
them the value of the deeds brought about through resolve and
resoluteness.

In the adult version, those events are interlarded with excerpts
from Robinson's Logbook where he meditates about and comes to
appreciate some of the basic values of the West and where he also
explores the relationship between sexuality and death. Indeed, after
assuming a fetal position in one of the island's coombs, he initiates a
sexual and fecund union with one of her flowers. Tournier excises
that last event from the children's version in much the same way he
says society bans sex from the eyes of the young.

Friday's arrival on the island is the occasion of another discrep-
ancy between the two versions, apparently to spare children what
they might find to be unsettling behavior by Robinson. In the adult

version it is his intention to kill the fleeing Friday in order to avoid the eventual wrath of his pursuers; in the children's version, he aims his gun at one of the pursuers. In both texts, Friday's ensuing time on the island is spent being submitted to the ways of Robinson's civilization. As in Defoe's novel, he is sometimes recalcitrant; but in both of Tournier's texts his obduracy leads to disaster, for, fearful of being discovered smoking Robinson's treasured pipe, Friday tosses it behind him. It lands in the powder magazine; the resultant explosions bring down everything Robinson has constructed on the island and also cause his dog to die of fright.

From this point on, though the basic story remains the same in both, the two versions begin to differ in profoundly significant ways. In the original, Robinson's temptation not to start all over again is at first presented in a vocabulary which suggests that to succumb would be retrogression; he would thereby rid himself of the burden of an administered life and island. Gradually, however, Robinson's decision to embrace Friday's way of life becomes a transformation, a purgation, rather than a retrogression; it is not a question of having exchanged a laboriously established civilized life for a savage condition, but rather of having acceded to a higher perception of and participation in the universe, more particularly in the reign of the sun.

In the derivative version, Robinson makes the decision immediately and confesses that he is happy to be rid of a routine which at bottom bored him; once the decision has been made, he asserts that they are now free and moves on to become an attentive witness of Friday's existence. The subtitles clearly point to this difference; the "limbos" of the first version imply that Robinson has moved beyond civilization, the "savage life" of the second that he has reverted to a precivilized state. That variation in ideological tone continues until the very end of the book. Yet both texts invite the reader to consider a form of existence that is better than the repugnant ways characteristic of civilization; it is a condition which, when internalized, leads Robinson to stay on the island.

Friday's decision to abandon the island, without telling Robinson beforehand, is shattering in several ways. In the original text, no explanation is given for it, probably because it raises questions that are too unsettling. In the second version, Robinson says that Friday has seen the frigate, which could have carried both of them back to England, as a novel, irresistible toy, thereby using a child's instinctive reaction to the enchantingly new to explain a catastrophic event. In both texts, its arrival causes Robinson to think about moving swiftly to his death. But, in the first version, before doing so, he ruminates at length over the several stages of his existence on Speranza; death becomes the path to follow only when he finds he has neither the emotional nor psychological strength to pursue some other recourse. Oddly, he never raises, as many readers must, the matter of the *meaning* of Friday's decision to abandon him and thus to become a part of the civilized world. The child reader is given a cause, if not a reason; the adult reader is given nothing, and so is left to his own speculations. That is a challenge Tournier will repeat more than once in later texts.

The final event in the story, Robinson's discovery of the ship's cabin boy who has sought refuge on the island from his unhappy maritime existence, is presented in remarkably different ways in the two texts. In the children's version, Robinson is extraordinarily happy:

> He now had this little brother whose hair—as red as his own— was beginning to blaze in the sun. They would invent new games, new adventures, new victories. A new life was going to begin, as beautiful as the island which was waking up in the mist at their feet. [152]

Since Friday's life consisted of more than games, adventures, and victories, one can reasonably say that Robinson's vision of the future is the second step in his retrogression. Because the cabin boy has never seen him in the role of an adult, Robinson can recreate daily with the youth a child's world. Growing and aging will, until debility sets in, have no meaning. One can say that the child's version of his novel represents Tournier's description of a world in which the differences between children and adults no longer matter. We are not told what the cabin boy thinks about a life devoted to devising new games.

The original text offers a much more unsettling ending, unsettling because it is really a beginning whose outcome we cannot reliably predict. When Robinson sees the child he has an epiphany:

the boy is a postulant from the solar realm, sent to allow Robinson to initiate him into the ways of that form of existence. In the face of that challenge, he feels himself assuming gigantic proportions. The scene is not unlike that of Bacchus arriving on Ariadne's island. Robinson tells the boy, "Henceforth, you will be called Thursday. That is Jupiter's day, the god of the Heaven. It is also the children's Sunday" (205). That announcement is fraught with meaning. For years, Thursday was a half-holiday for French schoolchildren, and many of them devoted it to receiving religious instruction, over-whelmingly in Christian religions. Robinson is thereby announcing a new dispensation and incorporating the boy into it by baptizing him with a new name, chosen for him by Robinson. The lessons contained in Friday's departure no longer count now that Robinson can play the role of God. One of the ways in which that role can be carried out is described in Tournier's next novel, *Le Roi des Aulnes*, where the protagonist, moved by a belief that he is called to serve children, ends up witlessly participating in the slaughter of some of them.

Tournier's later and shorter works for young readers are more directly related to the experience of children and are presented through their eyes. In *La Fugue du petit Poucet* (Tom Thumb's Escape), we follow the adventures of a young Parisian boy who is disturbed by his father's desire to be thoroughly abreast of modern ways of living; the father is an advocate of shopping malls, car parks, and tall buildings.[14] Indeed, as head of the tree-cutters of Paris, he makes a steady contribution to the creation of those spaces and is proud of his participation. When he announces his intention of moving his family to the twenty-third floor of a building whose climate is completely controlled and where the family can profit from the joys of color television, Pierre rebels, gathers his rabbits together, and runs away from the family abode in the direction of some milieu better suited to his vague aspirations. Warmed by wine he receives from a truckdriver, who has given him a lift out of the city, the boy finds himself in a forest where he is soon surrounded by enchanting young girls.

They lead him off to their home, where he finds a world quite different from that enjoyed by his father. Here he finds a place of marvels, where the father stays home and the mother goes to work;

here he sees a poster on the wall which urges its viewers to make love instead of war; here he meets the girls' father, Logre, who turns out to be a more genial ogre than others in some of Tournier's works. Indeed, unlike Robinson, and unlike the main character of *Le Roi des Aulnes*, he acts as a source of counsel for the young rather than serving as the provider of diversions and dangers. From him, Pierre learns that the grand curse of men is that "'they have left the vegetable kingdom. They have fallen into the animal kingdom. . . . What you find there is hunting, violence, murder, fear. In the vegetable kingdom . . . you find the calm growth in the union between the earth and the sun" (57). The idea recalls some of Robinson's thoughts in *Vendredi*, especially in the version for adults. Logre goes on to say that a good example of that union is a tree: it needs sunlight in order to grown and raise its branches toward the heavens, but it also needs to be ever more deeply rooted in the earth in order to remain sturdy. He derives a counsel from the tree's example: "The more you want to raise yourself up, the more is it necessary to have your feet on the ground. Every tree tells you that" (58).

The authorities do not approve of such sentiments; they approve even less of trying to indoctrinate young, impressionable children with them; and so they come to charge Logre with corruption of youth and to take him off to jail. Before being carried off, he tells Pierre to take a gift from the house. The boy chooses a pair of oversized boots like those his father had promised but failed to give him. Obliged to return to his parents' newfound high-rise flat, Pierre is not completely discouraged, for he has learned, as did Rousseau two centuries earlier, to have recourse to his imagination. While his parents watch television in an adjacent room, he stretches out on his bed, his newly acquired boots close by him; and there he dreams of being an immense tree and also, probably, of growing tall enough to fit into those boots.

La Fugue du petit Poucet recalls Tournier's detestation of his own childhood years in Paris, his belief that Paris is not a city for children, and his suggestion that a history of cities would be also the history of the possibilities of growth they have made available to the young, and of the good and the harm they have done.

Tournier's next tale, *Amandine ou les deux jardins* (Amandine, or

the Two Gardens) has a similar didactic cast.[15] As its subtitle indicates, it is meant to be a story about initiation, one of Tournier's
recurrent preoccupations in those interviews where he has discussed
the formation of children; it is such, though, only by way of absence.
Initiations suggest rites and ceremonies, carefully prepared by someone, so that their intent will be known and eventually assumed by
those being initiated. What happens to Amandine is that she makes a
series of discoveries and undergoes a few events which lead her
toward evidence of another world from that she has known—a
world she must try to put together on the basis of the new data she
has acquired. In the absence of established initiation procedures,
she must assume the initiative in putting things together.

   She lives comfortably enough in the two realms represented by
her parents. Her mother's world is inside, in the house she keeps;
her father's is outside, in the garden he patiently tends. In her
diary, where she writes entries only on Sundays and Wednesdays,
Amandine inserts descriptions of novel events in her life. Her
cat has kittens. Amandine is able to give the male kittens away,
but no one wants the sole female. The mother cat begins to show a
certain distance from the girl; the remaining kitten is indifferent
to Amandine as it goes about exploring the precincts. The child
eventually perceives that the kitten's explorations lead it away from
Amandine's sphere and into stretches she has never examined; she
concludes that the kitten is living in two worlds, the domesticated
world of Amandine's home and the wild world found in the other
garden.

   When Amandine finally climbs over the wall, she finds a space
entirely the opposite of the one her father tends—it is a virgin forest,
no garden at all, really. On her return to her garden, she exclaims:
"How clear and well-ordered everything is here!" (43). Some hours
later, having cried long and hard over nothing, she discovers some
drops of blood on her leg; when she looks into the mirror, she
notices that she no longer looks like the young ten-year-old she had
been. In the entry for the following Wednesday, she tells us that she
has discovered that her kitten has become a full-fledged cat and is
expecting a litter of its own.

   Tournier's points are all clear enough; they profit from being
stated mutely, by which I mean that he presents the phenomena of

the onset of puberty in ways which would not upset those who had not made Amandine's observations and which might help those who had, but who had been baffled by their meaning. Even the implicit criticism of an order which tends its homes and gardens better than its children is presented indirectly. In a way, that criticism is not present until the reader makes it and derives some wisdom from it, which may lead to more attentive ways of helping children understand more clearly what they see all around them.

La Mère Noel (Mother Christmas) is little more than an anecdote with ambition.[16] It tells of the Christmas-time rivalry between secular and religious forces in a small French village who conduct competing ceremonies at the same time. For years the local curé has been celebrating a vigil Mass at 6 p.m. on Christmas Eve; its highlight is a live Nativity scene. For years, at the same time, the local schoolteacher has been impersonating Father Christmas and distributing gifts to the schoolchildren. When the teacher retires and is replaced by a divorced woman with two children, the villagers begin to wonder if the longstanding rivalry will now come to an end. It does not. The woman announces her intention to continue the tradition and to take the part of Father Christmas. She also agrees to have her baby play the role of the Christ Child in the Nativity scene. There is some perplexity in the village over the situation, and there is consternation when the baby begins to cry, as the Mass gets underway, and cannot be satisfied except by the arrival of his mother, summoned from her distribution of gifts in order to nurse her hungry child and thereby to add another vital element to the live tableau. With the hindsight provided by one of his later novels,[17] one can discern larger reaches in this brief tale, for the infant's need of his mother and the instant response on the part of both congregation and mother to that need point to the power of a child to effect harmonies and perhaps to remind rivals of what the coming of Christ was for a long time taken to mean: the establishment of peace on earth as an ideal worthy of being pursued by human beings.

Tournier's next book, *Pierrot ou les secrets de la nuit* (Pierrot, or the Secrets of the Night), is, he says, his favorite book, and one which he worked on for six or seven years. (It is published in translation in this issue of *Children's Literature*.)[18] He says it is an example of what he would have liked to do had he continued with his early career in philosophy. "I would have liked to teach philosophy to children of 10, and that is what I am now trying to do in my books for children."[19] He told another interviewer that the teaching of philosophy to the young "is not done and that's a shame. My little book *Pierrot ou les secrets de la nuit* is metaphysics for 10-year-olds."[20]

What is often made deliberately obscure or ambiguous in Tournier's writings for adults is presented straightforwardly here as a matter of choices and values. The story is also an extension of the concerns expressed in *Amandine*, for here it is a question of how couples are formed in social partnerships and of the information which guides the decisions by which those partnerships are set up.

Tournier's story deals with a Pierrot who succeeds, not only in drawing Columbine back from Harlequin and vagabondage, but also in bringing about a victory for his own stable and domestic values. When he writes to the absent Columbine in his effort to win her back, he tries to explain the meaning of the colors of his world in order to allay her belief that they are sinister hues.

Columbine inspires Pierrot to create a lifesized brioche in her image, which reveals to her other dimensions of her being. Before 1979, Tournier had not written anything so forthright in defense of the values and continuities of the domestic order. In fact his *Météores*, published four years earlier in 1975, had raised serious questions about the attractiveness and viability of that order. Yet this apparent defense of the domestic life—of the washing of linen and the baking of bread—does not go as far as the reader might have expected—though it may go further. We do not read at the end of a marriage between Pierrot and Columbine. Instead we have what appears to be a reconciliation of all the opposed elements in the story. Harlequin returns to ask for the warmth and the hospitality of Pierrot's hearth; his request is honored; the two men watch with fascination as Columbine touches the breasts of the brioche portrait of herself and then invites them to join her in tasting and eating the good Columbine. The text tells us at its conclusion: "They are happy. They would like to laugh, but how can you do that with your cheeks swollen with brioche?"

Tournier is settling a number of matters in this tale which he has not settled as assuredly in his adult texts: the pacification of the nomad as a result of admiration for the security and strength of the sedentary baker, the celebration of the domestic and admiration for the maternal, the union of opposites which is often expressed in the difference between night and day, the absorption of cannibal instincts, whether physical or psychological, in eucharistic ceremony. But he sidesteps one of the main problems he has seen to be of central importance in the world of his readers—their initiation into sexual understanding and performance. What does a young reader make of this conclusion, which either suggests a union of the three or leaves unresolved Harlequin's more distant future? There is something of Marie Antoinette's alleged indifference to the people's hunger in a conclusion which suggests that youthful sexual rivalries can be satisfied by proximity to hot ovens and by the joyous consumption of tasty brioche. In Plato's world, one was encouraged to move from image to form; the same can be said of the world of sex; and Tournier chooses to remain silent about how that passage will occur and whether what it leads to will last.

What Tournier is trying to do in *Barbedor* (Goldenbeard), his recent book for children, puzzles me, though, as we shall see, it has some direct ties to the conclusion of the adult version of *Vendredi*.[21] It is an oriental tale about a not too earnest king who sports a luxuriant golden beard, which each day is brushed and waved by a woman barber; male barbers have been excluded from service because their manner of care involves trimming and cutting. One day the king discovers a single silver whisker in his beard; it is a sign of his age which reminds him that, after two infertile marriages, there is no heir to his throne, and that he has not paid adequate attention to that matter. He thinks of adopting a little heir "who will look strikingly like me . . . like a little twin brother." During his siesta, he feels something like a bite and, on awakening from his nap, discovers that his silver hair has been plucked. The same event happens day after day, reducing the richness of his beard and serving to remind him that his life is passing by. Eventually, he discovers that a bird is the ravisher of his beard. When the last hair has been taken, the bird leaves behind a feather from its plumage; it turns out to have the properties of a compass and leads Barbedor to the nest the bird has made from his beard. There he finds a beautiful gilded egg which he takes from the nest with the intention of bringing it back to the seat of his kingdom. He is stopped by one of his own foresters, who accuses him of a form of poaching. Barbedor discovers at that moment that he has become quite little and is easily able to elude his accuser. He continues on his journey and, as he nears the city, takes note of a great funeral procession in an outlying cemetery. When he arrives at the gates of the city he finds them closed. As he stands before them, the egg begins to open, and a white bird flies out, singing: "Long live the king! Long live our new king!" The transformed Barbedor thus becomes his own successor and repeats fully the events of his earlier reign, even in the matter of marrying the two barren women. At the point in his second reign where his golden beard begins to sprout, he forgets the history of the boy before the gates, the bird flying up from the egg, and the ensuing cry of "Long live the king!"

There were traces of that kind of longing in Robinson's aspiration to become part of the solar reign, to introduce the cabin boy to it, and thus to find a line leading toward immortality. A similar hankering led Paul, one of the narrators of *Les Météores*, to spin out extravagant theories in an attempt to project himself as an integral part of meteorological events. Here Tournier is going even further in his description of the process whereby an undeserving man is visited by renewal and restoration; here he allows for the possibility of a cyclical return of youth. He does not at the same time resolve the problem of how youth can move on to a purposeful, energetic adult life. One ought not to push that reading too far. Perhaps one should assume that what Tournier wanted was something simpler: to turn his hand to the creation of a magical, languorous world where troubling events become marvels, even for those who have not taken full advantage of their own promise and who have not wholly met their responsibilities.

There is a progression discernible in Tournier's works for children and an ever more visible commitment to particular values which are not as certainly appreciated in his writings for adults: sane integration into the natural world, the reconciliation of adversaries who need not be in conflict, the celebration of routines and rituals which enrich understanding of the worth of a serene life, an appreciation of enchantment as opposed to insanity. When Tournier writes about children, rather than for them, he depicts a world in which such values are absent or have been set seriously askew.

Fortunately, one has the children's works as the assurance of Tournier's belief that those absences and dislocations are the results of abuses and that the child's world does not have to be a place of suffering and confusion, especially if adults attend to their obligations and writers attend to filling in whatever gaps may be created by negligence of those duties.[22]

Notes

1. See, for example, Roger Shattuck, "France's Best Novelist?," *New York Review of Books*, April 28, 1983, 7–15; also, "Michel Tournier," special issue of *Sud*, 1980.

2. *Le Vent Paraclet* (Paris: Gallimard, 1977).

3. Escoffier-Lambiotte, "L'Ecrivain et la société," *Le Monde*, October 8–9, 1978, 32. All translations in this article from materials that originally appeared in French are mine.

4. Mary Blume, "A Laughing Provocateur Is Launched in Britain," *Herald-Tribune* (Paris), December 30, 1983, 7.

5. "Comment écrire pour les enfants," *Le Monde*, December 21, 1979, 19.

6. In *Le Vent Paraclet*, he writes: "The reader of a good writer ought not to discover new things in reading him, but ought to recognize, find again truths, realities which he believes simultaneously at least to have suspected right from the start" (198).

7. See, for example, "En Marge du romantisme allemand. Les Voyages initiatiques," *Le Monde*, January 19–20, 1977, 1 and 22; "Point de vue d'un éducateur," *Le Monde*, December 20, 1974, 20; "Emile, Gavroche, Tarzan" in *Le Vol du vampire* (Paris: Gallimard, 1981), 169–89.

8. *Des clefs et des serrures* (Paris: Chene/Hachette, 1979), 40. Mélanie, the central character in Tournier's "La Jeune Fille et la mort" (in *Le Coq de bruyère* [Paris: Gallimard, 1978], 159–83), shares that kind of expectation and so is disappointed when the Cuban missile crisis is peacefully resolved. *Le Coq de bruyère* appears in English translation as *The Fetishist* (New York: Doubleday, 1984).

9. Escoffier-Lambiotte, 32. Wednesday is now a half-holiday for children in France's state schools.

10. Ibid.

11. "The Prophet of Unisex," *The Observer* (London), January 30, 1983, 43.

12. *Le Roi des Aulnes* (Paris: Gallimard, 1970). Published in the United States as *The Ogre*, in the United Kingdom as *The Erl-king*.

13. *Vendredi ou les Limbes du Pacifique* (Paris: Gallimard, 1967). The folio edition (Paris: Gallimard, 1969) contains an essay by Gilles Deleuze, "Michel Tournier et le monde sans autrui," 255–81. *Vendredi ou la vie sauvage* (Paris: Flammarion, 1971; Paris: Gallimard (folio junior), 1977), with illustrations by Georges Lemoine. My references are to the 1967 and 1977 editions respectively. The English-language edition published in the United States bore the title *Friday, or the Other Island*.

14. *La Fugue du petit Poucet* (Paris: Editions G. P., 1979). First published in *Elle*, December 1972, as "Le Détournement du petit Poucet"; it also appears in *Le Coq de bruyère*, 45–61.

15. *Amandine ou les deux jardins*, illustrated by Joelle Boucher (Paris: Editions G. P., 1977). First published in *Elle*, November 1974. Tournier discussed the book with an

interviewer from *Le Monde*: "Le Sang des fillettes," December 9, 1977. That text appears as a long note in *Le Coq de bruyère*, 305–08.

16. First published as "Le Réveillon du petit Jésus" in *Elle*, December 1974. It appears in *Le Coq de bruyère*, 27–29.

17. *Gaspard, Melchior et Balthazar* (Paris: Gallimard, 1980). The novel recounts the reactions of three kings and a young prince to the birth of Christ.

18. *Pierrot ou les secrets de la nuit*, illustrations by Danièle Bour (Paris: Gallimard, 1979), unpaginated.

19. Zeldin, 43.

20. Blume, 7.

21. *Barbedor*, illustrated by Georges Lemoine (Paris: Gallimard, 1980), unpaginated.

22. In "Tupick," which Tournier calls his cruellest story and which he says he intended to be a tale for children, he tells the story of a boy who castrates himself because of his frustrations over the efforts of adults to impose on him gender roles he finds intolerable.

Varia

Pierrot, or The Secrets of the Night

Michel Tournier

Two little white houses faced each other in the village of Powder-snap. One was the laundry. No one could remember the real name of the laundress; because of her snow-white dress everyone called her Columbine the White Dove. The other house was the bakery of Pierrot.

Pierrot and Columbine had grown up together, sitting next to each other on the benches in the village schoolhouse. They were so often together that everyone imagined they would get married later on. But their paths separated when Pierrot became baker's boy and Columbine laundress. Obviously, a baker must work at night, so that the village will have fresh bread and hot rolls in the morning. A laundress works during the daytime. All the same, they could have met at dusk, either in the evening when Columbine was getting ready for bed and Pierrot was getting up, or in the morning when the day of Columbine was beginning and the night of Pierrot was coming to an end.

But Columbine avoided Pierrot, and the poor baker's boy was eating his heart out. Why did Columbine avoid Pierrot? Because her old friend reminded her of all sorts of unpleasant things. Columbine loved only the sun, birds, and flowers. She blossomed only in the summer, in the heat. But the baker's boy, as we have said, lived mostly at night, and for Columbine, night simply meant darkness peopled by frightening beasts like wolves or bats. She preferred at that hour to close her door and shutters and to curl up under her down quilt to go to sleep. That wasn't all. For Pierrot made his living from two dark realms that were even more disturbing: his cellar and his oven. What if he had rats in his cellar? And don't we say, as black as soot?

It must be said, moreover, that Pierrot had the looks of his trade.

Perhaps because he worked at night and slept during the day, he had a round, pale face which made him look like a full moon. His large, attentive, and astonished eyes made him resemble an owl, as did his loose clothes, floating and all white with flour. Like the moon, like an owl, Pierrot was timid, silent, faithful, and secretive. He preferred winter to summer, solitude to society. Rather than talk—which he found hard and was not good at—he preferred to write, which he did by the light of a candle with an immense pen, addressing long letters to Columbine that he never sent, convinced that she would not read them.

What did Pierrot write in his letters? He tried to set Columbine straight. He explained to her that night was not what she thought it was.

Pierrot knows the night. He knows that it is not a black hole, no more than his cellar or his oven. At night, the stream sings a higher and clearer note, and it shimmers with thousands and thousands of silvery scales. The foliage that the large trees shake against the dark sky sparkles with stars. The winds of night are more profoundly perfumed by the sea, the forest, and the mountains, than the winds of day, which are laden by the labors of men.

Pierrot knows the moon. He knows how to look at her. He knows that she is not a disc as white and flat as a plate. He looks at her with enough attention and friendship to see with his naked eye that she is modeled, that she is really a ball like an apple, like a pumpkin—and that, besides, she is not smooth, but sculptured, dimpled, undulating— like a landscape with its hills and dales, like a face with its wrinkles and smiles.

Yes, Pierrot knows all that, because after he has kneaded his dough a long time and leavened it with the secret of yeast, it needs two hours to rest and rise. That is when he leaves his kitchen. Everyone is asleep. He is the clear conscience of the village. He tours all its streets and alleys. His large round eyes open wide on the sleep of others, the men, women, and children who as soon as they wake up will eat the hot rolls he has prepared for them. He passes under the closed windows of Columbine. He becomes the watchman of the village, the guardian of Columbine. He imagines the girl sighing and dreaming in the cool whiteness of her big bed, and when he raises his pale face toward the moon he asks himself if this sweet roundness that floats above the trees in a veil of mist is that of a cheek, a breast, or even better, a bottom.

Undoubtedly things could have gone on like this for a long time, if one fine summer morning, all bright with flowers and birds, a funny vehicle had not entered the village. Drawn by a man, it was a bit like a gypsy van and a bit like a fair booth. It was clear that someone could take shelter and sleep there. At the same time this dwelling gleamed with bright colors, and richly painted curtains floated like banners all around. A varnished sign crowned the vehicle:

Harlequin. Housepainter

The man, lively and supple, with rosy cheeks and red curly hair, wore tights decorated with a mosaic of gaudy little diamonds. There were all the colors of the rainbow and some others, too, but not one diamond patch was black or white. He stopped his wagon before Pierrot's bakery, and examined with pouting disapproval its bare, sad facade, which bore only these two words:

Pierrot. Baker

He rubbed his hands vigorously and began to knock at the door. It was the middle of the day, as we have said, and Pierrot was sleeping like a log. Harlequin had to drum a long time before the door opened on a Pierrot paler than ever and staggering with fatigue. Poor Pierrot! All white, rumpled, bewildered, his eyes blinking in the pitiless light of noon, he looked so much like an owl that even before Harlequin could open his mouth, someone behind him burst out laughing. It was Columbine, who was watching the scene from her window, with a big iron in her hand. Harlequin turned around, caught sight of her, and burst into laughter in return. Pierrot found himself alone and sad in his moonlike smock opposite these two children of the sun brought together by their shared gaiety. Then he became angry. His heart stung by jealousy, he brutally slammed the door in Harlequin's face and went back to bed, but it is not likely that he was able to sleep again very soon.

Harlequin, however, turns to the laundry where Columbine has disappeared. He looks for her. She reappears, but in another window, and disappears again before Harlequin has had time to come close. It looks as if she is playing hide-and-seek with him. Finally, the door opens, and Columbine comes out carrying a large basket of clean wash. Followed by Harlequin, she goes toward her garden and begins to hang her flat work on the lines to dry. There are only white linens. White like the outfit of Columbine. White like that of Pierrot. Yet this white wash is hung up not in moonlight but in the sun, the sun which makes all colors glow, particularly those of Harlequin's outfit.

Harlequin, the fine talker, makes speeches to Columbine. Columbine answers. What do they chat about? They talk clothes. Columbine talks white. Harlequin talks colored. For the laundress used to bleaching linens, white is a matter of course. Harlequin tries to make Columbine think in color. Indeed, he succeeds a bit. The invasion of white sales by mauve towels, blue pillowcases, green tablecloths, and pink sheets dates back to this famous meeting in Powdersnap.

After hanging out her wash in the sun, Columbine returns to the laundry. Harlequin, carrying the empty basket, offers to repaint the facade of her house. Columbine accepts. Harlequin starts to work at once. He takes apart his van and with the sticks and pieces builds a scaffold against the front of the laundry. It is as if the van when taken apart took possession of Columbine's house. Harlequin perches nimbly on his scaffold. With his many-colored tights and his crest of red hair, he looks like an exotic bird on its perch. And to make the resemblance even closer, he sings and whistles with zest. From time to time Columbine leans her head out of a window, and they exchange jokes, smiles, and songs.

Soon Harlequin's work takes shape. The white facade of the house disappears under a many-colored spectrum. There are all the colors of the rainbow and a few more, but no black, white, or gray. Best of all, however, Harlequin has hit upon two changes that would prove, if anyone ever doubted it, that he is really the boldest and sauciest of housepainters. First, he has drawn on the wall the figure of a lifesized Columbine carrying on her head her washbasket. That isn't all. Instead of representing her in her usual white clothes, Harlequin has given this Columbine a dress with little many-colored diamonds, just like those on his own tights. And there is something else. He has, of course, repainted in black letters on a white background the word *Laundry* but he has added at the end in letters of every color, *Dyer!*

He has worked so quickly that everything is done by sunset, even though the paint is far from dry.

The sun goes down and Pierrot gets up. The basement window of the bakery lights up and reddens with hot reflections. An enormous moon floats like a milky balloon in the phosphorescent sky. Soon Pierrot comes out of his oven room. At first he sees nothing but the moon. She fills him with happiness. He runs toward her waving his arms with love. He smiles at her, and the moon returns his smile. Really they are like brother and sister, with their round faces and their filmy garments. But as he dances and turns, Pierrot catches his feet in the paintpots that litter the ground. He bumps against the scaffold erected against Columbine's house. The shock jolts him out of his dream. What is going on? What has happened to the laundry? Pierrot no longer recognizes this gaudy facade, especially not this Columbine in a harlequin's costume. And the barbarous word coupled to *Laundry: Dyer!* Pierrot stops dancing. He is struck dumb. The moon in the sky grimaces in pain. So Columbine has let herself be taken in by Harlequin's colors! From now on, she is going to dress like him, and instead of soaping and ironing fresh white linens she is going to steep faded, worn clothes in vats of dirty, nauseating chemical colors.

Pierrot goes up to the scaffold. He feels it with distaste. Above, a window is lit up. Scaffolding is terrible, because it makes it possible to look in the windows upstairs to see what is going on in the bedrooms! Pierrot climbs up on one board, then on another. He goes toward the window that is lit up. He glances in. What has he seen? We will never know! He jumps backwards. He has forgotten that he was perched ten feet above the ground on the scaffold. He falls. What a fall! Is he dead? No. He gets up painfully. Limping, he goes back to the bakery. He lights a candle, dips his big pen in the inkpot. He writes a letter to Columbine. A letter? No, only a brief note. He goes out, envelope in hand. Still limping, he hesitates and looks a minute, then decides to attach his message to one of the struts of the scaffold. Then he goes back inside. The light of the basement window goes out. A big cloud comes to mask the sad face of the moon.

A new day begins under a glorious sun. Harlequin and Columbine bounce out of the Laundry-Dyer's holding hands. Columbine is no longer wearing her usual white dress. She has a dress made of little colored diamonds, in every color except black and white. She is dressed like the Columbine painted by Harlequin on the facade of her house. She has become a Harlequinette. How happy they are! They dance together around the house. Then Harlequin, still dancing, turns to an odd task. He takes down the scaffold set up against Columbine's house. At the same time he reassembles his funny vehicle. The van takes shape again. Columbine tries it out. Harlequin seems to think their departure is natural. For the painter is a real nomad. He lives on his scaffold like a bird on his branch. He sees no point in dallying. Besides, he has nothing else to do at Powdersnap, and the countryside is bright with all its charms.

Columbine seems willing to go. She carries a light bundle into the van. She closes the shutters of her house. Here she is with Harlequin in the van. They are going to leave. No, not yet. Harlequin gets down. He has forgotten something. A large sign which he paints with flourishes, then attaches to the door of the house:

Closed for wedding trip

Now they can leave. Harlequin harnesses himself to the van and pulls it along the road. Soon the countryside surrounds them and welcomes them. There are so many flowers and butterflies that the landscape seems to have put on a harlequin's costume!

Night falls on the village. Pierrot ventures out of the bakery. Still limping, he approaches Columbine's house. Everything is shut. Suddenly he catches sight of the sign. This sign is so awful, he cannot read it. He rubs his eyes. Yet he must accept the evidence. Then, still hobbling, he returns to his oven room. Soon he comes out. He too has a sign. He hangs it on his door before slamming it shut again. It reads:

Closed for broken heart

Days pass. Summer is ending. Harlequin and Columbine continue to tour the country. But their happiness is no longer the same. More and more often now, it is Columbine who drags the van while Harlequin rests inside. Then the weather takes a turn for the worse. The first rains of autumn patter on their heads. Their fine, many-colored costumes begin to fade. The trees turn red, then lose their leaves. They go through forests of dead trees, plowed fields that are brown and black.

One morning, a magical change! All night the sky has been filled with whirling flakes. When day breaks, snow blankets all the country-side, the road, and even the van. It is the great triumph of whiteness, the triumph of Pierrot. As if to crown this revenge of the baker boy, that evening an enormous silvery moon floats above the icy land-scape.

Columbine thinks more and more often of Powdersnap and also of Pierrot, above all when she looks at the moon. One day she finds a little note in her hand. She does not know where it comes from. She wonders if the baker boy passed by recently to leave his message. In fact he wrote it for her earlier and attached it to one of the struts of the scaffold that has now become part of the van. She reads:

> Columbine!
> Don't leave me! Don't let yourself be taken in by the superfi-cial chemical colors of Harlequin! These colors are toxic, smell bad, and peel. But I too have my colors. Only mine are true and deep.
> Listen carefully to these marvelous secrets:
> My night is not black, it is blue! And it is a blue that you can breathe.
> My oven is not black, it is golden! And it is a gold that you can eat.
> The color I make rejoices your eyes, and besides, it is thick and solid, it smells good, it is warm, and it nourishes you.
> I love you and I am waiting for you.
>
> Pierrot

A blue night, a golden oven, true colors that one can breathe and eat, are these the secrets of Pierrot? In this icy landscape that looks like the baker's costume, Columbine reflects and hesitates. Harle-quin is asleep in the back of the van without a thought of her. In a while, she will have to put back on the harness that bruises her shoulders and chest to pull the vehicle on the frozen road. Why? If she wants to go back home, what is keeping her with Harlequin, since the fine sunny colors that attracted her are faded? She jumps out of the vehicle. She collects her bundle, then takes off with a light foot in the direction of her village.

She walks, walks, and walks, little Columbine-Harlequinette whose dress has lost its bright colors, without becoming white for all that. She flees in the snow which makes a soft flurry ruffling under her feet and fluttering in her ears: flight-flip-flight-flop-flight-flip-flight-flop. . . . Soon she sees in her mind's eye a swarm of words beginning with *F* which gather into a dark, hostile army: frigid, foolish, feeble, famished, failing, foul, fainting. About to fall down, poor Columbine luckily is rescued by a host of other words in *F*, fraternal words, as if they had been sent by Pierrot: flour, flame, feast, fire, flower, fairy, forward.

Finally she arrives at the village. It is deep in the night. Everything is asleep under the snow. White night? Black night? No. Because she has come closer to Pierrot, Columbine now has eyes to see: the night is blue, the snow is blue, as clear as day! But this is not the loud and toxic Prussian blue that Harlequin has in his pot. It is the luminous, living blue of lakes, glaciers, and the sky, a blue which smells good and which Columbine breathes deep into her lungs.

Here is the fountain imprisoned by ice, the old church, and here are the two little houses opposite each other, the laundry of Columbine and the bakery of Pierrot. The laundry is dark, as if dead, but the bakery gives signs of life. The chimney smokes and the basement window of the oven room casts a shaky golden glimmer on the snow of the sidewalk. Pierrot certainly told the truth when he wrote that his oven was not black but gold!

Columbine stops bewildered before the basement window. She would like to crouch before this mouth of light which blows warmth and an intoxicating smell of bread up under her skirts, but she does not dare. Suddenly the door opens and Pierrot appears. Is it by chance? Did he sense his friend's arrival? Or did he simply see her feet through the window? He holds out his arms to her, but just as she is about to throw herself into them, he stands aside afraid, and draws her down into his oven room. Columbine has the feeling that she is stepping down into a bath of tenderness. How good it feels! Though the doors of the oven are shut, the flames are so intense inside that they leak through all kinds of holes and slits.

Pierrot, tucked into a corner, drinks up with his round eyes this fantastic apparition: Columbine in his oven room! Columbine, hypnotized by the fire, peeps at him out of the corner of her eyes and finds that he looks just like a night bird, this good Pierrot plunged in the shadow with the large white folds of his shirt and his face like a moon. He should say something to her, but he cannot. The words stick in his throat.

Time goes by. Pierrot lowers his eyes to his dough trough where the large ball of pale dough is resting. Blond and tender like Columbine. . . . During the two hours that the dough has rested in its wooden trough the yeast has brought life to it. The oven is hot, it will shortly be time to put the loaves in the oven. Pierrot looks at Columbine. What is Columbine doing? Exhausted by the long road she has traveled, cradled by the gentle warmth of the kitchen, she has fallen asleep on the flour box in a pose of delicious abandon. Tears of tenderness spring to Pierrot's eyes in front of his friend who has taken refuge with him to flee the harsh winter and her dead love.

Harlequin had painted a portrait of Columbine-Harlequinette in a many-colored costume on the wall of the laundry. Pierrot has an idea. He is going to sculpt a Columbine-Pierrette in his own fashion in his dough. He sets to work. His eyes go back and forth between the sleeping girl and the loaf resting in its trough. His hands would like to caress the sleeping girl, of course, but it is almost as much fun to pat and make a Columbine out of dough. When he thinks his work is done, he compares it with the living model. Naturally, the dough Columbine is becoming a bit pallid! Quick, into the oven!

The fire roars. Now there are two Columbines in the oven room of Pierrot. At this moment timid knocks at the door wake up the real Columbine. Who is there? The only answer is a singing voice made weak and sad by the night and the cold. But Pierrot and Columbine recognize the voice of Harlequin, the performing singer, even though he no longer hits the triumphal notes of summer—far from it! What does this numbed Harlequin sing? He sings a song that has since become famous, but whose words can only be understood by those who know our story:

Au clair de la lune,

Mon ami Pierrot.
Prête-moi ta plume,
Pour écrire un mot.
Ma chandelle est morte,
Je n'ai plus de feu.
Ouvre-moi ta porte,
Pour l'amour de Dieu.

"My friend Pierrot, lend me your pen to write a word in the moonlight. My candle is out, my fire is out. Open your door, for Heaven's sake." Poor Harlequin had found, fallen amid his paint-pots, the note by which Pierrot had persuaded Columbine to return to him. So this fine talker could measure the power of writers, as well as of people who have an oven in the winter. And naively he was asking Pierrot to lend him his pen and his fire. Did he really believe he had a chance of winning Columbine back that way?

Pierrot takes pity on his unhappy rival. He opens his door for him. A pitiful faded Harlequin hurries toward the oven whose doors continue to leak warmth, color, and tantalizing aromas. How comfortable it is at Pierrot's home!

The baker boy is transfigured by his triumph. He flourishes with his long floating sleeves. Theatrically, he opens the two doors of his oven. A flood of golden light, maternal warmth, and delicious baking smells bathes the three friends. And now, with his long wooden baker's peel Pierrot slides something out of the oven. Something? Someone, rather! A girl with a golden crust, crisp and steaming, who looks like a sister of Columbine. This is no longer the flat many-colored Columbine-Harlequinette painted in chemical colors on the facade of the laundry, it is a Columbine-Pierrette, modeled in bread with all the shape of life, her round cheeks, her pouter-pigeon chest, and her cute little round bottom.

Columbine has taken Columbine in her arms, at the risk of burning herself.

"How lovely I am, how good I smell!" she says.

Pierrot and Harlequin observe this extraordinary scene with fascination. Columbine lays Columbine out on the table. With greedy gentleness she spreads the two brioche breasts of Columbine apart. She plunges her eager nose, her tongue wriggling, into the soft gold of her neck. She says, with her mouth full, "How delicious I am! You too, my loves, come taste, eat this good Columbine! Eat me!"

And they taste, they eat the warm Columbine of soft melting bread. They look at each other. They are happy! They would like to laugh, but how can you laugh, when your cheeks are puffed full of bread?

Margaret Higonnet, translator

Writer Devoured by Children

Michel Tournier

The letters come from every corner of France, from Belgium, Switzerland, and Senegal, letters signed with twenty or thirty first names, decorated with garlands and little designs, almost always on lined school paper. "We are students at X. . . . We have read your novel *Friday* at school. We liked it, in spite of many little flaws, and have some questions to ask you. . . . " Sometimes I propose a simple exchange of cassettes. The recording produced by their collective labor is often tumultuous, enriched by musical interludes and recitations, and I can easily imagine the festive atmosphere in which it was born. I return it, answering out loud: the personal message of the author. I am used to this kind of exchange. I have friends that I have corresponded with in this way for a long time. A cassette carries not only the sound of the voice, but household noises, church bells, the purr of the cat that has just jumped on my lap, the tick-tock of the grandfather clock. It is more than a letter, it is a slice of life.

Whenever I can, I go there in person.

Many visits have convinced me how extraordinary is the variety of education today. There are old buildings from the last century, as repellent as a prison, functional cubes cut out as if with a knife, little school-cities as colorful and whimsical as an African village. The atmosphere also changes from one city to the next. In one the children belted into uniform blue smocks stand up at attention, with their arms crossed, as soon as a teacher enters the classroom. Another evokes instead the barricades of May 1968; I am greeted by cheers mixed with boos. How many times I have found the "schoolmaster" nostalgic for his past of '68, settled down and furious about it! The Sartrouville lycee had prepared a different surprise for me. A festival: masks, streamers, carnival heads, primitive music. Under a thick coat of aggressive makeup, I recognized Patrick Grainville, that young genius devoured by an inner fire. In 1976 I fought to have his fine novel *Les Flamboyants* awarded the Goncourt prize. I had been warned when I entered the Goncourt Academy that I would often remember the terrible saying of Louis XIV: "When

I confer a position, I create one ingrate and one hundred discontents." Grainville is an exception to the rule.

In general, a visit begins by a brief introduction in the principal's office. The principals sometimes attend the session, on the pretext of not wanting to miss so rare a meeting. I am not duped, but I understand their anxiety. They are responsible for everything that goes on in their institutions. A modern writer on a visit to the seventh grade is disquietingly like a fox in a chickencoop.

Robinson, Friday, the island, the dog, the goat, and the parrots often seem to have completely invaded and taken over the classroom. Drawings cover the walls. Clay models reproduce the desert island with its gum tree forest, its swamps where Robinson goes to "soil" himself like a boar when things are going badly, the cave where he returns to the womb, and the beach where lies the tragic and grotesque wreck of the Virginia, the Dutch boat on which he arrived. The main traits of Friday's adventure—the man of air, the eolian genius—are reproduced lifesize: the bow and arrow, the kite, the eolian harp.

Certain drawings glow with genius, a word that seems strong but that we should not hesitate to use. An important study could be made of children's drawings, one that would give immediate insights into great painting. "Yes, they show genius," an art critic once said to me, flipping through children's drawings. "They show genius, but they have no value. . . . " And Picasso: "At ten, I drew like Ingres. I have spent thirty years learning how to do as well as my little friends did then." In short, there is a rough, primitive genius that we should not study, since it "proves" nothing—that is, it has the gratuitous, ephemeral, and futureless beauty of a sunrise.

All the same, there is a shock when you push the door open. Vannes left me two special memories. The children had covered three walls of the classroom with a series of drawings showing, like a comic strip, the main episodes of the story, with a frieze beneath recording something like the temperature curve of Robinson's state of mind. The curve plunges when everything is going badly and when our hero drowns his despair in a muddy pond with a couple of peccaries as companions; the curve rises when, reinvigorated by Friday's presence, he sends aloft a feathered and beribboned kite.

Also at Vannes: another class had put together a soundtrack and slides made from 200 drawings telling the whole story. The richly colorful spectacle lasted more than an hour. Yet I did not miss the opportunity to scold the artists a bit. One episode in the story was missing. One day Robinson realizes that because he has lived alone, he no longer knows how to smile. He looks at himself in a mirror and can only grimace horribly as he tries to recapture the gentlest expression of the human face. Despair possesses him, and he curses once again in his terrible solitude. Then he notices that his dog is lifting his head toward him, cocking it to one side, and oddly drawing back his ragged black lips from his teeth. He is obviously trying to smile, and, thanks to him, bit by bit Robinson will be able to do so in turn.

My little artists had recoiled from this terrible technical problem: how to show a dog smiling (it can happen!). I went home, but my lesson had not fallen on deaf ears. Two weeks later, the mailman brought me a packet of drawings: as many smiling dogs as there were schoolchildren at Vannes!

But the best parts are the theatrical presentations with exotic orchestra and noises. These have no connection to the superb spectacle based on my novel put on by Antoine Vitez a few years ago at the Palais de Chaillot. But I note all the same that the role of Friday is often played by a child from the Maghreb, Portugal, or Mali, proof that the children grasp the contemporary significance of my novel: the confrontation, through Robinson and Friday, of West and Third World, and that of Frenchman and immigrant worker.

These are only the hors d'oeuvre. The heart of the matter comes in the interplay of question and answer.

"How long did it take you to write this book?"

The schoolchild, who feels he has sweat blood and water on homework that takes an hour, is overwhelmed by respect for the writer who confesses he spent four years on his manuscript. Everything enters these young heads through a process of identification and comparison.

"How does one become a writer?"

In response to this ritual question, I ask another question: "Do any of you want to become a writer?"

There are always a couple of fingers raised, timidly, more often by girls than boys.

"Well now. . . . It is at your age that one becomes a writer, and as with everything else, admiration is what makes the difference. Admiration counts most at your age. If some among you are so unfortunate as to admire nothing, it is too bad, for they will never do anything in life. They are failures even before they have begun. A calling is a question of admiration. You admire a doctor, a boxer, a pianist, an architect, and that is what decides your future. Thus you become a writer by admiring certain books you have read. When I was your age, I read *The Adventures of Nils Holgerson* by Selma Lagerlöf. I was so dazzled, I decided that if one day I could do what I wanted, I would write a book like that one."

But there are always children who bring you right back to earth. "How much do you earn a month?"

On this point, I think you shouldn't hide a thing from children. At home they hear enough about money matters, so that you needn't bother with excessive modesty. When I tell them that an author's royalties range from 5 to 15 percent, and average 10 percent, so that when they buy a book for ten francs, only one goes into the author's pocket, their astonished indignation is a delight to see. So little! Oh, Messrs Flammarion, Stock, Seuil, Grasset, Gallimard, and others, where are you? The inverse proportion—nine francs for the author, one franc for the publisher and bookstore—would surely have seemed more equitable to them! I sense hesitation in the literary vocations I was encouraging. I have no difficulty in showing them, with figures, how hard it is to live by the pen. Today in France there are only about fifty writers who succeed in this feat. Not even one per million inhabitants.

Suddenly the enthusiasm of those who wanted "to write" chills. Nonetheless, I continue to address what I say to them. I treat them as my future colleagues. I explain to them how you prepare a manuscript. One should say "typescript," since it is imperative that the text be typed. It has been ages since publishers accepted real manuscripts, which they find hard to read and are afraid of losing. I take the occasion to recommend they ask for a typewriter as soon as possible and learn how to use one. In modern life, you cannot do without one. It is indispensable, and besides it is fun.

Then you must choose a publisher. Generally you go by the books you have liked. You send the work and wait. . . . I have had enough odd jobs with different publishers to enable me to retrace the path of a manuscript that arrives in the mail. Oddly enough, it is often Tuesday at 5 p.m. that the readers' committees meet at the publisher's to cut through the avalanche of mail with a yes or no. One can hardly help feeling bitter at seeing growing piles of manuscripts that will be returned to the authors; the more inexorably negative the reply, the more amiable the letter. How many hours of fevered labor, how many calls, cries, confessions, dreams lie buried in these pages! True, when you venture onto the paths of creativity and publication, you look forward to some irreplaceable joys, but far more surely you expose yourself to disappointments, attacks, innumerable misunderstandings, and hardest of all, without a doubt, the soft and impenetrable obstacle of indifference and ignorance. You must know and accept all this in advance.

I am never so cruelly frank with my green little writers. I refrain from giving them advice. Advice is useless and is never followed, even by those who ask for it. After this prudent preface, nonetheless I hurry to give them two pieces of advice. First, my dear little ones, write every day. Remember that everything you do *seriously*, you do every day. If you are serious about speaking English, riding horseback, playing chess, or becoming a singer, you must not practice once a week or twice for that matter. You should set aside a few minutes every day for your specialty. In a large notebook, then, you should keep a kind of diary. Every day, without exception, you should write down something, an event, a reflection, the weather, it doesn't matter what. When you reread what you have written, you will see over the course of a year or so how your style changes and your linguistic tools sharpen. An easy and fruitful type of diary is one in which you record your readings. What you read will give you double profit if you keep an account of it in your diary.

Then I recommend dictionaries. Begin with the *Petit Larousse* or the *Petit Robert*, but begin to dip more and more into encyclopedias. The dictionary is the panoply, the attic, the arsenal of the writer, and not just for writers. After all, we think with our language, we reason with our words, whether we are writers or dentists, butchers or bakers. When you run into a word you don't know, get into the habit of looking it up to see what it's all about. I myself never work without several dictionaries within reach. Sometimes I just look up the spelling of a word.

I have just let the cat out of the bag. They are quick to respond. "Speaking of that, when you hand in a manuscript, what does the publisher say if there are spelling mistakes?"

I talk about proofreaders, eccentrics to be found at every publishing house, gifted with encyclopedic erudition, with an exceptional power of attention, and poorly paid, poorly esteemed. . . . But above all I refute the idea that a writer is necessarily someone who earlier had been good at composition, first in grammar, or a superintellectual. No. Moreover, at their age, I was a very mediocre student. I feel at once that my popularity is rising, but some teachers have complained to me about what they take to be a "demoralizing" revelation. Some great writers today, however, never went on to advanced studies: Bernard Clavel began as a baker's boy, and Alphonse Boudard was more familiar with prisons than universities.

"How many pages do you write a day?"

Wait a minute! Do you realize that if I were to write only one page a day, that would make a big book every year? Very few writers obey this rhythm, and generally those who do are wrong. It is far too much. In fact, I write as often and as long as my strength permits, that is to say, very rarely. But you see, writing is only part of the work, the last phase. When I sit down at my table, my book is already almost finished, I need only copy what is in my head. For me everything happens before then. I think about it constantly. I carry my workshop in my head. That is why I never lose any time. A dentist, a grocer, and a mason leave their work when they go home. Not the writer. Whatever the writer does, his work follows him, haunting him. For him there is no Sunday, no vacation, no retirement, and even at night when he is asleep, his work is ripening invisibly. And that is marvelous, because when I say that I never take a vacation, I could also say that I am always on vacation, the ideal vacation, since I am doing just what pleases me most: thinking about and writing a book.

Questions ricochet. The most treacherous is asked by a little snip wearing glasses.

"When you drive, do you pick up hitch-hikers?"

Ready for anything, I collect my wits. Let's be careful!

"That depends on what they look like. I am like anyone else. I have my likes and dislikes . . ."

"Well then, how should they look?"

I am put on the defensive. I make a great effort of memory and imagination: How should they look?

"Well, for example, I don't much like people with beards."

"Why don't you like people with beards?"

A new challenge to cope with.

"When I was your age, I had a grandfather with a big beard. Every morning and evening, I had to give him a kiss. I didn't like it. It prickled."

"But sir, when you pick up hitchhikers, you don't have to kiss them!"

A low blow! Down on the mat for the count!

They come back to better subjects:

"Do you have animals?"

"I used to have some. But I take trips. I am gone five months out of twelve. And you can't just leave animals behind. Then there is something else. An animal doesn't live very long. When you love a cat or a dog, in the end you always lose it. Its old age is often pitiful. I know people who adored their dog or cat. The animal died. Well, they decided never to begin again."

To go on with animals: I see an extraordinary number of children with a call to become veterinarians. Approximately 10 percent, it seems, dream, will dream, or have dreamed of taking care of animals. I warn them with a frankness that may seem cruel. When you love animals—or simply respect them—you are revolted by their mass production in batteries. For chickens, calves, and pigs, this method inspired by the desire for extravagant yields is an abomination that dishonors our society. I recommend that children go see this for themselves as soon as they can. Such batteries inevitably need veterinary services, since the animals are always at the limit of survival. Veterinarians may then become accomplices to this ignominy. If children want to become veterinarians, they should be careful about what they will be made to do. They should orient themselves toward irreproachable specializations, horses or dogs, for example. And they should be prepared to fight with all their strength for the disappearance of battery culture.

We pass from animals to nature, to ecology, to the quality of life, and then, quite simply, to happiness. Children are not afraid of the big questions. In fact they do not order problems hierarchically. What do you eat for breakfast? Or, How can one be happy? They throw out such questions without making any distinction. One must know how to answer. We may skip breakfast. But what about happiness? "Happiness? Very simple. There is only one condition, but it is absolutely essential: you must passionately love something or someone. If you love nothing or no one, you are lost, your life has ended before it has begun. You might as well die right away—it makes no difference. If on the contrary you have a passion for botany, Indian music, rugby, or stamps, if you want to know absolutely everything about Pharaonic Egypt, if you spend nights with your eye glued to a telescope because you are fascinated by the stars, if you adore above all else a woman, a man, or a child (or all three at once), and if you are ready to make all the sacrifices demanded by your passion . . . then you might become a great writer, a famous painter, or a world renowned botanist, but one thing is altogether certain: your life will be worth living."

Margaret Higonnet, translator

Reviews

Childhood's End?

Janice M. Alberghene

The Rise and Fall of Childhood, by C. John Sommerville. Volume 140,
    Sage Library of Social Research. Beverly Hills: Sage Publications,
    Inc., 1982.
Children of War, by Roger Rosenblatt. New York: Anchor Press,
    1983.
Children without Childhood, by Marie Winn. New York: Pantheon
    Books, 1981, 1983.
The Disappearance of Childhood, by Neil Postman. New York: Dela-
    corte, 1982.
Family Politics: Love and Power on an Intimate Frontier, by Letty Cottin
    Pogrebin. New York: McGraw Hill Book Company, 1983.

Promising to reveal the secrets of childhood, the books above reveal
instead the secret concerns of adults. In these volumes, childhood
per se often seems less important than childhood as a vehicle for
discussing other issues—war and peace, social change, patriarchal
power structures. It is fortunate, then, that *The Rise and Fall of
Childhood*, the first of the five books, offers a perspective from which
the reader can view the remaining four. Sommerville explicitly
defines his subject as "an abstraction, 'childhood,' which is made up
of the expectations, hopes, and fears societies have expressed with
regard to their youngest members." A cultural history of childhood,
Sommerville's work is "a study of adult attitudes as much as of the
actual lives of children" (7). With few exceptions, the other authors
present their arguments as relating to real children. Yet each page
bears the firm imprint of various "adult attitudes" toward children.
Time and again the writers turn to literature and myth—not life—to
shape their texts. The reader is forced to conclude that for these
adults, and perhaps for many others as well, "childhood" is an idea, a

188

cultural construct dependent upon time, place, and the concerns of grownups, rather than upon universal and verifiable fact.

These ideas and the concerns that shape them are nonetheless important. They determine behavior and policies regarding children. Recall the issues the books discuss: war and peace, social change, patriarchal power structures. Although at first these issues look diverse, the ways in which the authors treat them reveal the common denominator of concern for the future. This future will be both *shaped by* and *shaper of* today's children.

Once again Sommerville strikes a keynote. His very title, *The Rise and Fall of Childhood*, identifies the worry the five writers share that "children are in danger of becoming a thing of the past" (7). He sets that worry in context by surveying childhood from Mesopotamian, early Greek, and Hebrew culture up until the present day, but his main focus of attention is on the past 450 years and on the major Western countries: England, Germany, France, and the United States. *The Rise and Fall of Childhood* can be seen as complementary to Philippe Ariès's earlier *Centuries of Childhood*, which primarily examined the family and child in France and the shift from a medieval to a modern sensibility. The two books belong on the same reference shelf for anyone seeking particulars of the cultural context in which a given work of children's literature was produced or received.

The Rise and Fall of Childhood is valuable for another reason. It shows us that worried as we may be about the ways in which we treat young people, we do care about children; earlier eras would have wondered what all the fuss was about. This is not to say that Sommerville ignores contemporary uncertainties so acute that they make us wonder if childhood exists anymore. He links these uncertainties to adults' fears of a future characterized by long-term economic depression, a situation that would be exacerbated by a rise in population (9). Heirs are assets when the future looks rosy, liabilities when it appears grim. Economic decline, however, is not the only specter on the horizon. Nuclear destruction is a distinct possibility, although Sommerville does not raise the issue. The "fall" of childhood may be a function of contemporary adults' inability to imagine any future at all.

The future was very much on Roger Rosenblatt's mind as he interviewed children from five of the world's war zones: Northern

Ireland, Israel, Lebanon, Cambodia, and Viet Nam. *Children of War*
records the two-part odyssey Rosenblatt began with the hope that
the endangered children would give him a sense of the future of the
strategic areas in which they live. He also hoped to gain insight into
the meaning of war and to learn "why violence grows in the heart"
(17). Midway through his first trip, in a chapter entitled "Pausing
with Telemachos," Rosenblatt stops in Athens to consider what he
has seen. The children of war are serious, gentle, and they believe in
God. Despite their losses and the bellicose adults around them, the
majority of the children do not seek revenge. Rosenblatt then wonders if revenge is an "adult invention" adopted primarily by children
who see it as a "sure sign of adulthood" (119, 120). At any rate,
he "began to realize that most of the children in the war zones
patronized their parents. . . . They tolerated things in their parents,
like the idea of revenge, which they did not accept in the abstract or
for themselves . . . they loved their parents, but they did not believe
in them" (120–21).

The idea of children patronizing their parents with good reason is
disquieting. Nobody wants to be the sort of mother or father who
deserves that response, least of all Rosenblatt. Six months after he
wrote a cover story for *Time*, he made a second journey and revised
his initial assumption—"that children were important to grownups
because grownups saw in them all they had lost in the process of
becoming grownups." In a radical about-face, Rosenblatt decided
that he would not have heard the children's gentleness if he had
not had some of his own, a gentleness apparently generic to all
grownups: "Every adult responds to the gentleness of children. . . .
Children matter so much to adults because they remind us that we
never lost any of the virtues of childhood. . . . Astonished by Khu [a
Vietnamese child], . . . I was astonished by me" (205–06).

It is difficult not to see the above as solipsistic. Rosenblatt clearly
makes childhood in his own image. A further complication is that
the image derives as much from literature as it does from experience. While "pausing with Telemachos," Rosenblatt noted that Telemachos expresses surprise when Odysseus tells his son to slay
Penelope's suitors and thereby start a series of blood feuds. Although Rosenblatt acknowledges that Telemachos might simply be
doubting his own prowess, he would like to think that Telemachos is

opposed to the idea of revenge. The journeys in *Children of War* are ultimately epic attempts at finding a reason to reaffirm peace.

In contrast to Rosenblatt, the next two authors believe that we have already lost many of the virtues of childhood and are in danger of plunging back into a medieval state of mind in which we will fail to differentiate children from adults. Marie Winn, author of *Children without Childhood*, sees many reasons for our current peril. She blames Judy Blume, books such as Fran Arrick's *Steffie Can't Come Out to Play* and John Donovan's *I'll Get There: It Better Be Worth the Trip*, *Mad* magazine, movies such as *Raiders of the Lost Ark*, and television (both its content and parents' use of it as a babysitter). Like Vance Packard in *Our Endangered Children*, she thinks that divorce and women entering the work force blight our youngsters. Even more at fault, she finds, are parents who are so afraid of being authoritarian that they fail to be appropriately authoritative.

According to Winn, the problem is that we have moved from a golden "Age of Protection" to an "Age of Preparation." Although never clearly defining or dating the "Age of Protection," Winn seems to link its demise with the protest movements publicizing society's ills in the 1960s. These movements contributed to the belief that early exposure to adult problems fosters the ability to deal with them. Winn disagrees and cites early childhood expert Annie Herman to explain the importance of protection from adult problems: "The child *needs* to feel dependent on the adult, has a *right* to this feeling" (199). The child also has the right to a period of "unselfconsciousness." Winn turns to "our myths of Paradise to teach us the truth about childhood. There must be an Eden at the beginning, just as there is in every creation myth" (204). This poeticizing does not address issues such as the anxieties children feel when they sense hidden tensions or the length of time that children should stay in their Edens. Winn's fear that the "Age of Preparation" gives children information they are not yet ready to know can also be read as an attempt to postpone their control of their futures for as long as possible.

Neil Postman's *The Disappearance of Childhood* turns Winn's fear into a moot point. He argues that we simply cannot keep information from children. Television, seen by Winn as just one cause of the "disappearance of childhood," is *the* cause for Postman. He maintains that the modern concept of childhood depended upon literacy (the encoding of information in print), education (learning how to decode), and the idea of shame (declaring information about sex, violence, or adult fallibility unsuitable for children to decode). In other words, childhood is a function of adults' ability and desire to keep secrets from children. Postman argues that books take great skill to decode and therefore make such good hiding places for adult secrets that they are largely responsible for creating childhood. Television, on the other hand, makes secrets impossible. No formal education is necessary to decode its images, and access to those images is only a fingertip away. Television effects our return to the Middle Ages where there is "no need for the idea of childhood" because everyone lives in "the same information environment and therefore . . . the same social and intellectual world" (36). Postman's argument is provocative, but *access* to information is not identical to *understanding* information. Mankind's return to the Middle Ages may still be a few weeks away.

Letty Cottin Pogrebin is the author who finally embraces the decades ahead. She opens *Family Politics* with a declaration of faith: "Very simply, I hope to preserve family life by saving what is best about it and changing what isn't" (x). The best is the family's ability to humanize. The worst is the pedophobia it must combat: "*America is a nation fundamentally ambivalent about its children, often afraid of its children, and frequently punitive toward its children.* As a society, we love children when they are *under control*" (42). We control them by supporting a patriarchal model of the family in which Dad's work produces money that he brings home to his consumer family in exchange for power over their lives. Even though relatively few households conform to a strict patriarchal model, this "obsolete ideology" persists because it is necessary to our economy (66).

The changes Pogrebin proposes begin with our attitudes and carry through to the policies implemented by our institutions. Central to her recommendations is the belief that we should stop thinking and acting as if families were simply consumers. *All* families should be "redefined as *producers* engaged in the production of social attitudes, moral and ethical capacities, mental health, decision-making skills, interpersonal competence, and other human resource development" (67). Families are, however, more than just producers. Prefacing her discussion with a reference to Robert Frost's "Death of the Hired Man," Pogrebin argues that families should think of themselves as "friends—not to invalidate family's special status, make parents into pals, or eliminate the boundaries between childhood and maturity (as so many fear), but rather to hold family relations to the highest possible standard of human relations" (217). Pogrebin adds a footnote reference to Winn and Postman; if we have not come full circle, we have at least traced a parabola.

So, what is the reader to conclude? If childhood is about to disappear, can children's books be far behind? Asking this presupposes that childhood comes first, and children's books follow. The five authors' responses to myth and poetry and novels suggest otherwise. They use literature to formulate their ideas about childhood, family, and society. Perhaps children's books help create childhood for us, not the other way around. Maybe we should turn to a different question: if children's books disappear—if they are less and less frequently read—can childhood itself survive?

Looking Backwards

Hugh Keenan

Signposts to Criticism of Children's Literature, edited by Robert Bator (Chicago: American Library Association, 1983).

In this anthology of criticism, Robert Bator attempts to survey judiciously the often contradictory views taken of children's literature. To do so, he has culled essays principally from journals or annuals devoted to the field such as *Signal*; *Children's Literature in Education*; *Phaedrus*; *Children's Literature*; *The Lion and the Unicorn*; *Children's Literature Association Quarterly*; *Horn Book*; and *School Library Journal*. As a result the reader finds essays by many familiar writers and critics. It is a cosy family circle whose members occasionally squabble among themselves as all families do, while perpetuating their mutual interest. Missing are outside voices—those of trade publishers or of provocative social critics such as Ariel Dorfman (*The Empire's Old Clothes*). Despite these serious limitations, the first part of the anthology raises three basic questions: What is children's literature? What is its stature? How should it be criticized? This section shows that the criticism of children's literature has moved beyond plot summary or classification by age. Part 2 gives varied appraisals of eight major and occasionally overlapping subgenres of children's literature: picture books, fairy tales, poetry, fiction, fantasy, historical fiction, science fiction, and the young adult novel.

Because the second section is more specific than the first, the strengths and faults of the volume are most obvious there. Discussions of the fairy tale by Catherine Storr, Brian Hooker, and Perry Nodelman are worth reading; Nodelman wittily argues that the literary flaws of the Grimms' "The Golden Bird" provide its strengths as children's literature. The essays on fiction, fantasy, and the young adult novel are solid but not inspiring. Disagreement arises especially about the newest subgenre, the young adult novel: its value as fiction and its distinction from adult fare. Jane Abrahamson contrasts such works' pretensions to realism with their "glib assurances" (321). Though associated with pulp fiction, young adult

194

novels (most of these critics agree) are better written and more topical.

Unfortunately, Bator's introductions are often more probing than the essays he has selected. Thus the current popularity of science fiction is certainly not illuminated either by Thomas Roberts's attacks on its scientific content, "sentimental lard," and unsophisticated style or by Eleanor Cameron's demurral that fantasy, not science, is the real heart of her Mushroom Planet series. All in all, one wonders why critics write on these subgenres if they think so many are trivial.

Important as the questions are, many of the more general essays comprising the first section are also disappointing. These essays fail to agree on how children's literature is different or what its values are. Apparently to demonstrate the fluctuation of tastes, Bator has juxtaposed selections from Sara Kirby Trimmer's *Guardian of Education* (1802–05) and an anonymous review from the *British Quarterly Review* (January 1868). Mrs. Trimmer trumpets the case for moral fiction. Sixty years later, the reviewer calls for more imaginative writing. In many ways, modern children's literature is still pulled between two poles—moralism on the one side, unfettered imagination on the other.

To define the nature of children's literature of Clifton Fadiman gives an urbane if concise survey (eleven pages) of the world history of children's literature, with examples of its distinctive forms and themes. Then Bator tosses the whole matter into a cocked hat by following it with a brief (two-page) comment by writer/critic John Rowe Townsend. Townsend's pragmatic definition boils down to two points. Children's literature is that which is placed on the shelves by "a consensus of adults and children" (19). And before that, the publishers make the initial determination. So much for the critical definition of children's literature.

Likewise the critics are evasive about the low status of children's literature. Rather than evaluate the mode, they attack the evaluators. Thus, in her essay, Felicity Hughes blames the restriction of novels to an exclusively adult audience in the nineteenth century. And we are all familiar with those cautionary tales about young girls ruined by reading novels. Francelia Butler blames the sexist and age bias of society. As it values women and children less, so it values children's literature less because women principally write it and children read it. Paradoxically, Butler argues that adults may need it more than children "to restory" their lives. Certainly Bettelheim (*The Uses of Enchantment*) would agree.

Defending the value of children's literature, I. B. Singer asserts: "It's easier to force university students to eat literary straw and clay than [it is] an infant in a kindergarten" (52). He believes that children are superior critics because they want an interesting story first of all. Less encouraging, Aiden Chambers denies that "good story-telling" is peculiar to children's literature (55) or that didacticism has been expunged. Hugh Crago argues that children's books are old-fashioned and peripheral in many ways, including their content, style, and intent. Further isolated by inappropriately sophisticated criticism, they will atrophy.

To judge by the sharp exchanges of letters in Bator's volume, the critical warfare of the little magazines is often more emotional and personal than logical and objective. Thus Paul and Ethel Heins of *Horn Book* wrangle about progress in children's books with Lillian N. Gerhardt of *School Library Journal*, who caustically asserts that this literature is the "last bastion of yesterday's literary methods and standards." The reliance on "episodic novels, first-person narration, and the unresolved plot" (91) explains in part for Gerhardt the exclusion of children's literature from the National Book Awards and the essay topics of the National Book Critics Circle. Her charges of critical "hogwash that induces self-defeating complacency" (94) and Heins's disingenuous belief in the "intellectual honesty" of children's literature have a gossipy interest, but as answers to Bator's question about the proper kind of criticism such exchanges are nearly worthless.

Everyone is defensive about the criticism of children's literature. Author Susan Cooper (like Singer later in the volume) takes the critics to task for their "earnest psycho-analytical approach," their use of jargon, and abstruse and awkwardly written analyses (101). Critic and teacher Lois Kuznets replies to this attack by asking for a definition of good criticism. She defends her own close reading of texts as a way of "honestly trying to discover the author's answers" (113). She argues that "the reader has the right to ask questions and penetrating ones about how and by what methods and for what reasons that world [of the book] is being depicted. . . . I believe teachers should teach readers to ask questions" (113).

Yet assuming criticism is desirable, the appropriate kind is not clear. Peter Hunt's "Criticism and Children's Literature" offers a survey of various critical approaches. A reviewer of Roger Sale's *Fairy Tales and After* argues with Aiden Chambers about whether the implied reader in such criticism is to be an adult or a child. Peggy Whalen-Levitt's "Pursuing 'The Reader in the Book' " would have the critic use "recent developments in literary theory" (136), especially that of reader response, but her essay is itself wooden. Marilyn Kaye would advance on all fronts, using a critically eclectic approach to form, audience, and varying subgenres.

It should be clear by now that Bator risked certain inherent strengths and weaknesses in attempting to cover so much in one volume. The general essays about definition, status, and critical approaches found in part 1, "The Wide Domain," do not really belong with those mechanically arranged in part 2, "The Territories." The latter belong in a separate book. Bator chose assertive essays to give the sense of a lively debate, but they sometimes give instead the impression of an adolescent quarrel. Only Bator's paternal introductions make sense of such squabbles. In fact, his introductions are superior to most of the essays.

No reader is likely to accept Bator's invitation either to be "a sidewalk superintendent or . . . to pick up hammer and nails to construct [his] own signpost" (xiv). This volume already has too many opposed signposts and the reader cannot be confident either that their labels are accurate or that the posts point in the right direction. A better title for the book might have been "A Tournament of Critics."

What this anthology lacks is extended specific criticism of particular children's books. Nodelman's essay on the Grimms' fairy tale is a notable exception. Because Bator's anthology concentrates on the critics rather than on children's literature, few outside the circle of the American Library Association which published it are ever likely to open its pages.

Bator's volume fails to take children's literature seriously enough. The reader will look in vain for the provocative statement or that which relates children's literature significantly to the main culture, such as we find in Ariel Dorfman's *The Empire's Old Clothes*. In his essay "Of Elephants and Ducks," Dorfman shows how the Babar books are prophetic of "the theory of neocolonialism" (40) and observes that Disney's Donald Duck and nephew ducklings effectively neutralize the "natural rebellious energies" of children (59). He is concerned not only with "the adult values and hidden interests that shape and infect fiction for young reader" but also with the "infantilization" of adults by the mass media (204). An age when soaps dominate the television screen and movies such as *E.T.* and the *Star Wars* series fill the movie houses should call forth more perceptive comments on the mainstream relevance of children's literature than are generally found in Bator.

One of the paradoxes of our time is that much children's literature has become more sophisticated and realistic at the same time that mass media for a general or adult audience has become more simplistic and escapist. Though various writers in the anthology glimpse this paradox, none grapples with it. A work like Dorfman's will lead the reader back to the works in question to validate an argument. *Signposts to Criticism* will only lead him to sleep or ennui.

The Power of the Tale

Roni Natov

The Trials and Tribulations of Little Red Riding Hood: Versions of The Tale in Sociocultural Context, by Jack Zipes. South Hadley: Bergin and Garvey Publishers, Inc., 1983.

In the broadest and perhaps most fundamental sense, *The Trials and Tribulations of Little Red Riding Hood* is a study of what happens to an oral folk tale once it is immortalized in print: how, honed and shaped by the imaginations of its literary authors, it absorbs and reinforces in its retellings the values and norms of a given society. Zipes traces the literary evolution of "Little Red Riding Hood" and demonstrates how its history and reception, as it spread throughout Western Europe and America, reveal significant "shifts, conflicts, and ruptures in the Western civilizing process." Zipes focuses on the changes in the tale engendered by the class and sex biases of its literary authors. A tale like "Little Red Riding Hood," he points out in his preface, "can reveal to what extent the boundaries of our existence have evolved from male phantasy and sexual struggle for social domination.

The book has two parts. It opens with a long introduction which traces the historical and political contexts of the tale from its early folk origins, through its literary appearance in the work of Charles Perrault and the Grimm brothers, and finally through contemporary experimental versions. The second and major part of the book includes thirty-one variants of the tale. The major constellation of the wolf, grandmother, and young girl is seen, therefore, from a variety of points of view. Zipes makes us aware of the significance of the changes in motifs from story to story. The oral version, for example, significantly entitled "The Story of the Grandmother," makes no mention of the red cap or hood. Perrault's addition of the red hood suggests some association with "sin, sensuality and the devil." According to Zipes this strongly cautionary variant (witness the finality of the ending where Little Red Riding Hood and the grandmother are eaten by the wolf) reflects Perrault's rigorous

199

aristocratic morality, which compelled him "to improve the minds
and manners of young people" through making the child "responsible for her own rape" by virtue of her vanity and lack of self-
control. If this at first seems far-fetched to the reader, Zipes makes a
strong case. He goes beyond Bettelheim's suggestion in his earlier
study, *The Uses of Enchantment*, that Perrault makes Red Riding
Hood appear stupid or the willing victim of her seduction as she
makes no move to escape or fight back. What we learn from this
study—what all earlier interpretations, including Bettelheim's,
neglect—is that in the early, seminal oral tale spread throughout
France and northern Italy between 1400 and 1700, and first recorded by Paul Delarue in 1885, the young girl rescues herself from
the werewolf (replaced by the wolf in Perrault's version), after the
famous seduction ("Oh, Grandma, what big eyes, ears, teeth you
have . . . "), by claiming that she has to relieve herself. The werewolf
attaches a rope to her foot to let her go outside; the girl cleverly reties
it to a tree and escapes unharmed. There are other wonderfully
rich and revealing details, but essentially, the victory of the little
girl over her would-be seducer/devourer is what was repressed by
Perrault, who, according to Zipes, must have been familiar with this
widespread oral version.

   In his discussion, Bettelheim found the significant details of early
oral variants vulgar (where, for example, the wolf tells the girl to eat
of the grandmother's flesh and drink of her blood) and approves
their removal by Perrault from the tale. He claimed that the two
paths through the forest, the path of needles and the path of pins,
symbolize the girl's choice between the pleasure principle and the
reality principle, and that "taking the easy way of using pins instead
of needles was readily understood as behaving in accordance with
the pleasure principle" (Bettelheim, 171n). Zipes properly reinter-
prets these details from a historical and sociological point of view.
He argues, referring to recent studies, that the eating of flesh and
drinking of blood symbolize the replacement of the grandmother
by the young girl and suggest a natural inheritance of her body
and spirit. He further notes that the references to the pins and
needles "were related to the needlework apprenticeship undergone
by young peasant girls, and designated the arrival of puberty and
initiation into society in specific regions of France where the oral tale

was common." As Zipes pointed out in his earlier book, *Breaking the Magic Spell: Radical Theories of Folk and Fairy Tales* (London: Heinemann, 1979), there are dangers in treating the tales (as psychological studies such as Bettelheim's have done) as if they were only stories about the inner psychological life of children or more generally of all of us; these interpretations suggest that external reality is isolated from the inner life. Essentially they ignore social context and therefore distort the meaning and importance of the tales. In a recent article by Robert Darnton, "Mother Goose's Secrets" (*New York Review of Books*, February 2, 1984), Zipes's political and historical view received support, as Darnton pointed out that psychoanalysts from Erich Fromm to Bettelheim have strayed far from any kind of valid interpretation of the story because of their "blindness to the historical dimension of folk tales."

Zipes goes on to develop the sociological context of the story by showing how the Grimm brothers made further moralistic modifications in the tale. Their alternations, which include the mother's warnings to the girl to stay on the straight and narrow path and not to talk to strangers, as well as the girl's fascination with the natural pretty things of the forest, reinforced the moral of the tale: that the little girls' natural instincts need to be curbed. Of course, the addition of the male savior in the form of the hunter who rescues Little Red Riding Hood and her grandmother from the belly of the wolf further reduces the power and cleverness of Little Red Riding Hood until she is hardly recognizable as the original, spunky peasant girl. According to Zipes, the various nineteenth- and early twentieth century variants seem to stress "either the French erotic elements of play and seduction or the German concern with law and order." The American mixture of the Perrault and Grimm versions produced a "Victorian middle-class" Red Riding Hood "whose virtue is threatened because she forgets to control her sensual drives and disobeys her good super-ego mother."

Especially striking in this book is the collection of post–World War II versions, which are essentially original stories that use the major motifs of the popular Perrault or Grimms' version. Zipes includes these experimental tales to reflect the questioning of traditional male values by the civil rights, labor, and women's movements. Some of them, such as Catherine Storr's "Little Polly Riding Hood" and Anneliese Meinert's "Little Red Cap '65," are merely light and humorous; others such as Iring Fetcher's "Little Redhead and the Wolf" and Tony Ross's "Little Red Hood," seem contrived. But the best of these, for example, Anne Sexton's poem from her book *Transformations*, are challenging with their ironic stance and deep sense of disillusionment expressed through parodies of the Grimms' version. Sexton focuses on the theme of deception and extends it in her idiosyncratic series of free associations to include the many delusions of modern life, particularly for women. Angela Carter, in her nightmare narrative, "The Company of Wolves," remakes the story into a gothic tale of mutuality between the wolf and the maiden. The sexual initiation of a bold and brave virgin tames the appetites of the murderous "carnivore incarnate." Innocence cannot remain so nor should it, Carter seems to suggest, and sexual depravity can be transformed. "See!" she writes. "Sweet and sound she sleeps in granny's bed, between the paws of the tender wolf."

These two versions, however, will not speak to children, nor were they meant to. The strongest contemporary "Red Riding Hood," which portrays the heroine achieving a strong identity without total dependence upon males, is a story collectively created by a group of feminists in Liverpool, the Merseyside Fairy Story Collective. The child and her great-grandmother overpower the wolf with their courage and strategy. The old woman encourages the child to trust her instincts and to overcome her fears of the forest by preparing to confront them. There is none of the slickness or preciosity of some of the other versions here. This story treats seriously children's fears. The old woman says to the child, after the parents laugh at her fear of wolves:

> "Not everyone can hear that howling; they think it is only the wind in the trees. One winter day when I was a girl, out alone chopping wood for the stove, I was attacked by one of the grey wolves which speak."
>
> Oh, great-grandmother!" whispered Red Riding Hood. "What did you do?"
>
> "I fought the wolf with my hatchet and killed it," replied the old woman, "for I was strong and agile when I was young."

This tale encourages children to "grow brave" as Red Riding Hood shares her cloak, the sign of her bravery, with other children. The story ends with Red Riding Hood wearing the cloak herself "as she explored deeper and deeper into the great forest."

Zipes's book is a testament to the symbolic power of our richest tales to reverberate over the centuries. The "Red Riding Hood" tale, with its warnings against the dangers of strangers and of deception, has inspired the forces of conservatism and reaction, radicalism and liberalism, to reinterpret some basic conceptions about girls, sexuality, and the coming of age; about the individual and her place in society; about the child and the balance of innocence and experience, which by necessity must lead to a "higher innocence" or an ability to incorporate visions of good and evil into a balanced wisdom. Role models are established, confirmed—and in the parodies, questioned, debunked and replaced by new ones.

In the final analysis, what remains a serious challenge is how to replace the deep and penetrating dreamlike states produced by the Perrault and Grimm versions with equally profound stories which reverberate with the seriousness of their predecessors, but with new, strong, life-affirming values for children.

Cott im Himmel

Perry Nodelman

Pipers at the Gates of Dawn: The Wisdom of Children's Literature, by
Jonathan Cott. New York: Random House, 1983.

According to Jonathan Cott, children's books contain the wisdom
of the ages, *the* truth about life; they are sacred texts of biblical
stature. Children's writers are prophets, deep drinkers in the wells
of truth—gurus, in fact. Cott's faith in the spiritual significance of
his subjects makes this book of interviews of prominent children's
writers a prime candidate for consideration as the silliest book about
children's literature ever written.

At one point in his discussion of William Steig, Cott says, "It
would, of course, be egregiously reductive and slighting of Steig's
remarkable literary and pictorial style . . . to see *Dominic* as simply
some kind of mouthpiece for Wilhelm Reich's ethical and social
ideas." But he goes on to do just that, in an egregiously reductive
discussion that equates the dog Dominic not just with Reich, but with
the heroes of Homer, Whitman, Tolstoy, and Emerson, and finally,
with Jesus Christ himself. For Cott, Mary Poppins relates to Taoism,
Zen, and the poetry of Kenneth Rexroth; the works of Dr. Seuss
evoke the ideas of Wordsworth, Italo Calvino, Georg Groddeck,
Erik Erikson, Piaget, Berlyne, Bateson, Brian Sutton-Smith, the folk
mystic expert Charles Wolfe, and the psychologist D. W. Winnicott.
Sendak reminds Cott of Heraclitus and Kafka, and for him, "It is
clear that Pippi Longstocking *is* Émile—the perfect fictional embodi-
ment." Cott also believes that not just Steig's Dominic, but also Pippi,
Mary Poppins, Sendak's Ida, in fact, just about all the important
characters in every book he discusses, are exactly like the cured
patients of the psychoanalyst Reich. Cott probably finds Reich's
ideas lurking on the backs of cereal boxes.

Cott's theorizing would be less distressing if the writers he interviewed were less willing to adore the pseudo-depth he discovers in
their work. In his interview with Astrid Lindgren, Cott says, "I read
her Reich's statement about the child of the future" and reports

Lindgren's reply: " 'That's Pippi!' she exclaimed." Later, he quotes Bachelard to her, and she says, "That's wonderful!" Even Maurice Sendak finds Cott's comparison of his work to that of Heinrich von Kleist "extraordinary," although he admits, "I don't know for sure what Kleist really meant." The world at large has so little respect for children's writers that they seem to have a deep need to be considered respectable—real writers with profound ideas, not just rich but dumb purveyors of shallow-minded kiddie-lit.

Cott's flattery reaches a crescendo in his interview with Pamela Travers—an astonishing document that is not so much an interview as a report of a visit to the Gateways of Heaven. According to Cott, "At the time I visited P. L. Travers in July, 1979, I was feeling perplexed and confused about several things in my life, whose murkiness contrasted sharply with the clarity of the pictures in her study. Everything she showed me in her house somehow seemed to help me put things in perspective." For Cott, Travers is "giving, healing, and wise. And doesn't *Sophia*—the Greek feminine term for 'wisdom' and the personified Divine Mother of the Gnostics (teacher, guide, and source of insight)—suggest many aspects of both Mary Poppins and P. L. Travers?"

One important aspect of Travers's wisdom is her high regard for Cott's wisdom. As he inundates her with quotations, she says, "You're really teaching me my book" and "Please, let me have a copy of that" and "It's wonderful! I must have that quotation!" And when he asks the creator of Mary Poppins, "And have you noticed the first initials of the words 'Mighty Prophet?' " she says, "Oh, I never thought of that! How perceptive of you!"

Happily, not all of Cott's subjects are always open to flattery. Even though Sendak obviously enjoys being compared to Kafka, when Cott says, "Maurice, this is as good a time as any to ask you about the idea of incorporation in your work," he snippishly replies, "While I'm eating a sandwich?" And Cott gets no respect from the ineffably practical Dr. Seuss, who responds to Cott's suggestion that he produces his books according to the Zen precept of emptying his mind and being always a beginner by saying, 'But to create a book . . . you have to have an ability and a technique, which you don't have in any empty mind."

Cott's gassy theorizing would be funny if it were not so sad. What is

saddest about it is that *Piper at the Gates of Dawn* seems to represent
the only sort of attitude toward children's literature that gets children's literature any respect in the corridors of literary power. Its
writing was supported by a Guggenheim fellowship. It was published by a prestigious mainstream publisher, advertised widely, and
reviewed in all the right places. Apparently, people who take literature seriously share Cott's attitude that children's literature can only
be important if it isn't really for children at all but actually secret
pop-Zen for fuzzyminded grownups.

For that is the depressing message of this book: children's literature is actually for adults. "Children's books can enable us to recapture and re-enter our earliest worlds: a sudden word or phrase or
description—or a beloved illustration—may cast light on a darkened
past." Or again, "Children's literature . . . helps us to wake up. It
brings us back to experiencing our earliest and deepest feelings and
truths. It is our link to the past and a path to the future. And in it we
find ourselves." Such a description of children's literature is a tre-
mendous insult to child readers, who presumably don't need to go
looking very hard for their childhood and therefore surely must
read children's books for other reasons.

Furthermore, any adult with any real memory of his own childhood must acknowledge that the sort of imaginative books for children Cott admires do not really evoke childhood with any degree
of accuracy. Accurate descriptions of childhood make good adult
fiction—novels like Joyce's *Portrait of the Artist as a Young Man* and
Dickens's *Great Expectations*, stories like Philip Roth's "Conversion of
the Jews" and Faulkner's "Barn Burning." But if we compare such
books with good children's books, we see an immediate difference.

The adult works I've mentioned constantly reveal how the presumably delightful innocence of childhood is also a dangerous ignorance; such books seem accurate to anyone who is no longer
innocent, and who must therefore view the delights of innocence
with some ambivalence. But most children's books are not particularly accurate simply because they are not ambivalent; they present
the events they describe from the unqualified viewpoint of innocence, a viewpoint which never doubts the impossible or notices
moral ambiguities. Therefore, the climax of many good children's
books is that exact moment in the life of a child when he or she ack-

nowledges that the world is more complex and more subtle than he or she had been willing to admit—when the child admits that innocence is actually ignorance, and often dangerous.

Certainly, many children's books present a simpler view of childhood than do many adult ones, at least before their climaxes; they are books which allow the simplicities of innocence. That's why Cott insists they are wise, for he's one of that breed who believe that complexity is just too damned confusing to be real; after all, if God had wanted us to think, he would have given us minds. But Cott is so determined to admire children's books for their simplicity that he ignores their complications. He dwells on the positive value of the ignorance of many of the characters he discusses and disregards those moments when they realize how ignorant they have been, and he sees books that clearly attack childish egocentricity as celebrations of childlike freedom. In fact, he perceives too little in children's books and admires that little too much.

Furthermore, Cott constantly confuses the simplistic qualities he finds in children's literature with the qualities of childhood itself, and he makes it quite clear that he thinks children are wonderful exactly because they are limited. Blessed by a lack of knowledge and experience, he suggests, they can transcend the petty demands of good sense, social responsibility, logical thought, and history.

Children, I trust, are not as ignorant as Cott insists they are—even though he gives that ignorance prettier names. Their innocence is rarely as unqualified as is the innocence of some children in books they read. Even the very youngest of children know that life can be cruel and disorderly, that parents can be unreasonable, even that they are sometimes unreasonable themselves. Many of them even enjoy books that reflect that knowledge—books like some of those Cott distorts and misinterprets; many of them particularly enjoy the aspects of those books that Cott disregards.

In fact, however, children also enjoy books that make life seem distressingly uncomplicated—as do adults, who read as many mysteries and romances as they do subtle attempts to evoke life as it is. We enjoy such books exactly because they make no attempt to evoke life as it is; and many children enjoy many of the books that Cott admires for their supposed profundity because they know that these books, too, make no attempt to evoke life as it is—that they are the

exact opposite of profound. To see *Pippi Longstocking* as offering
scriptural insights is akin to finding the meaning of life in James
Bond.

But if adults are supposed to be retrieving childhood from children's books because childhood is wise, then children ought to be
wise enough to have excellent taste in books. At one point, Cott
suggests they have: "It is exactly in those books that children have
adopted as their own that our deepest wishes and fantasies are most
simply expressed." But he also speaks of a youngster who, "if he
weren't watching TV, . . . might well be reading a 'Young Adult'
novel like *Dinky Hocker Shoots Smack*, while his sister, in her turn,
might be absorbed in a 'Teen Romance' like *Superflirt*." According to
Cott's theory, therefore, *Dinky Hocker* and *Superflirt* ought to be
"wise" books, in which our deepest wishes are expressed. I suspect
they are; but for Cott they aren't, of course, because they don't evoke
Cott's namby-pamby vision of childhood. For him, in fact, the pleasure children take in these books is not a flaw in his theory, but a
failing of contemporary children, who, he says, are growing up too
soon.

Finally, that's the most horrifying aspect of this book. Not only
does Cott wish to make children's literature respectable by misrepre-
senting its messages and by taking it away from children and making
it a health-giving medicine for adults sick of too much maturity; he
also wants to say that only adults are wise enough to understand
what childhood really is; today's children are too stupid to know how
to be children. Cott wants to deprive children, not just of children's
literature, but of childhood itself. That this version of "the wisdom
of children's literature" should be the one that finds expression and
support in the literary world at large reveals a deep and terrifying
bias against real children, and against the reality of childhood in
contemporary culture—the kind of bias that loves to wax nostalgic
about the good old days of bubblegum cards and ten-cent movies
but finds real children distastefully crude, disturbingly grubby, too
childish to be considered genuinely childlike. This life-denying bias
makes the silliness of *Pipers at the Gates of Dawn* a source more of
tears than of laughter.

To Undress Innocence

Hernan Vera

The Empire's Old Clothes: What the Lone Ranger, Babar, and Other Innocent Heroes Do to Our Minds, by Ariel Dorfman, translated by Clark Hansen. New York: Pantheon Books, 1983

In this collection of bold studies on literature for children and the "infantilization of adults, " Dorfman wants to explore "some of the major cultural myths of our time" as they have been expressed in comic books, magazines, and children's books to "map out their concealed social and political messages." From Dorfman's point of view comic books, for instance, are not mere entertainment; they give us "a constant secret education" on how not to rebel. He argues that the world of children constitutes the "axis of all process of domination," in that children are universally required to accept unquestioningly the status quo of their parents: childhood is, in essence, a form of underdevelopment parallel to that of Third World countries. Dorfman challenges the United States to examine "the myths and popular symbols that it exports to its economic and military dominions" as a way of coming to terms with itself. He avowedly takes "an insolent point of view, an underdog, ironic, proud point of view."

Thus Dorfman underscores the fact that his insights are those of a foreigner. Indeed, a strength of this work derives from its "objectivity," not the detachment and neutrality claimed by some scientists and other purveyors of "truth," but that active kind of engagement attributed to "the stranger." According to Georg Simmel, the stranger "is freer practically and theoretically; he surveys conditions with less prejudice; his criteria for them are more general and more objective ideals; he is not tied down in action by habit, piety, and precedent." Simmel also notes that this "objectivity" is considered dangerous, subversive, and offensive by some. In a very real sense this objectivity is that of the legendary child who dared say that the emperor was wearing no clothes.

Dorfman's deliberate avoidance of what he calls "uncomfortably neutral" and dispassionate critical postures allows a fuller appraisal of his observations and a closer examination of his conclusions. It is crucial for the understanding of this book to know that the author is a Chilean exile, a professor of literature and journalism, who wrote these essays between 1970 and 1973, while he was exploring alternatives to mass-market fiction in a project set up under the democratic socialism of Salvador Allende. Few will fail to admire Dorfman's intellectual courage and integrity. Even where his contentions will not compel agreement, they will compel in everyone the recognition of one's own stance.

The first study, "Of Elephants and Ducks," uses a wealth of comparative material from folklore, mythology, adventure narratives, economic theorists, and even Ronald Reagan's speeches to show how the 1930s French stories of Babar the elephant and Disney's comics present children with "a theory of history, an unconscious method for interpreting the contemporary economic and political world." Staying close to the text, Dorfman debunks the colonial French myth of a civilizing mission in vogue when Babar was being written as well as the corresponding contemporary American myth expressed in Disney comic books. Babar is adopted by a European "Old Lady" who teaches him how to dress and behave in a proper manner. In turn, Babar will dress and Europeanize other animals, thus enacting the colonialist dream "where nature and civilization could live side by side, where technical advances would not corrupt but bring contentment." Babar succeeds in this mission as well as in growing up, because of his intellectual and spiritual resources. In Babar's books adulthood is presented as the desirable state, whereas childhood is assimilated to savagery. In contrast, Donald Duck must constantly be rescued by his nephews; he is cowardly, egotistical, disorderly—in short, a worthless adult. In Disney's world "children represent goodness and intelligence. . . . They are more mature than their elders." The foreign places to which Donald and his nephews travel are full of danger, but the savages are eventually appeased when they are freed from their fears and shown the fairness of some exchange.

In this key essay Dorfman follows some ideas first developed in his widely acclaimed *How to Read Donald Duck: Mass Communication and Colonialism* (now available in thirteen languages). He argues that

Disney fantasies unconsciously imitate the way in which world capitalism has constructed reality. Children's literature inscribes the ideological patterns of a society. For example, a consistent pattern in the adventures of Donald Duck is the danger of losing property, whereas in Babar the danger of losing one's life prevails. In Babar's stories there is a civilizing crusade that modifies habits of thought and mores; for Disney, civilization means learning how to do business and "education [is] the process which accompanies the interchange of goods and services." Children might miss the contempt expressed in the way Disney names the rest of the world: Asteclano, Chiliburgeria, Brutopia, Hondorica, San Bananador, South Miseryland, Foola Zoola, Unsteadystam, or Footsore. Dorfman, however, finds the caricatures "a disheartening panorama of the majority of mankind as viewed by a minority." Moreover, these derogatory names were created between 1945 and 1967, when the newly decolonized nations appeared to be fair game to the United States, a country that considers itself also a recent arrival on the international scene and which "is renewing and reformulating its own past all the time."

The second essay is a study of the Lone Ranger and other heroes such as Batman, Zorro, the Phantom, and Superman (who unlike the others does not wear a mask but lives nonetheless disguised as Clark Kent). These characters express the rebellion and appeasement proper to class societies. Oppressed groups project onto their heroes the idea of an underdog who breaks the status quo and rises from obscurity to construct a better world. These democratic and rebellious impulses are domesticated, so to speak, by those sectors in control of written memory who assign a stabilizing function to the hero. The principal difference between action comic books and older heroic sagas is that the masses that consume the modern heroic myth do not participate in its creation, development, or modification: "the superhero descends upon their brains just as magically and ubiquitously as the mass media penetrate their homes." If the analytical task of the essay on Babar and Donald Duck was to winnow out French and American colonial political philosophies, then the task of this essay is broadly speculative: to discover the psychological needs to be fulfilled by these literary heroes and their adventures. Thus, the mask is seen as "the emotive mechanism that allows projection. . . . Such fiction provides a way for the reader to have the experience of overcoming his condition of being an object, his alienation."

According to the ideological critique in "The Infantilization of the Adult Reader," the *Reader's Digest* exemplifies the media that treat adults as children. These publications offer their readers "the wisdom of maturity without any of its dilemmas . . . life without death; digestion without evacuation. . . . The *Digest* responds to the illusion of the child who does not want to die." As in the previous essay, Dorfman speculates about the psychologically regressive mechanism by which the magazine reassures its adult readers: it repeats that North American humanity is superior and delivers them from evil thoughts, from "the abyss and the boredom."

Dorfman does not dodge the methodological and theoretical problems that typically scourge studies of this sort. The last analytic essay, "The Innocents March into History . . . and Overthrow a Government," engages the problem of what constitutes an explanation in the analysis of literature and the arts. Dorfman applies his assumption that "fictional forms influenced people, especially youngsters, through a code of half-hidden values." What he examines is the interplay of historical events, literature, and its creators in the case of a children's magazine story published on the eve of the overthrow of Chile's constitutional government in 1973. The magazine *Mampato*, named after the hero of the story run in its four central pages, contained staple semieducational material such as nature stories, historical vignettes, and puzzles. In the days when right-wing factions and their press were calling President Allende a tyrant, the weekly series depicted an adventure of the year 4000, when the boy-hero Mampato overthrew a tyrant ruling, with the help of foreigners, over beautiful and peaceful telepaths. Elements in the weekly installments, such as the physical landscape, the alliances between military forces and government, the parts played by giants, rats, mutants, and an enslaving "yellow race," correspond to phenomena and events in Chile between May and October 1973. While "the fact that the very story people were reading in a magazine was also being enacted in the streets may be no more than a surprising coincidence," Dorfman writes, "the parallels between the story and the history are too many to be dismissed."   .

Yet Dorfman rejects intentional fallacies that make the author a conspirator along with other types of explanation he finds reductive or slothful. The position taken by Dorfman is more complex but also more enlightening. In stories like *Mampato*, artists, who already have mechanisms of expression and established interpretations of the world, respond to the conflicts that they experience along with their readers. In producing the story, these artists work out their dilemmas and make them intelligible to others. Essential to this process is "the purported freedom to create stories without 'interference.' "

The other essays in the book ask how one can explain the success of certain characters or the recurrence of elements in heroic myths. Drawing on scholars such as Bettelheim, Barthes, Bachelard, and Marx, he examines why children's stories are more important and perhaps more strategic for the study of ideology than other forms of literature. Dorfman takes positions that will not always be acclaimed. For my part, I object to the imputation of psychological processes in the essays on the Lone Ranger and the *Reader's Digest*. Such psychologizing ironically stifles the type of open dialog Dorfman wants to provoke, since there is no way to check the fit of the theory with responses by the mass of readers.

The concluding chapter also seems to me perplexing. In it the alarmist ghost of Frederick Wertham's *The Seduction of the Innocent*—the 1950s psychoanalytic study of comic books that was so instrumental in the comic book industry's self-censorship—is resurrected when Dorfman describes his work as having attempted "to determine the adult values and hidden interests that shape and infect fiction for young readers." One might recall that Wertham, a psychiatrist, was alarmed by the discovery that the juveniles he was counseling in a New York penal institution were given to the avid reading of comic books. His analysis of these texts showed a wealth of ethnocentric, unwholesome, violent, and sadistic images. Wertham attributed his subjects' delinquency to the reading of comic books. Yet at the same time some 50 million other youngsters were reading the same comic books. Dorfman's mistake is similar to Werthman's "clinical sample fallacy," as social scientists call it. Dorfman draws sweeping generalizations about American culture from a narrow sample of texts, giving little or no attention to the question of competing media and institutions—such as other magazines,

books, and school and religious instruction. He does not demonstrate that his selected texts are uniquely representative of the dominant ideology.

Most perplexing is Dorfman's basic question: "How do we save
the children?" Often brandished by those interested in removing
books from school libraries, this question suggests imposing forms
of censorship. The aphoristic style of the conclusion makes it hard to
determine Dorfman's intention when he suggests that "more democratic societies would automatically limit or perhaps even cancel
the sway that these pseudo-imaginings have upon us." Clearly the
conclusions in the final chapter do not flow from the analytical work
nor fit the stated purposes of the book. Rather, one would have
expected a conclusion that called for the opening of new paths and
media for collective expression.

In spite of these problems—in fact, because of them—and the
debate that they are bound to generate, this book deserves careful
reading. Literary critics, social scientists, teachers, librarians, and
parents will all find in this spry, jargon-free book much to provoke
thought and to encourage a reexamination of the ideological "old
clothes" that they may find hanging in the closet.

Mountains out of Mole Hills, a Fairy Tale

Jack Zipes

One Fairy Story Too Many: The Brothers Grimm and Their Tales, by John M. Ellis. Chicago: University of Chicago Press, 1983.

When it comes to his case against the brothers Grimm, John Ellis does not mince his words. Indeed, he claims to shake the foundations of Grimm scholarship by charging that the Grimms did not gather oral tales from peasants and common workers, and that they did not record them faithfully as documents of the quintessential German folk tradition. Ellis insists that "the sources of the material the Grimms used were not older, untainted, and untutored German peasant transmitters of an indigenous oral tradition but, instead, literate, middle-class, and predominantly young people, probably influenced more by books than by oral tradition—and including a very significant presence of people who were either of French origins or actually French-speaking. Second, knowledge of the sources shows that they were largely limited to the brothers' family, friends, and acquaintances in their home area, which indicates both a very narrow base for the collection and that the brothers devoted little interest to collecting. Third, the Grimms deliberately deceived their public by concealing or actually misstating the facts, in order to give an impression of ancient folk origin for their material which they knew was utterly false. Fourth, the essential facts which show all these first three conclusions to be true have long been available. And fifth, scholars have shown considerable reluctance to admit that the evidence leads to the first and second conclusions, and complete universal reluctance to admit that it must lead to the third" (35–36). Given the seemingly meticulous research conducted by Ellis, one is almost compelled to join in his accusations against the Grimm brothers and Grimm scholars and to demand that they be punished for their "crimes." Almost.

Upon closer examination, it appears that one could also accuse Ellis himself of foul play, for his book is set up like a mock trial, and the jurors do not have a chance to reach a fair verdict unless they know how Ellis went about building his case. As an expert lawyer, he divides his seemingly open-and-shut case into six chapters investigating the problem and status of the tales, the origin and development of misconceptions about the status of the tales, the character of the Grimms' sources, the Grimms' treatment of their sources in the preparation of the first edition, the further development of the text of the tales, and the status of the tales and their historical context. His conclusion makes the Grimms into crypto-fascists and counterfeiters, while his appendix contains the revised texts of *The Frog King, Sleeping Beauty*, and *Hansel and Gretel*, which allegedly provide evidence of the Grimms' crimes against the general public.

Whether one agrees with Ellis or not, it would seem that we owe him a great debt for uncovering so much "new" material about the Grimms' dubious methods of work. Yet there is absolutely nothing new or original in Ellis's findings. They are based almost entirely on the remarkable sleuth work of Heinz Rölleke, who in *Die älteste Märchensammlung der Brüder Grimm* (1975) revealed that most of the so-called uneducated storytellers from the folk whom the Grimms used as their sources were actually from the educated middle class and strongly influenced by French culture. It is also Rölleke who was the first to draw attention to the major textual variations and who has continued to do this in his recent publication of the Grimms' *Kinder- und Hausmärchen (KHM)* based on the second edition of 1819. This work, which appeared in the fall of 1982 and contains valuable information about the Grimms' method of work and their sources, refutes many of Ellis's claims and is never quoted by Ellis, even though it appeared fully one year before his own book. Moreover, he neglects the work of Renate Steinchen in "Märchen—eine Bestandsaufnahme" (1979), Hermann Bausinger in "Anmerkungen zu Schneewittchen" (1980), Ulrike Bastian in *Die "Kinder-und Hausmärchen" der Brüder Grimm in der literaturpädagogishcen Diskussion des 19. und 20. Jahrhunderts* (1981), and myself in "Who's Afraid of the Brothers Grimm? Socialization and Politicization through Fairy Tales" (1980). These studies have examined the stylistic and substantive changes made by the Grimms and seek to explain the Grimms' changes and the general reception of the tales from a careful study of sociohistorical conditions.

Ellis, on the other hand, is more concerned with toying with history and making the Grimms into outright liars who did not care much about methods of research and deliberately sought to deceive their public. The fact of the matter is that the Grimms, though untruthful about some of their sources, were never as duplicitous as Ellis maintains, and their interest in the scientific study of folklore, myth, and linguistics grew as they matured. Ellis never mentions that the *Kinder- und Hausmärchen* was the Grimms' first major endeavor in folklore research and that they were among the pioneers in this field. They believed firmly in the romantic approach to their material and thus intended to make it seem that all their tales emanated from the *Volk*. For them it was vital to their work to give adequate expression to the German *Geist*, and thus they did not think they were distorters but rather exponents of a German cultural tradition rooted in the common people, even if they did rely on middle-class storytellers.

The issue of motivation is central to the charges made by Ellis. Behind the "unscrupulous forgery" of the Grimms, Ellis sees nationalism rear its ugly head. "The Grimms appealed strongly to German nationalism because their *own* motives were nationalistic; and so this factor is dominant both in the brothers' fabrications and deceit, and in the strong reluctance of later scholars to acknowledge what they had done when the evidence emerged. The Grimms wanted to create a German national monument while pretending that they had merely discovered it; and later on, no one wanted to seem to tear it down" (100). Ellis concedes that the factor of nationalism has been discussed by other scholars—and again he omits certain ones such as Hans-Wolf Jäger, who in "Trägt Rotkäppchen eine Jakobiner Mütze?" (1974) refutes his case—but he firmly believes that "there is no longer any reason to treat the *KHM* as having been authored by a nation" (102).

The issue of nationalism and the *KHM* is a complex one. The Grimms were indeed nationalistic but not in the negative sense in which we now tend to use the term. When the Grimms began their folklore research, Germany, as we know it today, did not exist. Their "country," essentially Hessia and the Rhineland, was invaded by the French. Their desire to publish a work which bespoke a German cultural spirit was part of an effort to contribute to a united German front against the French. They also felt part of the nascent national bourgeoisie trying to establish its own German identity in a more democratic manner than the aristocratic cliques which controlled the 300-odd German principalities. Certainly, the Grimms "lied," if you will, in their programmatic statement published in the first volume of the tales when they stated: "We have tried to collect these tales as faithfully as possible.... No particular has been either added through our own poetic recreation, or improved and altered, because we should have shrunk from augmenting tales that were so rich in themselves by adding passages analogous to or reminiscent of what was already there, they cannot be fabricated" (13–14). But they did retract this statement and never sought to conceal it later. Ellis feels that the Grimms were embarrassed by their original statement. Yet he does not provide proof for his assertions or deductive accusations. On the contrary, if the Grimms had felt their actions dishonest, they would have tried to cover up their "lies" in a more stealthy manner in the second edition, in which they admitted to changing the tales. Moreover, they would have asked Clemens Brentano to return their handwritten manuscripts, which have been used by present-day scholars to reveal the authentic sources of the Grimms. The lies and fabrications which Ellis discusses—"lies" and "fabrications" which German scholars have openly discussed over the years—emanate ironically from an *honest* belief held by the Grimms that they were tapping a German cultural tradition which they wanted to nurture. And they came to view themselves as midwives, who, perhaps due to a strong affection for their material and the German people, were over-protective in their desire to cultivate the tales in the interest of nationalism.

If the issue of nationalism is at the crux of the Grimms' fabrications, then Ellis does not pursue many exciting avenues he could have followed instead of pointing his finger at the brothers like a moralistic schoolteacher. For instance, he never discusses the significance of the subjective selection of the tales and the changes made in terms of the "republican" ideology of the Grimms. (There is also the psychological factor of the Grimms' patriarchal attitudes.) Nor does he consider the major reason for the revisions made mainly by Wilhelm, who felt that all the editions after 1819 should be addressed toward children. As Wilhelm Schoof in his book about the origins of the Grimms' collection of tales has maintained, Wilhelm

was "guided by the desire to endow the tales with a tone and style
primarily for children. He created a literary art form for them
through the use of rhetorical and artistic means. This form is a
synthesis based on faithful and scientific reproduction and the folk-
loristic (*volkstümlich*) narrative style. Given his own ability to capture
the appropriate childlike tone, he created a uniform fairy-tale style
which has prevailed in the course of time and has become known as
the classical or Grimm fairy-tale style" (*Zur Entstehungsgeschichte der
Grimmschen Märchen*, 147). In other words, the Grimms were totally
conscious and open about their endeavors to make their material
more suitable for children and to incorporate the political ideals
they shared with like-minded people, their notion of family, and
their sense of a "folk" aesthetic. What is most interesting about their
"fabrications" is the manner in which the brothers "Germanicized"
their material to stay in touch with the sensibility of the German
people. And, indeed, the German people responded in such a way
that the Grimms' collection has become second only to the Bible in
popularity throughout the past 150 years. That the nationalist reception became more narrow and reactionary in the late nineteenth
century and first part of the twentieth century is no fault of the
Grimms. One must make a clear distinction between the Grimms'
republican nationalism and the rise of fascism and the use which
fascists made of the Grimms' collection. Implicit in Ellis's critique of
the Grimms is the distorted charge that the roots of German fascism
can be traced to the Grimms and the German romantics.

If Ellis has not uncovered anything new, one must ask at this point
what the significance of his critique is. Perhaps, for the English-
speaking reader, he does provide a compilation of material docu-
menting the changes made by the Grimms. As I have mentioned, the
latter part of his book, about eighty-five pages, contains texts of
three of the tales from the handwritten manuscript to the seventh
edition so that readers can see the types of changes made by the
Grimms. Otherwise, Ellis stretches his case against the Grimms to
such an extent that, instead of arguing there is "one fairy story too
many," about the Grimms, one might argue that, with the publication of his book, we have one study too many about the Grimms that
does not enrich our understanding of the complex origins and
development of their tales.

Dissertations of Note

Compiled by Rachel Fordyce

Alford, Sandra Elaine. "The Portrayal of Black Characters in Children's Literature." Ph.D. diss. University of Pittsburgh, 1982. 117 pp. DAI 44:90A.

Alford surveyed 163 books that would normally appeal to children between the ages of five and twelve to determine what personal traits were assigned to black characters. She hypothesizes that bias would be more prevalent in books published before the 1954 Supreme Court ruling on desegregation. In fact, she finds "no significant level of bias" and suggests that while some books do show bias "most black characters are portrayed nonstereotypically, not as a group but as unique characters." Where bias exists there is marked generalization of all black people.

Burston, Linda. "Fantasy Components of Sir James Matthew Barrie: A Study through Selected Plays." Ph.D. diss. University of Georgia, 1983. 203 pp. DAI 44:1245A.

Relying on the critical works of Tolkien, Norman Holland, Eric Rabkin, and others, Burston demonstrates how Barrie "incorporates varying fantasy features with his basic reality, creating plays at different levels of theatrical fantasy." In this instance, fantasy is defined as "some ideal wish fulfillment manifested in a comforting realm centered around the individual human being, thus providing a sense of escape from realistic problems, tensions, and/or ambiguities." Burston gives a detailed analysis of *Peter Pan* and discusses those features of Barrie's life that contributed to his creation of fantasy plays.

Bushnell, John Palmer. "Powerless to Be Born: Victorian Struggles in Romantic Landscapes of Adolescence." Ph.D. diss. Rutgers University, The State University of New Jersey (New Brunswick), 1983. 342 pp. DAI 44:1459A.

In individual chapters on *Great Expectations*, *David Copperfield*, and *Alice's Adventures in Wonderland*, Bushnell argues that "adolescence, especially as depicted in Wordsworth, Keats, Byron, and Shelley, functions as an appropriate metaphor for the Victorian period itself." Noting that Carlyle and Ruskin feared the "rebellious power" of adolescence, he stresses that the Brontës, Dickens, Carroll, and others "recognize the adolescent quest for selfhood as positive and exhilarating, similar to the national quest for identity and akin to their own life-creating, artistic energies." Throughout the dissertation Bushnell examines "the novelists' portrayals of youth's attractiveness as well as their recognitions of its frequent inability to escape the constricting forces of adulthood and an industrial age."

Carey, Bonnie Marshall. "Typological Models of the Heroine in the Russian Fairy Tale." Ph.D. diss. The University of North Carolina at Chapel Hill, 1983. 217 pp. DAI 44:1100A.

Using a structural and semiotic methodology, and predicating her work on the assumption that fairy tales are "reflections of ideologies and value systems," Carey demonstrates that "the patterns and messages that emerge from folklore texts are important to a definition of feminine roles and models." Moreover, she is concerned with a male-oriented critical scholarship. She feels strongly that the Aarne-Andreev-Thompson index, as a research tool, "perpetuates a scholarship that ignores, diminishes and misrepresents the heroine." While describing the conflict between matriarchies and patriarchies, Carey notes the subjugation of women to

220

marriages that they can either accept "fatalistically or struggle against." For the heroine in the Russian fairy tale "there is no happy ending."

Cariou, Mavis Olive. "Syntax, Vocabulary and Metaphor in Three Groups of Novels for Children in Grades Four to Six." Ph.D. diss. The University of Michigan, 1983. 206 pp. DAI 44:1613A.

This dissertation in library science is designed to analyze three groups of novels for middleschool children: Newbery Award books, novels children have acclaimed by vote, and "popular series novels such as the Hardy Boys and the Nancy Drew mysteries." Cariou's focus is on language as she studies various "aspects of syntax, vocabulary and metaphor." Newbery Award books were the most complex syntactically, choice books were the least complex, and "popular series novels had the highest means for vocabulary difficulty and diversity." However, Cariou suggests caution in overinterpreting these findings.

Corona, Laurel Ann Weeks. "Man into Beast: The Theme of Transformation in American and European Fiction from the 1860's to the 1920's." Ph.D. diss. University of California, Davis, 1982. 246 pp. DAI 44:161A.

Corona's dissertation in comparative literature demonstrates that "the particular popularity of the theme of transformation in the time covered was due in part to the influence of Calvinism as well as the ideas of Darwin and Freud." She focuses on "the fear of loss of control by a chance occurrence or freak accident" and "the loss of control through revelation of secret guilt or sin" in such works as *Dracula, The Strange Case of Dr. Jekyll and Mr. Hyde,* and *The Time Machine.*

Dodson, Janelle Slaughter. "A Content Analysis of Children's Picture Story Book Reviews Published in Selected Journals during the Year 1981." Ph.D. diss. Southern Illinois University at Carbondale, 1983. 135 pp. 44:1361A.

Dodson's main purpose is to determine to what extent reviews used by librarians to select picture books for primary and preschool children include "descriptive and evaluative information about the texts and the illustrations." The periodicals that are evaluated are *Booklist, Bulletin of the Center for Children's Books, The Horn Book,* and *School Library Journal.* Of the 625 reviews evaluated, fewer than half included descriptive statements. Rarely did reviewers compare works or make critical comments on content and illustrations although some sort of "evaluative statement about the total artistic effect was found in about 65 percent of the reviews." The journals did not "vary significantly" among themselves, although most individual reviews did include plot summary, character description, and a general comment on the illustrations.

Flores, Juan Manuel. "A Study in the Evaluation of Chicano Adolescent Literature." Ed.D. diss. University of the Pacific, 1983. 141 pp. DAI 44:1316A.

The purposes of Flores's dissertation are "to determine if there were significant differences in the way that selected samples of Chicano adolescent literature were perceived by a sample of Chicano adolescents and a panel of professional librarians" and to investigate "the current process of evaluating Chicano adolescent literature" to decide whether or not librarians are making choices appropriate to their audience. He concludes that there is no significant difference between the perceptions of the children and the librarians although there may have been differences "in their perceptions of authenticity and relevance."

Goodrich, Peter Hampton. "Merlin: The Figure of the Wizard in English Fiction." (Volumes I and II) Ph.D. diss. The University of Michigan, 1983. 471 pp. DAI 44:1798A.

Goodrich explores the interrelated treatments of Merlin as "Wild Man, Half-

Human, Poet, Prophet, Wizard, Counsellor, and Lover," as well as the various models for the character, and applies "Merlin's functional ambivalence . . . to the social and intellectual concerns" of different historical periods. He concludes that "Merlin's character and functions tacitly underlie all conceptions of the wizard in our culture, and his typology may be used as an analytical tool for examining other wizard figures in Western media."

Haunert, Rita M. "Mythic Female Heroes in the High Fantasy Novels of Patricia McKillip." Ph.D. diss. Bowling Green State University, 1983. 260 pp. DAI 44: 1085A.

Haunert points out that "the female rite of passage in high fantasy literature is virtually non-existent," although women's secondary roles might be predicted given their origins in myth and romance. As a contrast to Campbell's *The Hero with a Thousand Faces* and Frye's *Anatomy of Criticism* and *The Secular Scripture*, which focus on the male hero, Haunert explores McKillip's novels via Annis Pratt's *Archetypal Patterns in Women's Fiction* to examine how female heroes reach adulthood or "social autonomy" in a patriarchal society. Haunert contends that McKillip's female heroes break the "traditional stereotyped roles" and become "strong, autonomous women." She suggests that McKillip also treats male heroes as individuals who must combat the dictates of society and concludes that "McKillip stresses the need for the individual and society to understand and incorporate matriarchal belief in order to have a balanced world." She feels that McKillip's books "are important for both women and men in that they show what becoming an adult should mean."

Johnston, David Edgar. "Gifted Fifth and Sixth Graders' Preferences and Responses Regarding Contemporary or Classic Literature." Ed.D. diss. University of Washington, 1983. 176 pp. DAI 44:126A.

By comparing five acknowledged classics for children with five contemporary novels with similar themes, focus, and genre, Johnston notes that the gifted students he studied seemed to prefer contemporary works "but the trend was not statistically significant." This leads him to conclude that it might be beneficial to use "adapted classical works for gifted children."

Karrenbrock, Marilyn H. "Characteristics Discriminating between Most and Least Often Preferred Books of the Georgia Children's Book Award Lists, 1972–1981." Ed.D. diss. University of Georgia, 1983. 231 pp. DAI 44:411A.

Karrenbrock evaluates sixty books (the three most and three least often chosen over a ten-year period) to determine preferences. She found that Georgia children preferred "multiple focal characters" who were young and readily identified with, "a first person narrator who was highly engaged in the action," humor, "urban and suburban/small town settings," and uncomplicated, informal language. They did not like "Native American characters, rural or historical settings, violence, plots based on abstract ideas, and plots with multiple-interwoven story-lines."

Masiello, Lea. "Speaking of Ghosts: Style in Washington Irving's Tales of the Supernatural." Ph.D. diss. University of Cincinnati, 1983. 205 pp. DAI 44:1792A.

Focusing on "The Legend of Sleepy Hollow," "Rip Van Winkle," and other tales from *The Sketch-Book, Bracebridge Hall, Tales of a Traveller,* and *Wolfert's Roost,* Masiello observes that Irving "used figurative language to enhance characterization, create comedy, and reveal narrative *ethos*" while employing "military, agricultural, temperature, and disease" patterns. She notes that it is Irving's colorful and "enlightened" figurative language that frequently puts his stories in the realm of the American tall-tale.

Matthews, Kenneth Ernest. "C. S. Lewis and the Modern World." Ph.D. diss. University of California, Los Angeles, 1983. 188 pp. DAI 44:1451A.

Matthews attacks the critical assumption that Lewis is an "antimodernist and
neomedievalist" to show that "his response to the modern world is not simplistic,
escapist, or extreme, but is a complex, balanced, sane response based on a modern
perception of the human self." Matthews points out that while Lewis disliked
certain aspects of modern society, particularly its disregard for the past, he believed
in a "plastic" self, "unbounded by space or time, thus . . . capable of apprehending
and experiencing the past in a very immediate way."

Perilstein, Bette L. "An Historical Evaluative Study of Five Late Eighteenth-Century
English Didactic Children's Books." Ed.D. diss. Temple University, 1983. 277 pp.
DAI 44:1253A.

The works Perilstein examines are Maria Edgeworth's *The Parent's Assistant*
(1796), Mrs. Trimmer's *Fabulous Histories* (1786), Mrs. Barbauld's and Dr. Aiken's
Evenings at Home (1792–96), Dorothy Kilner's *The Life and Perambulations of a Mouse*
(1783?), and Mary Jane Kilner's *Jemima Placid* (1785?). Her object is to show that
despite their didactic styles, and contrary to contemporary criticism, these books
need not have been "automatically offensive to children." She feels "modern critics
have disregarded the documentary evidence as well as social, historical, philosophi-
cal, and literary trends" that influenced authors, children, and those who bought
the books. She contends that these books "fulfilled societal dictates" for a century of
readers, that they exhibited "novel literary devices," that "they were instrumental
in helping to define the developing genre of children's literature," and that they
are "far more than curiosities from the past."

Phelps, Henry Carr. "The Undiscovered 'Territory': Mark Twain's Later Huck and
Tom Stories." Ph.D. diss. The University of British Columbia (Canada), 1983. n.p.
DAI 44:1455A.

Shortly after Twain completed *The Adventures of Huckleberry Finn* he wrote *Tom
Sawyer Abroad*, "Tom Sawyer, Detective," and several unpublished fragments about
Tom and Huck in an attempt to keep their tradition alive. These latter works are
"generally considered to be greatly inferior to the earlier novels" but Phelps
contends that they have "hitherto undetected significance and value," especially
because they clarify Twain's thinking about such issues as "maturity, the Transcen-
dent Figure, the 'Matter of Hannibal,' . . . the folly of romanticism," and demonstrate Twain's willingness to "grapple with issues of profound complexity."

Sarumpaet, Riris Kusumawati. "An Analysis of Children's Books about Indonesia
Published in the United States 1960–1980." Ph.D. diss. The University of Wis-
consin-Madison, 1983. 272 pp. DAI 44:663A.

This dissertation in curriculum and instruction is an examination of "the evaluative tone (positive, neutral, negative) and the accuracy with which people in
Indonesia are portrayed" in fiction, nonfiction, and folktales for children written
between 1960 and 1980. Sarumpaet found that "stories and information about the
picturesque and exotic predominated," that "some otherwise fine books were
spoiled by overgeneralization, stereotyping, and inaccuracies in the text, illustration, or captions," but also that a number of works presented an interesting and
"extremely positive" view of Indonesia and Indonesians.

Scapple, Sharon Marie. "The Child as Depicted in English Children's Literature from
1780–1820." Ph.D. diss. University of Minnesota, 1983. 383 pp. DAI 44:762A.

Scapple examines moralistc fiction written for children between 1780 and 1820
"to discover how the child was depicted and to discover the relationships between
the portrayal of the child in literature and societal attitudes toward children. The
study goes beyond textual synopsis to provide details of the content of early fiction
for children and to show how writers and parents/adults regard children and

childhood." The ten works analyzed are *The Life and Perambulations of a Mouse, Fabulous Histories, Original Stories, The Parent's Assistant, The Keeper's Travels, Twin Sisters, Aunt Mary's Tales, Son of a Genius, The Adventures of a Donkey,* and *The Histories of the Fairchild Family.* (See also Perilstein, above.) Issues related to education, religion, class, family, manners, and morals are compared and Scapple concludes that "the moral tales realistically depicted certain segments of English life in the late eighteenth and early nineteenth centuries. The writer's intent to regulate the child's thoughts and actions and to employ narrative as a stimulus to learning are indicative of the adult recognition of childhood as an impressionable period of life, one which determined the kind of adult the child would become in later life."

Steveson, Lynn Bradley. "Lewis Carroll's *Through the Looking-Glass* as a Kaleidoscope of English History: A Critical Approach to Scripting Interpreters Theatre." Ph.D. diss. Southern Illinois University at Carbondale, 1983. 329 pp. DAI 44:1234A.

Steveson's dissertation in speech communication is a "historical allegorical exegesis" of Carroll's *Through the Looking-Glass, and What Alice Found There.* It includes a brief biography of Carroll "with special attention paid to his knowledge and attitude toward history and the theatre," and a discussion of allegory as a genre. The work "is based on the theory that the Red Queen may be interpreted as Elizabeth I of England, and that the White Queen may be interpreted as Mary of Scotland. The other main characters also are seen to have historical counterparts. The study also posits that the three nursery rhyme battles, 'Tweedledum and Tweedledee,' 'Humpty Dumpty,' and 'The Lion and the Unicorn,' may be based on historical battles." She then looks at "historical forerunners" of *Through the Looking-Glass* and "examines the chess structure . . . as it relates to the historical allegory with focus on the Dramatis Personae." She concludes with an evaluation of previous dramatic presentations of *Through the Looking-Glass,* including oral interpretations, and suggests areas for future research.

Tandy, Gary Lynn. "The Non-Fiction Prose of C. S. Lewis: A Rhetorical Analysis." Ph.D. diss. The University of Tulsa, 1983. 184 pp. DAI 44:488–89A.

Tandy's dissertation is relevant for information it can supply about how Lewis chose and treated his fictional material, and how he used his rhetorical style. Tandy feels that Lewis "both in his religious and literary pronouncements . . . projects the image of old Western man; he portrays himself as a representative of older patterns of thought, an embattled survivor in the midst of a century largely hostile to his beliefs and ideas." (See Matthews, above, for an alternative point of view.) Tandy focuses on Lewis's "elaborate structures and rhetorical figures," his use of humor, and how "syntactical mannerisms" create Lewis's tone.

Wahlstrom, Wanda Louise. "Developing Self-Concept through Bibliotherapy." Ph.D. diss. University of Toronto (Canada), 1982. n.p. DAI 44:669A.

This dissertation in elementary education explores "the effects of a literature program specifically designed as a treatment condition to ameliorate children's problems related to self-concept." Wahlstrom's work was with fifth-grade girls, and she found that both the girls and their teachers noted a marked improvement in self-concept and in grades after enlightening books had been read.

Ward, Nellie Charlene Meacham. "Realistic Adolescent Fiction: Characterization of the Anglo-American Male." Ed.D. diss. Arizona State University, 1983. 233 pp. DAI 44:724A.

Ward examines thirty-three characters in thirty novels written from 1967 to 1982 to determine "characterizations of Anglo-American adolescent males depicted in popular contemporary realistic" novels. The dissertation contains descriptions of the novels and characters as well as a discussion of "the characters' personal traits and self-images, relationship to others, and goals and barriers to those goals to determine the existence or lack of stereotyping and static characters." She found little of either but did discover that most characters were the eldest child in a family, that they felt a strong need to leave home and/or control situations, that they were often defeated, and that "author conventions for these characters included lack of happiness, apathy toward outsiders," although most characters had at least one friend, "and little overt rebellion." The novels dealt frequently with death and violence and characters were "typically intelligent, athletic, physically non-handicapped, and mature."

Winter, Ryoko Yamazaki. "The Role of the Teacher as Depicted in American and Japanese Literature for Children and Younger Adolescents." Ed.D. diss. University of San Francisco, 1982. 148 pp. DAI 44:747A.

Using samples of recent American and Japanese children's literature in which a teacher is either the "main character or a significant subordinate character," Winter demonstrates that there are definite differences in the portrayal of teachers in the two cultures. Winter found that Americans played "mostly primary" rather than secondary roles, that "Japanese teachers interacted with their pupils more extensively outside of school and school hours," and these interactions also tended to involve large groups of children as opposed to the American teachers' more personal interaction. While student-teacher relations are "generally positive . . . more American teachers were depicted negatively" and American students "appeared to be freer to criticize teachers."

Also of Note

Adair, Susan Anderson. "Science Fiction in Elementary Science Education: A Content Analysis of the Quantity and Validity of Scientific Referents in, and the Readability of, Selected Science Fiction Literature for Children Published between 1940–1959 and 1960–1980." Ed.D. diss. Temple University, 1983. DAI 44:68A.

Brand, Patricia Petrus. "The Modern French Fairy Tale: Aspects of *Le Merveilleux* in Aymé, Supervielle, Saint-Exupéry and Sabatier." Ph.D. diss. University of Colorado at Boulder, 1983. 208 pp. DAI 44:1468A.

Cooper, Janet Louise. "A Study of the Effects of Pre-Performance Materials on the Child's Ability to Respond to Theatrical Performance." Ph.D. diss. University of Georgia, 1983. 209 pp. DAI 44:323A.

Hertford, Bruce. "*John Brown's Schooldays*: A Musical Adapted from the Thomas Hughes Classic and Directed in Performance at Brigham Young University." Ph.D. diss. Brigham Young University, 1983. 354 pp. DAI 44:324A.

Martinez, Miriam Frances. "Young Children's Verbal Responses to Literature in Parent-Child Story Time Interactions." Ph.D. diss. The University of Texas at Austin, 1983. 650 pp. DAI 44:1044A.

Meacham, Margaret McKeen Ramsey. "*Alice in Wonderland*, A Chamber Opera in One Act." (Original composition) D.M.A. diss. University of Maryland, 1982. 88 pp. DAI 44:16A.

Myers, Margaret Teresa. "Subterranean Heroes: Children and Women in the Novels of Charles Dickens." Ph.D. diss. Indiana University, 1983. 157 pp. DAI 44:761A.

Page, Anita. "Children's Story Comprehension as a Result of Storytelling and Story Dramatization: A Study of the Child as Spectator and as Participant." Ph.D. diss. University of Massachusetts, 1983. 154 pp. DAI 44:985A.

226 RACHEL FORDYCE

Parchem, Georga Larsen. "The Paper Bag Players, A Theatre for Children, 1958–1982: Development, Creative Process, and Principles." Ph.D. diss. The Ohio State University, 1983. 506 pp. DAI 44:16.
Piercy, Sandra Lee. "The Cradle of Salvation: Children and Religion in Late Sixteenth and Early Seventeenth Century England." Ph.D. diss. University of California, Santa Barbara, 1982. 295 pp. DAI 44:1541–42.
Pinciotti, Patricia Anne. "A Comparative Study of Two Creative Drama Approaches on Imagery Ability and the Dramatic Improvisation." Ed.D. diss. Rutgers University, The State University of New Jersey (New Brunswick), 1982. 184 pp. DAI 44:442.
Van Hoorn, Judith Lieberman. "Games of Infancy: A Cross-Cultural Study." Ph.D. diss. University of California, Berkely, 1982. 333 pp. DAI 44:67.
Williams, Lyle Thomas. "Journeys to the Center of the Earth: Descent and Initiation in Selected Science Fiction." Ph.D. diss. Indiana University, 1983. 329 pp. DAI 44:746–47.
Wirtschafter, Carol Lavenstein. "Parent Involvement in a Literature Enrichment Program for Students in Grades Five through Eight." Ph.D. diss. University of Kentucky, 1983. 156 pp. DAI 44:1740A.
Young, Katharine Galloway. "Taleworlds and Story-realms: The Phenomenology of Narrative." Ph.D. diss. University of Pennsylvania, 1983. 463 pp. DAI 44:832A.

Contributors and Editors

JANICE M. ALBERGHENE teaches children's and adolescent literature at Bowling Green State University; she is currently completing a book on artist figures in American children's literature.

JEAN-MARIE APOSTOLIDES teaches French literature at Harvard University. He is author of *Le Roi machine* (1982) and *Les Métamorphoses de Tintin* (1984), as well as a play, *La Nauf des fous*.

RUTH BOTTIGHEIMER teaches comparative literature at the State University of New York, Stony Brook, and has received a DAAD fellowship to complete a monograph on the Grimms. She organized the Princeton conference on fairy tales held in 1984.

FRANCELIA BUTLER, founder of the journal, who teaches children's literature at the University of Connecticut, has just published an adult novel about child abuse, *The Lucky Piece* (1984).

JOHN CECH, past president of the Children's Literature Association, teaches at the University of Florida, Gainesville. He has recently written a play about H. C. Andersen, *From Inside a Swan's Egg*, which was performed at the 1984 World's Fair in New Orleans.

MARGARET R. HIGONNET teaches English and comparative literature at the University of Connecticut. She has published an English version of a Romansch folk song for children and is writing a book about the eighteenth-century French debate on suicide.

CONSTANCE B. HIEATT, who teaches English at the University of Western Ontario, is a medievalist whose publications include adaptations of medieval tales for children and a medieval cookbook for modern cooks.

RACHEL FORDYCE is associate dean of the College of Arts and Sciences at Virginia Polytechnic Institute and State University.

HUGH KEENAN, a medievalist who teaches at Georgia State University, has written various studies of children's literature including a book on Tolkien and a recent essay on Joel Chandler Harris.

U. C. KNOEPFLMACHER, who teaches English at Princeton University, has written extensively on the Victorians and is currently writing a book on Victorian fantasies for children.

JOSEPH H. MCMAHON, who teaches French at Wesleyan University, has just finished *Haunting Heroes: Sexuality, Death, and the Heroic Order* and a book on Anthony Burgess.

RONI NATOV teaches English at Brooklyn College, CUNY, and coedits *The Lion and the Unicorn*.

PERRY NODELMAN, who teaches English at the University of Winnipeg, is editor of the *Children's Literature Association Quarterly*. He is completing a book about how children's picture books tell stories.

HARRIET RITVO teaches in the Humanities Department at the Massachusetts Institute of Technology. Her article is part of a study of the role of animals in nineteenth-century English culture.

MICHAEL STEIG teaches English at Simon Fraser University. Author of *Dickens and Phiz* (1978), as well as articles on the Victorian novel, *Alice*, and Kenneth

227

Grahame, he is working on a book about authorial intention, reader-response, and interpretation.

MARIA TATAR, who teaches German literature at Harvard University, has published *Spellbound: Studies in Mesmerism and Literature* and numerous essays on German Romanticism. She is currently writing a book on folktales and literary fairy tales.

HERNAN VERA teaches sociology at the University of Florida, Gainesville. His fields are sociology of knowledge, occupations and professions, and marriage and the family. He has published on the families of Disney.

JACK ZIPES, who teaches German and comparative literature at the University of Wisconsin, Milwaukee, is a coeditor of *New German Critique*. His work on children's literature and fairy tales includes *Fairy Tales and the Art of Subversion* (1982) and *The Trials and Tribulations of Little Red Riding Hood* (1983).

The editors of *Children's Literature* are planning a future issue focused on literature of any era which presents a response to violence or disaster and is intended for an audience of children or adolescents. Submissions on this topic are particularly encouraged.

The Networking Committee of the Children's Literature Assembly of the National Council of Teachers of English is compiling an international directory of professionals in the field of children's literature. Librarians, teachers, writers, researchers, critics, speakers, reviewers, performers or storytellers, publishers, and others will be included. Persons who want to share their interests and abilities and are willing to complete a survey should send their names and addresses to : Alice K. Swinger, Chair; Networking Committee of the Children's Literature Assembly; c/o College of Education and Human Services; Wright State University; Dayton, OH 45435 USA.